LITERATURE AND MORAL UNDERSTANDING

LITERATURE AND MORAL UNDERSTANDING

*A Philosophical Essay on Ethics, Aesthetics,
Education, and Culture*

FRANK PALMER

CLARENDON PRESS · OXFORD
1992

Oxford University Press, Walton Street, Oxford OX2 6DP
Oxford New York Toronto
Delhi Bombay Calcutta Madras Karachi
Petaling Jaya Singapore Hong Kong Tokyo
Nairobi Dar es Salaam Cape Town
Melbourne Auckland
and associated companies in
Berlin Ibadan

Oxford is a trade mark of Oxford University Press

Published in the United States
by Oxford University Press, New York

British Library Cataloguing in Publication Data
Data available

Library of Congress Cataloging in Publication Data
Literature and moral understanding
p. cm.
1. Literature—Philosophy. 2. Literature, Modern—20th century—
—History and criticism. 3. Literature and morals.
PN49.L4999 1992 801'.3—dc20 92–9977
ISBN 0–19–824232–8

Typeset by Cambridge Composing (UK) Ltd
Printed and bound in
Great Britain by Bookcraft (Bath) Ltd,
Midsomer Norton, Avon

To
Diana, Melanie, and Sophie,
and to the memory of my father,
Arthur Palmer

Art is a tribute to man's own humanity.
(Herbert Read, *The Meaning of Art*)

PREFACE

The purpose of this book is to investigate how and in what ways our understanding and appreciation of literary works call upon and further our capacities for moral understanding. Nearly all the questions this task gives rise to have their root in the perennial problem of the relation between art and life. That problem, it seems to me, should not only be of concern to philosophers working in some now (alas) unfashionable corner of philosophy known as aesthetics. It also provides meat for moral philosophy, epistemology, philosophy of mind, and what bears the amorphous title 'social philosophy'.

There is a tendency among some recent philosophers to treat the topic of 'fiction and reality' as though it were just a technical matter to be sewn up with the incisive needle of logical theory. This is symptomatic of the impoverishment of contemporary philosophy, which, both in its narrowing range of specialist interests and in its professional jargon, has yielded to the temptation to cut itself off from the human problems that matter deeply to the intelligent layman. As far as the arts are concerned, this intellectual myopia has proved disastrous. Artists of any art do not simply produce. They are profoundly affected by theoretical conceptions of the nature and importance of the activity in which they are engaged. And while mainstream analytical philosophy has turned its nose in other directions, absurd and destructive theories of art and criticism have flourished in its absence, protected from its searching demands. Indeed it is quite paradoxical that some of these theories are far more abstract and less 'humane' than they perhaps would have been had they received more critical attention from analytical philosophers.

Though what I have written is intended to be a philosophical essay, I have endeavoured, perhaps not always successfully, to avoid needless technicalities in the hope of speaking to a wider audience, which it is hoped will include those with an interest in literature and criticism, in the educational value of art, and in the moral dimension of language and culture. The general reader may find the first three chapters more technical than the remaining five, but their inclusion is necessary for the wider matters I go on to explore. My starting point in Chapter 1 is modern literary theory, which has not only failed to leave room for, but has in some cases actively eschewed, the idea that fictional characters are to be regarded as human beings. It is only a small step from a 'dehumanized' conception of character to a view of literature as devoid of moral ideas, and to a conception of criticism as a scientific or political exercise. However, if in understanding and responding to the representational content of literary works we are to regard fictional characters as persons, we must then take issue with those philosophers whose theories preclude us from talking about or 'referring to' characters as persons, and who make a huge fuss about the ontology of fictional existence. I am thus compelled to confront prevailing theories of reference and argue for their inapplicability to literary fictions.

Having analysed the similar inadequacy of accounting for our experience of and discourse about fiction in terms of pretence and make-believe in Chapter 2, I then proceed in Chapter 3 to a philosophical digression on the moral attitudes. The purpose of that chapter is to argue that moral attitudes necessarily enter into our understanding of persons. Chapter 4 investigates some problems about moral responses to fictional characters, while Chapter 5 considers how far the form of such responses is guided by our experience of fictional representation, which is neither purely subjective nor objective but, instead, is governed by a kind of bargain between the author/playwright and the reader/spectator.

There is a long-standing prejudice based upon genuine insights that, unexamined, can be misleading: that life is one thing and art another. At the opposite extreme there is the politicization of art which expects and demands that it be 'relevant to life', even conveying social truths and social messages. Chapter 6 argues that there is *a* distinction between art and life, but this does not mean that life in art is a different kind of life. Rather, the difference consists in the way that our interest and attention is directed, shaped, and organized.

Chapter 7 contends that agreement with the moral vision of a literary work is neither a necessary nor a sufficient condition of our perception of its merit. That does not mean, however, that art has nothing to do with morality (a view found in for instance the 'aestheticism' of Oscar Wilde). For not only would such a view make the idea of literary merit or aesthetic qualities quite vacuous, it would run counter to our experience of literature.

The final chapter raises questions which should be of interest to anyone who is troubled by fashionable ways of thinking about education and culture. It is argued that literature (and indeed painting) is a source of non-propositional knowledge (knowledge by acquaintance, rather than knowledge by description). In order to defend that idea there is an examination of the distinction between 'telling' and 'showing'. I also examine some non-propositional features of moral understanding and show how it differs from knowledge of matters of fact or theoretical knowledge. I then suggest how it is possible for literature to deepen our moral understanding without giving us information. The part played by imagination in moral and practical reasoning is here explained, and it is suggested that literature can be a source of understanding not provided by actual life. This debate, however, is not restricted to a consideration of how the individual learns from the individual text (a tendency in recent analysis which in my view involves a short-sighted view of the significance of literature and of the cultural, perhaps even spiritual, content of moral understanding). The discussion is therefore widened through an exploration of how culture, and in particular language, is enriched by art and what this contributes to the moral life.

A slightly shorter version of this work was presented as a doctoral dissertation to London University in February 1988. I am greatly indebted to my supervisor, Professor Roger Scruton, not only for his encouragement and support, but for criticisms which forced me to attend to some matters it would have been easier to pass over in silence. I also wish to thank my examiners, Dr Malcolm Budd and Professor Anthony O'Hear, for their kind and helpful suggestions regarding revisions for publication. Professor O'Hear has also been generous enough to read and discuss some new material I have added to the book. The thesis, which I completed at Birkbeck College, actually began life some years ago (at King's College, London) as an incidental chapter to a topic which was not to be about literature at all, but about interpersonal understanding. My interest in the philosophy of fiction was greatly encouraged by my supervisor at that time, Professor Peter Winch, whose influence on me has deepened over the years—though I do not suggest that he would necessarily agree with what I have written here. That chapter in turn was originally stimulated by a chance remark made to me by Professor Stuart Brown on an interesting similarity between failing to understand a person and finding a fictional character implausible. I owe more to that chance remark than Professor Brown could possibly know. Finally I must record my appreciation for the kind advice given to me by the philosophy editor of Oxford University Press, Mrs Angela Blackburn, both about content and about matters of style. I am also grateful to the copy-editor and to the desk-editing department for their suggested improvements.

CONTENTS

1
Fictional Persons and Fictional Worlds

Characters in fiction are mostly empty canvas. I have known many who have passed through stories without noses, or heads to hold them; others have lacked bodies altogether, exercised no natural functions, possessed some thoughts, a few emotions, but no psychologies, and apparently made love without the necessary organs. (William. H. Gass, *Fiction and the Figures of Life*, 45.)

FICTIONAL PERSONS

Any normal reader or theatre-goer is perfectly well aware at all times that the characters depicted in novels and plays do not really exist. Yet we refer to them by name, have conversations about them, reflect upon their plights and predicaments, and even blame or admire them for their non-existent deeds. If we are to regard literature as having moral significance and powers of edification— and it is the purpose of this volume to defend and elucidate this conception of literary art—then how do we justify placing such value on works of literature in view of the fact that the personages and circumstances such works contain do not actually exist?

Philosophical debate about fictional existence has tended to concentrate on one or other of the following questions. There is first the matter of the rationality of emotional responses to fiction: in other words how our emotions can be 'about' things we do not even believe to be actual. This topic will be taken up in Chapter 4, where I shall be expressly concerned with the *moral* emotions we have towards fictional characters—something which has received little attention in recent debates about fiction and emotion. Second, there is the problem of the intelligibility of fictional discourse: the logical status of statements or propositions apparently referring to or describing fictional characters or entities.

To some readers the latter may seem an arid or even irrelevant matter. Indeed it is a defect in some analyses that the second problem has been treated in isolation from the first: as though we could construct an adequate theory of fictional discourse out of 'pure logic', so to speak. Yet it is for that very reason that the subject demands attention here. It is a central contention of this book that literature would have little or no interest or significance for us as human beings if we did not regard fictional characters as morally responsible agents: i.e. as persons. To regard characters in this way is to be able to talk about *them* and enter into disputes about *their* actions—an implication which is denied by some theories of reference which, as I shall show, tell us that in referring to or describing fictional characters we are really referring to something else (e.g. the author or the work, or even a bundle of abstract qualities or properties).

Two quite different, or even mutually opposed, 'schools' or approaches to criticism nevertheless converge in their agreement that literary characters should not be regarded as human beings. For the sake of convenience, I shall refer to these as the semiotic school and the symbolic poem school.

(a) The 'semiotic' school

Both structuralism and post-structuralism are quite dismissive not only of the idea of characters as persons but more generally of the idea that the meaning of a literary work is reached through a humane interest in the representation of a human world. In so far as structuralism has made an impact on Anglo-Saxon countries, its origins can be traced to the work of the Russian formalists, roughly between 1915 and 1930, who rejected the idea that the meaning and value of a literary work lies in its representational content and turned attention instead to a more theoretical preoccupation with abstract linguistic features of its form or structure. However, structuralism's chief impact has been mediated through the French connection (having escaped to Paris, Todorov was instrumental in founding the structuralist school of criticism there). In the 1960s structuralist theory aspired towards the status of a science, relying for its authoritative aura on the work of the Swiss linguistician Ferdinand de Saussure, with his general theory of 'signs' ('semiology'). On any orthodox structuralist view the literary work is no longer a human voice expressing human experience to those with the imagination, sensitivity, and 'humane literacy' to respond to it, but a linguistically constituted 'object' or 'text' to be deciphered by those with the necessary theoretical equipment (possessed of course only by those who happen to be propounding the theory at the time).

Post-structuralism (equally known as 'deconstruction') is a supposed revolt against structuralism (though sharing some of its premisses) and has come about largely through the more radical French thinkers such as Barthes, Derrida, and Lacan. Ideological in orientation, it is heavily influenced by Marxism and psychoanalysis. And it is largely as a result of this phenomenon, which has stretched Saussure's 'arbitrariness of the sign' into implying utter detachment from the world and from concepts, that it has become fashionable in some academic circles to believe that 'texts' can only have whatever meaning is imposed upon them since, in themselves, they are meaningless marks on a page. Since language never refers to the world or to 'reality' (a 'bourgeois' notion) and since 'texts' are only composed of words (or, better, 'signs' without reference) any written object constitutes a 'text' and is therefore as worthy (or unworthy?) of attention as any other, and there are no constraints upon interpretation. This is a useful conclusion for those who wish to depart from 'reading' good or great works of literature and 'deconstruct' them in accordance with Marxist or feminist ideologies.

While subscribers to either persuasion would be eager to point to the differences between structuralism and post-structuralism, both are united in their rejection of the view that what concerns us in a literary work of art is the quality of the representation of human experience. As one might expect of an approach to literature that reduces it to bloodless technical abstractions, structuralist treatment of character has been sparse and perfunctory. Characters are merely 'devices' having a purely functional role in relation to other abstract, if not quantifiable, units of plot or narrative. Some would-be defenders of the structuralist approach, e.g. John Sturrock, insist that this abstract 'functionalist' approach to character does not rule out humane 'evaluation' of character.[1] However, this insistence is unconvincing and certainly lacks demonstration. The question that needs answering is how it is possible to move from a purely functional evaluation of an abstract 'element', in its system-

---

[1] See John Sturrock, *Structuralism* (London, 1986), esp. ch. 4.

atic relation to other abstract elements, to an ethical evaluation of something even remotely resembling human conduct. It explains nothing merely to say that a structuralist interpretation should 'come first': '. . . we ought to remember that in the first instance the "characters" of a fiction belong together, as elements in that particular fiction, and that whatever evaluations we submit them to subsequently, the first evaluation is a functional one.'[2] But if we begin with a conception of fictional characters that falls so far beneath the idea of human personality that the word 'characters' can only appear, rather grudgingly, in inverted commas, what does it mean to speak of submitting 'them' to further evaluations? For, by definition, 'they' are no more logically capable of bearing moral or psychological predicates than is a quadratic equation.

This confusion, however, is linked to further misconceptions about the very nature of moral and personal 'evaluation', which is different in kind from purely functional 'evaluation':

If we again take the example of the 'characters' in a narrative, a first interpretation of what each character 'means' should be made in terms of the place which that character is seen to occupy within the scheme of the narrative as a whole. Only in that way can we work towards the 'value' of the character. Most readers of fiction probably do this anyway; they compare the characters one with another and reach certain ethical or other conclusions about them: that they are likeable or unlikeable, good or bad, and so on. Such comparisons are made possible by our experience as readers, by our 'competence' that is, but they function within the perimeter of the structure that encloses them.[3]

It is important to note that Sturrock's reference to the 'value' of a character seems to be intended in the Saussurian sense: that is to say that when Saussurian linguistics is taken as a model for literature the text consists of a set of symbolically charged 'signs' and the value of a sign is no more than its place or role in the sign system. (It is in accordance with this vocabulary that Sturrock refers to the Bennet family in *Pride and Prejudice* as a 'small system' within the 'larger system' of the novel.[4]) In so far as Sturrock wishes to say that a structuralist approach describes what the common reader is up to, one is left wondering what structural-

---

[2] Ibid. 125.   [3] Ibid. 124.   [4] Ibid.

ism has to contribute to our understanding of literary practice. For if, beneath the technical jargon, all we were being told is that ordinary though literate readers form their ideas about the characters in relation to the narrative (and surely it would have to be in relation to their *understanding* of the narrative), then it would require no great structuralist returned from the grave to tell us this.

If Sturrock is right that 'most readers compare the characters one with another and reach certain ethical or other conclusions about them' he is already appealing to a different notion of character, and one which is rather more full-blooded than the functional ciphers arrived at, or presupposed in, structuralist discourse. In order to 'compare the characters one with another' not only must we be thinking of the characters as bearers of personal qualities (i.e. persons), but we must also already have come to know and understand something of those personal qualities, otherwise there could be no basis for comparison. Furthermore, to speak of ethical evaluation as Sturrock does as one among other 'conclusions' we 'reach' is to imply that our first perception of the characters is value free and that 'ethical or other' values are subsequently added on. Hence the simplistic way in which he sums up the content of our 'ethical or other' conclusions about characters as amounting to nothing more than deciding whether they are 'likeable or unlikeable, good or bad, and so on'. Such epithets sound like labels pinned on *ex post facto*. Precisely what is wrong with this way of thinking about 'evaluation' will be explained in Chapter 3, where I shall argue that understanding human action is saturated with moral concepts.

It is consequential upon that argument, and upon our actual experience of fiction, that we do not, and cannot, 'work towards' an evaluative understanding of characters by first thinking of them as functional devices, such as pieces on a chessboard. Not only can there be no passage from the latter to the former, but since mere devices cannot fornicate, commit murder, or save a damsel in distress the very idea of their 'function' is called into question. The idea seems to be that we approach a text by considering characters as mere 'roles': a 'role' being a 'place' within a narrative scheme. But those secondary abstractions could only begin to acquire descriptive force in relation to the concrete actions and events that are experienced by the reader as the representational content. Duncan is stabbed to death by a man called Macbeth, not by a role or a place in a narrative scheme. And without a human understand-ing of Macbeth's deed, which includes some understanding of the man who performs it, there cannot be a place in a narrative scheme for the deed to occupy. Far from 'functional' interpretations 'coming first', we must think of characters as persons from the very beginning to obtain any idea of their function within the literary work as a whole.

A similar point needs to be urged against the concept of character which emerges from post-structuralist analysis (or 'deconstruc-tion'). For within the perspective of the latter—especially from the 'ideology-hunting' that it has licensed—any interest we have in literary characters can never be analogous to the interest we have in human beings: an interest which thrives upon our perception of human beings as individuals. Rather, 'characters'—already reduced by structuralism to a type of technical apparatus—become little more than illustrations or tools of ideology. It is notable for instance that in Terry Eagleton's book *Marxism and Literary Criticism*, the only mention of 'character' (predictably in grudge-quotes) occurs on one page, where he endorses the view that the rise of the novel in eighteenth-century England reveals 'in its very *form* a changed set of ideological interests'. One of the ways this is shown is by 'a concept of life-like, substantial "character"; a concern with the material fortunes of an individual protagonist who moves through an unpredictably evolving linear narrative and so on.'[5] Eagleton's contempt for the very idea of a character as a human being (and the 'increasingly confident bourgeois class' of which this idea is the 'product'[6]) is evidenced in his own critical practice. In his book *William Shakespeare*—which the preface describes as 'an exercise in political semiotics'—we read that Cordelia is 'spokeswoman for the material bonds of kinship' and that *Coriolanus* is the 'study of a bourgeois individualist'. In *Macbeth* Duncan is a 'symbol of the body politic', Macbeth is a 'floating signifier in ceaseless doomed pursuit of an anchoring signified', while the witches are not the evil hags we thought but 'signify a realm of non-meaning and poetic play' and call for our approval since they 'deconstruct the political order'.

Now Eagleton and his fellow political semioticians may be the

---

[5] *Marxism and Literary Criticism* (London, 1976), 25.   [6] Ibid.

extreme example of a fashion which finds it 'difficult to read Shakespeare without feeling that he was almost certainly familiar with the writings of Hegel, Marx, Nietzsche, Freud, Wittgenstein and Derrida'.[7] But one does not have to seek within a semiotic approach to literature to find examples of literary theory which reduce characters to symbolism. It is essential to the impulse of modernism to reject 'naturalistic' conceptions of character. As John Bayley objected, in a book which *The Times* described as 'profoundly subversive of the current orthodoxies of literary criticism':

Criticism does not interest itself much today in the old idea of character. Where the drama is concerned we have quite stopped asking whether a character is 'convincing' or not, or discussing what he is 'really like'; and we more and more assume that the novelist, too, need not start out by making his characters like 'real life', but will subordinate their individuality to the general atmosphere and purpose of the work . . . On the new view of character a man with a wooden leg, say, is given it by the author not to individualize him but to reinforce a controlling theme—the impotence of modern society or something of the sort.[8]

(b) The 'symbolic poem' school

For reasons which have nothing to do with the scientific and political orientations of a semiotic approach, this debilitated view of character has also been promoted by a tradition in literary criticism which emerged in the earlier part of this century as a reaction against what was considered to be an overemphasis on character analysis as a technique of criticism. This reaction is most clearly illustrated through consideration of the change in the nature of Shakespeare criticism, though the implications of course were much wider: the general thesis being that one's 'total response' to a literary work, which is seen as symbolic or metaphorical, overrides a concern with character. As this pertained to Shakespeare the 'revolution' in criticism (most often supposed, rather misleadingly, to be against the approach to character typified by A. C. Bradley) took the form of concentrating on the plays not so much as depictions of the 'actions of men' but as poems containing rich textures of symbolic images (see for example Caroline Spur-

---

[7] *William Shakespeare* (Oxford, 1987), pp. ix–x. (Eagleton is the general editor of the 'Re-Reading Literature' series.)

[8] John Bayley, *The Characters of Love: A Study in the Literature of Personality* (London, 1968), 36.

geon's *Shakespeare's Imagery* (1935) and G. Wilson-Knight's *The Wheel of Fire* (1930)). It was in explicit acknowledgement of this school of criticism that C. S. Lewis, in his lecture 'Hamlet: The Prince or the Poem?', declared of the *Merchant of Venice* that 'the real play is not so much about men as about metals'.[9]

Even F. R. Leavis, the modern critic one most associates with a firm insistence on the link between literature and morality, lent his support to the iconoclastic blast against what now has to be called, in Bayley's phrase, 'the old idea of character'. This can be seen for instance in his response to C. H. Rickword, who in 'A Note on Fiction' argued that 'character' (taken to mean 'an imagined portrait of a human being') provides a dangerous focus for literary criticism since it invites 'extra-literary scrutiny'. 'Character', Rickword maintained, is an 'illusion' or 'symbol', for it is 'merely the term by which the reader alludes to the pseudo-objective images he composes of his responses to an author's verbal arrangements'.[10] In *Towards Standards of Criticism* Leavis expressed approval for Rickword's suggested link between fiction and poetry: 'A novel, like a poem, is made of words; there is nothing else one can point to. We talk of a novelist as "creating characters" but the process of "creation" is one of putting words together.'[11] This, together with his sympathy for Wilson-Knight's view in *The Wheel of Fire* that Shakespeare's plays are ultimately symbolic poems, gave rise to the idea of 'the novel as dramatic poem' and of Dickens as 'the Shakespeare of the novel'.[12] This dictum found further expression in the well-known essay by L. C. Knights (himself a pupil of Leavis) entitled 'How Many Children had Lady Macbeth?' The essay correctly pointed out the futility of some forms of speculation about aspects of the lives of characters not revealed by the playwright, but did so at the unnecessary expense of denying that characters are to be regarded as human beings. Thus Knights endorsed G. Wilson-Knight's view that 'the persons ultimately are not human at all but purely symbols of a poetic vision'.

---

[9] In C. S. Lewis, *Selected Literary Essays*, ed. W. Hooper (Cambridge, 1979), 96–7.

[10] 'A Note on Fiction', in F. R. Leavis (ed.), *Towards Standards of Criticism: Selections from the Calendar of Modern Letters 1925/27* (London, 1976), 16.

[11] Ibid.

[12] See for instance, F. R. Leavis and Q. D. Leavis, *Dickens the Novelist* (London, 1970).

The unreasonable choice foisted upon us by arguments of this type is that the only alternative to regarding characters as 'critical counters' (in L. C. Knights's phrase) is to commit oneself to the view that the main task of a novelist or dramatist is to spawn 'interesting characters' and that our sole interest in his work amounts to a thirst for portraiture. And since A. C. Bradley is popularly supposed to be a fitting target for this line of attack, it is as well to point out that Bradley himself was acutely aware of the status of Shakespeare's tragedies as 'dramatic poems'—even to the point of claiming that *King Lear* is 'one of the world's greatest poems'.[13] Being tragedies, however, they depict 'tragic action' which, as Bradley pointed out, is not a matter of random happenings but the actions of men:

The 'story' or 'action' of a Shakespearean tragedy does not consist, of course, solely of human actions or deeds; but the deeds are the predominant factor. And these deeds are, for the most part, actions in the full sense of the word; not things done ''tween sleep and wake', but acts or omissions thoroughly expressive of the doer—characteristic deeds. The centre of the tragedy therefore, may be said with equal truth to lie in action issuing from character, or in character issuing in action.[14]

Moreover, to say that Shakespeare's main interest lay here is not to claim that it was an interest external to the artistic purpose: 'To say that it lay in *mere* character, or was a psychological interest would be a great mistake, for he was dramatic to the tips of his fingers'.[15]

It is also wrong to suppose that this debunking of character has a precedent in Aristotle, as for instance C. S. Lewis does when he says, 'Aristotle has long seemed to me simply right when he says that tragedy is an imitation not of men but of action and life and happiness and misery. By action he means, no doubt, not what a modern producer would call action but rather "situation".'[16] While a selective reading of the *Poetics* may fasten on Aristotle's claim that there could be tragedy without character but not without action, this remark should not be taken to imply that there could be action without the human beings who engage in it. Rather,

---

[13] *Shakespearean Tragedy: Lectures on Hamlet, Othello, King Lear, Macbeth* (London, 1985), 229.
[14] Ibid. 7.
[15] Ibid. (emphasis orig.).
[16] 'Hamlet; The Prince or the Poem?', *Selected Literary Essays*, 94.

Aristotle's subordination of character to plot simply means that as a question of priorities it is better to have a good story in which the characters are less well drawn than a story in which the characters are well drawn but the plot is unconvincing.

According to the *Poetics*, tragedy is indeed a representation of action, but this in no way implies that the nature of the actions is independent of the nature of the persons whose actions they are. This is made clear in Chapter 6 when he says that it is action brought about by agents who necessarily display 'certain distinctive qualities of nature and thought according to which we also define the nature of the actions'.[17] When Aristotle speaks of a requirement of the plot that the arrangement of incidents should be 'necessary' or 'probable' (in the sense that one event is not merely followed by another event but, instead, that what takes place develops out of the circumstances of the plot itself), this is not said in complete separation from the requirement that the characters should be 'lifelike and consistent' (Chapter 15). Although in fiction we may be presented with what is unexpected, or even impossible, what is represented must be something we can make sense of: in other words it must be credible that such and such a person would do or say such a thing in those circumstances. (We may regard it as impossible that the future can be foretold, for example, yet we are satisfied that if Macbeth could be told the future he would behave exactly as he does, and endeavour to fight to the death against fate.)

Far from regarding character as unimportant or eliminable, Aristotle thus indicates that an understanding of human nature is essential for the poet or playwright; and this cannot be separated from his view (against Plato) that poetry concerns itself with universal truths. This is not to say that poetry, like philosophy, is essentially concerned with what is abstract. The characters are not to be thought of as abstractions (after all in chapter 17 Aristotle explains that in composing his plots and characters the poet should keep the scene before his eyes as though he were witnessing what is taking place). Poetry depicts particular men in particular circumstances, though the representation only succeeds in so far as what is depicted is in accord with what we can recognize to be true of men. And as far as tragedy is concerned it should be remembered

---

[17] T. S. Dorsch's trans. in *Aristotle/Longinus/Horace: Classical Literary Criticism* (London, 1965), 39. (All quotations are taken from this edn.)

that the aim of the representation is not merely intellectual insight but the arousing and resolution of particular feelings (pity and fear). It is therefore strange that C. S. Lewis should invoke Aristotle in support of his own allegiance to the 'symbolic poem' school, especially in view of the fact that while Aristotle acknowledged that tragedy achieves its effects through the medium of poetry he considered the poet to be 'a maker of plots rather than of verses'.

In all of the approaches that I have so far discussed there seems to be a common consensus, however differently it is tricked out, that to regard characters as persons is to commit the cardinal sin of 'going beyond the text'. And with the 'symbolic poem' school in particular (though the thematic approach is also found in the 'semiotic' school) there is some reliance on the assumption that to understand or appreciate the metaphorical or symbolic significance of a literary work is flatly incompatible with a 'naturalistic' approach to character. I cannot say everything that needs to be said against those two contentions here and now because there are some general philosophical matters to explore which will eventually throw more light on why I think these to be mistaken and confused. I shall not ultimately challenge the principle that good criticism does not 'go beyond' or 'lead away from' the text, though that is only if a literary text is not simply 'words on a page' but a work of art having a representational content (or depicting a fictional world) that cannot be understood or appreciated without the imagination (imagination itself being grounded in some 'common expectations' of our experience of the actual world). Nor will it be my intention to undermine some of the genuine insights of the 'symbolic poem' school in drawing attention to the metaphorical or symbolic levels of meaning in a literary work 'conceived as a whole'. But I shall want to deny the tacit inference that seems to be drawn: that fictional characters are to be thought of as metaphorical people (i.e. figurative unpersons). Indeed I shall try to show (especially in Chapter 6) that metaphorical or symbolic levels of meaning in a literary work can only be appreciated by thinking of the characters as persons.

FICTIONAL EXISTENCE

It is all very well to say that it is absurd not to conceive of fictional characters as persons, yet it still must be explained how it is possible to refer to, to describe, or to engage in discourse about fictional persons, given that they do not actually exist. On prevailing theories of reference, statements of the form '*a* is *F*', where a predicate is asserted of a subject, seem to demand as a minimal requirement for their truth that *a* exists, otherwise the statement is either false (e.g. on Russell's view) or without truth-value and therefore neither true nor false (e.g. on Strawson's view). On such theories the immediate problem with such a statement as 'Uriah Heep has red hair' is that 'Uriah Heep' has no referent and therefore the statement as a whole is either false or incapable of being either true or false. Yet on the other hand it does not seem ridiculous to suppose that we can and do speak meaningfully about fictional characters and, at the very least, make true or false statements about them, such that it is true to assert that Mr Murdstone married Mrs Copperfield and false to assert that Mrs Micawber was childless. How can this be?

Unless we follow the most ruthless logicians in dismissing statements about fictions as some kind of pseudo-discourse, it seems that we have two broad options, which I shall distinguish as *A*-type approaches and *B*-type approaches. Under the first heading one may distinguish the attempt to deny that such statements involve bogus reference or failure of reference by endeavouring to show either (*a1*) that fictional persons or fictional entities do, after all, have some kind of existence and can therefore be referred to 'direct' or (*a2*) that statements about fictions which seem to refer to non-existent entities really refer to something else in the 'real world'. An alternative, still under the rubric of *A*-type approaches, would consist in the attempt to account for the existence of fictional persons in terms of the modal logician's 'possible worlds', though whether this option falls under (*a1*) or (*a2*) depends entirely on what one takes 'possible worlds' to be. Under the second heading, *B*-type approaches, one may try to sidestep the whole problem of reference by arguing that fictional statements belong to a special type of discourse which does not rely for its intelligibility upon satisfying the referential or descriptive functions of factual or information-giving discourse.

I shall examine the difficulties internal to *A*-type approaches, but a general and more crucial objection will be that they exhibit a kind of ontological desperation largely because they do not have the right sense of the problem. Paradoxically, they deny the fictionality of fictional objects: (*a1*) approaches insist that the objects exist (or, worse, have a *kind* of existence); and (*a2*) approaches frustrate and deform our utterances about fictional objects into utterances about what is non-fictional. I shall contend that it seems fruitless to assimilate statements about literary fictions to statements about actual objects or states of affairs and also misguided to fail to distinguish statements about fictions or about imaginary objects from statements about *literary* fictions. It seems therefore that the only hope lies in the direction of *B*-type approaches: that statements about literary fictions belong to a special sort of discourse. But this path also has its dangers. What must be avoided is the notion that statements about literary fictions employ a special sort of language. If literary fiction is to be intelligible at all, words must mean what they usually mean. In the sentence 'Micawber is impecunious', the predicate 'is impecunious' must mean whatever it would mean if asserted of an actual subject.

More promising is what may be derived from the idea of a 'language-game' (to use a term derived from Wittgenstein), according to which the force of particular utterances can only be understood against the wider context of shared assumptions, rules, conventions, and traditions circumscribing their employment in particular types of circumstances. Unfortunately, however, speech-act[18] and language-game approaches to the analysis of fictional discourse have, unnecessarily and incorrectly in my view, tended to promote the idea that statements within or about literary fiction are a matter of pretence and make-believe (a move which perhaps takes the gaming metaphor too far).[19] One of my several reasons for rejecting that analysis is that (apart from its philistinism) it fails to distinguish between different kinds of utterances about fictional characters—to say that Mr Micawber is impecunious is quite a different type of statement from the assertion that Mr Micawber is a fictional character or that Mr Micawber does not exist. Perhaps, then, we should not join in the misguided search for a single unitary phenomenon called fictional discourse but, instead, attend to different modes of discourse about fictional characters which

---

[18] On speech-act/pretence theory, see e.g. John Searle, 'The Logical Status of Fictional Discourse', *New Literary History*, 6. (1975), 319–32.

[19] The make-believe view is most associated with Kendall Walton (discussed Ch. 2.)

nevertheless depend for their sense on the implied connections between them.

Though the bearing of this upon the aesthetic attitude has yet to be explained, we should first note that the logical problem about literary fictions does not arise simply from the non-existence of fictional objects but rather from a deep-rooted and puzzling inclination to say of fictional entities, especially fictional persons, that they exist and that they do not. It is no solution to this supposed antinomy to postulate a strange realm of entities which in some way half-exist. This temptation must be resisted, not so much because it does violence to the way we regard characters in fiction (although it certainly does) but because it does violence to the logic of 'existence'. To discuss the ontological status of fictional entities in this sense is misleading if we are invited to believe that there are degrees of existence or that fictional characters enjoy a different type of existence from our own. As Ryle put it in his paper 'Systematically Misleading Expressions',[20] existence or non-existence is not the having or the not having of a specified status, since existence is not a quality, property, or attribute. Ontologically speaking, there are not two sorts of persons—existent and non-existent ones—and therefore to be a fictitious person is no more to be a person of a certain sort than to be a non-existent banana is to be a second type of banana. The problem, as posed by Ryle, is not what status fictional characters have but how we can 'seem' to make statements about them, given that there are no such persons to make statements about. Ryle's well-known solution (constituting what I have called an (*a*2) approach) is that since 'Mr Pickwick' is a 'pseudo-name' our statements about Mr Pickwick are really propositions either about Dickens or about *The Pickwick Papers*, and when Dickens seems to make propositions about Mr Pickwick he is pretending to do so, without lying because the propositions can neither be true nor false. This solution is counter-intuitive, for it is difficult to see how we could discuss *A Christmas Carol* without being able to make statements about Mr Scrooge that are not statements about the story. It is not the story which is miserly, works his employee hard, or pities Tiny Tim. Nor is it the story which can be accused of being a 'clutching, covetous old sinner'. Certainly statements about Scrooge are usually (though not always)

---

[20] In Gilbert Ryle, *Collected Papers*, 2 vols. (London, 1971), ii. 39–62.

made within the context of a discussion of the story, but that does not mean that the statements are about the story and not about Scrooge.

Ryle himself misleads by treating 'Mr Pickwick is a fiction' as the paradigm of all (attempted) statements about Mr Pickwick. Consequently, the classical problem of denoting non-existent entities obtrudes in such a way that we are not invited to consider the difference between saying 'Mr Pickwick is a fiction' and 'Mr Pickwick is *X*' (where *X* is a description or judgement derivable from an understanding of the story). It is ironic that the inventor of the 'category mistake' should not consider that those two statements belong to different 'categories'. Thus he wrongly concludes that all statements about Mr Pickwick fail to refer and are really about something else. What is needed is a way of showing that statements about the exploits of fictional persons belong to a different 'category' from statements affirming their fictionality (such as 'Scrooge raised Cratchit's wages' is true *of* Scrooge, yet is not equivalent to 'Dickens pretended that . . .' or 'on page so and so we read that . . .'). In other words, what is needed is a way of showing that

(1) There is no *X* such that *X* is Scrooge and *X* did *Y*

does not contradict

(2) Scrooge did *Y*.

The contradiction is not prevented by taking (2) to be about an imaginary object which has a different kind of existence from the existence denied in (1). Here Ryle's objection in his paper 'Imaginary Objects'[21] holds good, since this move would combine two fallacies: that there are different kinds of status of existence and that imaginary objects are a 'species' of object. From this it would follow that an imaginary elephant is not a different kind of elephant. Ryle, however, strangely concludes that an imaginary elephant 'has none of the attributes of an elephant'[22]—a conclusion which surely yields the paradox that if I imagine an elephant walking round Piccadilly Circus it is not an *elephant* I imagine. He would no doubt deny this by saying that since I only imagine this elephant to have attributes—such as a trunk, etc.—it does not

---

[21] Ibid. 65.   [22] Ibid.

'really' have such attributes, for there is no 'it' to have them. But this would reinstate the paradox. For I do not imagine an elephant with an imaginary trunk any more than I imagine a dragon to breathe imaginary fire. Dennis the dragon, as the intentional object of my thoughts, sees with real eyes and breathes real fire. The nearest Ryle gets to considering imaginary objects as intentional objects is in his dismissal of the idea that such objects occupy a kind of alternative existence 'in the head' (which is not an alternative way of existing). But to exist as an intentional object is not to exist 'in' somewhere. In articulating the intentional object of my thoughts I am expressing the propositional content of the thought, rather than assigning existence to a non-existent object. And, given that existence is not an attribute, my imagined elephant has all the attributes of an elephant. If nothing is added to the attributes of an elephant by its existence, then nothing is subtracted from those attributes when I imagine an elephant escaping from the zoo. Ask me to imagine that there is an elephant in the next room and I shall not imagine an imaginary elephant.

Moreover, ask me again tomorrow to imagine an elephant and it is perfectly feasible to say that I shall be able to remember the same elephant. What we have here is a case of what Geach has called 'intentional identity'. Suppose in sharing a joke with a friend I point to an empty corridor in Senate House and say 'Freddy's been here again today'. Neither my friend nor I believe that there is any such elephant. But that does not stop us from referring to the same elephant. For the identity we ascribe to Freddy is not a case of actual identity. It is not true of any elephant that it has been in Senate House or that it has been the subject of our jokes. As Geach puts it, 'we have intentional identity when a number of people, or one person on different occasions have attitudes with a common focus, whether or not there actually is something at that focus'.[23] While it may not be true of any animal that it is the Loch Ness Monster and has been discussed by me, I can nevertheless enter into arguments about the characteristics of the Loch Ness Monster, distinguishing it from, say, the Abominable Snowman.

But if this argument is right, all it establishes is that imaginary objects, *qua* intentional objects, do not for that reason alone lack the properties or attributes of 'real' ones. It is another question

[23] 'Intentional Identity', in Peter Geach, *Logic Matters* (Oxford, 1972), 147.

whether fictional characters differ in important respects from the kind of imaginary objects which Ryle seems to run parallel with these. Why should the way we speak about sea-serpents or imaginary elephants be assimilated to the way we speak about fictional characters? The latter are not, after all, simply the products of my imagination in the way that my imagined pink kangaroos are. Hamlet is not simply a man that I have imagined, such that someone can tell me to stop imagining things. (He is neither like Wilde's Bunbury nor Wyndham's Chocky.) The child who says of his imaginary friend 'Boozo would like some bread and jam' is saying something significantly different from 'Dennis the dragon would have liked to drink Daddy's lighter fuel'. The second is not the manifestation of a private fantasy, even though the child may not be repeating what it says in a book but engaging in counterfactual speculation about the dragon in the story. Indeed the ability of young children to project characters into situations not found in the story is testimony not to their indulgence in a fantasy but to a deeper understanding of the character they are considering. The distinction I am drawing here is not simply to do with the difference between fantasy and imagination—important though that is—but between different fields of discourse.

As a purely ontological question, fictional persons do not exist and there's an end on it. So anyone with Russell's 'robust sense of reality' may well conclude that talk about fictional characters is on a par with talk about the man in the moon. Yet these are different kinds of talk. For one thing, we do not have the same temptation to say of imaginary or mythical objects that they exist and they do not. The temptation to say this of fictional characters is quite a different kind of paradox from the notorious Meinongian inclination to say that non-existent objects must have some kind of 'being' in order to be talked about, for we have no emotional attachment to non-existent objects just because they can be spoken of. Yet we can and do have emotional attachments to fictional characters: we can despise, pity, admire, or even love them. The aesthetic enterprise demands what seem on the surface to be two opposed attitudes. It not only presupposes but requires the reader's full knowledge and awareness that the persons and events depicted in literary works do not exist (or if there is some correspondence in actuality that that is not an aesthetically relevant consideration). To fail to understand that would not only be to lack the concept of fiction but, as I shall later argue (especially in the final chapter), to be deprived of access to the value of literary art. Yet it seems to be at least a minimal requirement for anything approaching sensitive or genuine understanding of fine novels and plays that we are able to enter into some form of lived acquaintance with fictional persons, such that they touch our minds and hearts.

It is that apparent paradox about our experience of literary fiction, rather than some abstract logical consideration, which occasionally inspires a kind of semantic schizophrenia. To yield to the disease produces odd results. Consider for instance Jaakko Hintikka's putative counter-example to Descartes's *Cogito* argument: that Hamlet thought a great many things but does not exist.[24] There is clearly a sense in which it is true to say that Hamlet thought, and it is equally clear that, being fictional, Hamlet does not exist. Yet the combined assertion 'Hamlet thinks but Hamlet does not exist' is totally absurd. For the sense in which it is true to say that Hamlet had thoughts is one which would make it absurd to deny his existence. And the sense in which Hamlet does not exist would make it absurd to claim that Hamlet could think. The problem, then, is to give an account of these two different ways of speaking: otherwise there is a contradiction in asserting (1) 'Hamlet exists and thinks' and (2) 'Hamlet does not exist and does not think'.

For 'P and $\sim P$' to be a contradiction, P must be taken in the same sense when it is both affirmed and denied. 'This circle is not circular' is not contradictory if the circle referred to is for instance a child's clumsy attempt to draw a circle or if the circle is a 'circle of friends', and so on. Yet the distinction I am after is not to be brought out by saying (incorrectly) that in (1) 'Hamlet', 'exists', or 'thinks' have a different sense from the occurrence of the same words in (2). My point is rather that the contextual framework which permits our utterances about a man called Hamlet who thinks and acts must be distinguished from the context in which it is equally permissible to deny all of these things. We are concerned here with different 'fields' or 'modes' of discourse. The force of 'Hamlet accidentally stabbed Polonius' can only be grasped by appreciating the background against which the utterance is made.

[24] 'Cogito Ergo Sum: Inference or Performance?', *Philosophical Review*, 71/1 (Jan. 1962).

It is no more possible to consider such expressions in isolation than it is possible to assign a meaning to a physical movement independently of the social context that transforms mere movements into the different category of human action. This comparison deserves at least the following gloss. I do not mean to suggest that we start with the raw datum of a physical movement and then work backwards to an interpretation of the movement as an action. To regard human action as movement plus a meaning is as misleading as saying that persons are bodies plus minds and that we *infer* mental states from bodily behaviour. I may move my head as a way of saying 'yes' but the movement of my head no more enters into a description of what I have done than (to borrow J. L. Austin's point) the movement of my tongue enters into a description of what I have said. Certainly we may say 'he nodded his head', but nodding is an act, not simply a movement. Just as the nod of a head during an auction signifies a bid, so the words 'I will' in a traditional wedding ceremony signify the eternal vow not captured in the provisional 'I will' of common discourse.

'Polonius is pompous' and 'Dogberry is a bumbling fool' are not to be explained by saying that the individual words in these sentences are meant in a different sense from 'normal' utterance; there is a convention at work here which allows them to have the same sense—though not one which involves bogus reference, or failure of reference, to persons or states of affairs in the actual world. The convention which makes this possible has to do with the 'institution' of art. That is to say, if we understand what it is for something to be a story or play we inherit a freedom and a constraint: the freedom to engage in a mode of discourse which permits our statements about fictional characters to be no less intelligible than our statements about actual persons; the constraint that disciplines this freedom by insisting that our judgements be anchored to a grasp of the relevant literary text.

I said earlier that the statement 'Mr Micawber is impecunious' belongs to a different category from the assertion that Mr Micawber is a fiction. Another way of putting this, to avoid the problematic notion of a 'category', is to follow Wittgenstein in saying that confusion results from using words outside the language-game that is their home. What my suggestion amounts to is that there are at least two conventions, or modes of discourse, governing the way we speak about fictional characters. In a paper read to King's College

London Philosophy Society in 1977 I referred to these as 'internal' and 'external' conventions, and will retain that terminology here at the risk of confusion, not so much from the terms themselves but from the unfortunate coincidence that others writing in this field have subsequently employed similar terminology—each to a different purpose, and certainly distinguishable from mine. It will be easier to compare these different positions if I first state my own.

There are two conventions, or modes of discourse, governing the way we speak about fictional characters. According to one convention—which I shall call the internal convention—Hamlet not only exists, but has sword-fights, falls in love, and feigns madness. According to the other convention—which I shall call the external convention—Hamlet neither exists nor performs deeds. Neither convention is misguided, provided they are not jumbled together. Hintikka, however, places one foot in the internal convention in order to say that Hamlet thought and steps outside it in order to say that Hamlet does not exist. In commenting on Hintikka's alleged counter-example, Anthony Kenny tries to tread a middle path by saying that Hamlet's thoughts are imaginary, like his existence.[25] Here I am sure he echoes a common intuition, but one which, like many common intuitions, may mislead. Since there are no such things as 'imaginary thoughts' Hamlet could not be said to think them. He no more had imaginary thoughts than he had imaginary sword-fights. Hamlet's deeds are performed by a man of flesh and blood and, moreover, with a sword that could draw blood. Kenny might suppose that his remark is legitimate if made from the standpoint of the external convention. But the appropriate thing to say from the external convention is that Hamlet does not exist so there are no thoughts that Hamlet thought. Hence 'Hamlet's thoughts are imaginary' trespasses into the internal convention. But there is no home for it there either. The temptation to say that Hamlet's existence is imaginary is born of the attempt to give sense to expressions like 'Hamlet is the son of Gertrude and he is a man who . . .'. But we can only give a sense to these expressions by adopting the mode of discourse in which they do have a sense.

When we describe Hamlet as a fiction we are of course committing ourselves to saying that outside the play there is no Hamlet, no Prince of Denmark who wrote to Ophelia 'doubt thou the stars

---

[25] *Descartes: A Study of his Philosophy* (New York, 1968), 60–1.

are fire'. Outside the play there is no Hamlet at all, not even an imaginary Hamlet—still less a Hamlet with imaginary existence. But, then, there isn't an imaginary Hamlet within the play. Within the play Hamlet is no more imaginary than you or I. The statements 'Hamlet does not exist' and 'Hamlet thought the world to be weary, stale, flat, and unprofitable' do not contradict one another, because they do not belong to the same mode of discourse. We do not have to seek out some sort of average and say that Hamlet's existence falls halfway down the chart between Being and Not-Being. The modes of discourse those two statements presuppose do not compete with one another, any more than the conventions of utterance governing a wedding ceremony, a debate, or a high court trial rebel against, or are totally impervious to, the conventions governing informal speech. What I have called the external and internal conventions neither clash nor are wholly distinct. The internal convention resides within the external convention much as the conventions of utterance which permit me to describe a bag of wind as a football or a series of dots on paper as a melody exist within a wider framework of utterance. What is said about Hamlet or Pickwick with respect to the internal convention can only be said given that the external convention recognizes the existence of novels and plays.

The above needs to be strongly contrasted with the observation provided by Thomas G. Pavel, who has recently proposed that we distinguish between an 'external approach' and an 'internal approach' to discourse about fiction:

researchers of fiction can adopt two different courses. On the one hand they may choose an external approach that would relate fiction to a more general theory of being and truth; in this case, since the ontology of the nonfictional world would prevail, fictional names would lack denotata, fictional statements would be false or spurious, and metaphysical segrega-tionism would be vindicated. On the other hand, an internal approach is conceivable, which would not so much aim at comparing fictional entities and statements with their nonfictional counterparts . . . as at constructing a model that represents the *users'* understanding of fiction once they step inside it and more or less lose touch with the nonfictional realm. And, clearly, an internal approach should not avoid exploring Ryle's no-man's land and providing adequate housing for the entities wandering in it.[26]

[26] Thomas G. Pavel, *Fictional Worlds* (Cambridge, Mass., 1986), 16 (emphasis orig.).

The crucial difference between this argument and mine is that Pavel's 'external' and 'internal' approaches are offered as mutually exclusive options. This is because they are not themselves modes of discourse but rival theories or, more precisely, rival types of theory. In contrast, my 'internal' and 'external' modes of utterance are not in rivalry, because they are uses of language, not theories about such usage. To speak from the external convention is not necessarily to regard fictional statements as 'false or spurious' any more than to speak from the internal convention is to 'lose touch with the nonfictional realm' and postulate a collection of Meinongian entities. It is precisely to avoid such pitfalls that the search for a single form of discourse about fiction must be abandoned.

I must therefore draw an equally sharp distinction between my terminology and that of Peter Lamarque, who speaks of an 'internal perspective' (from within stories) and an 'external perspective' (from the 'real world').

Within stories, fictional characters are indeed ordinary people, at least those of the Miss Bridget and Mr Allworthy kind. Furthermore, within the story of *Tom Jones*, Mr Allworthy can refer to Miss Bridget and say true or false things about her, just as he can have breakfast with her. Within the story, that is from the internal perspective, the names 'Miss Bridget' and 'Mr Allworthy' function as ordinary proper names referring to ordinary people. Let us call this an *internal* use. Now an internal use is only possible for a speaker within a story. The appearance of these same names in an author's or informed reader's use ... must fall under an external perspective. This will be an *external* use.[27]

Lamarque's 'internal perspective' differs from my 'internal convention' in its being a perspective that we can never adopt, whereas it is crucial to my own argument that the internal convention is one *we* adopt. To say that Gertrude's behaviour offended her son is only intelligible if we conceive of Gertrude and Hamlet as persons—which on Lamarque's account is not possible for us since the internal perspective is, by his definition, only possible for speakers within a story (or play). I can make no sense of this notion of an internal perspective. Confined, as Lamarque confines us, to an 'external perspective', there is no alternative perspective for us to adopt, and the 'internal perspective' is as non-existent as the

---

[27] 'Fiction and Reality', in Peter Lamarque (ed.), *Philosophy and Fiction: Essays in Literary Aesthetics* (Aberdeen, 1983), 58 (emphasis orig.).

fictional persons who alone can adopt it. It is only in so far as *we* are in some way allowed to conceive of fictional characters as persons that it can make any sense to speak of them 'referring' to one another or having breakfast.

If Lamarque's 'external perspective' were to be understood in anything like the way intended by my use of the 'external convention', it would follow that outside the literary work the fictional persons, permitted by the internal convention to exist, do not exist (*tout court*). Lamarque's external perspective, however, is ontologically generous in allowing them to exist 'as characters'. Again, this is difficult to accept. He arrives at this conclusion largely because one of his central preoccupations is how names of fictional characters can be proper names and how we can be said to 'refer' to the bearers. His solution, following Frege, is to say that from 'our perspective' sentences containing names of fictional characters have to do with the 'sense' of the name, rather than its 'customary reference' (possible only for speakers in the story). To adumbrate his point, we might then say that 'Hamlet rejected Ophelia' neither refers nor fails to refer to a person called Hamlet, but refers to the character, Hamlet. Hence we refer to the 'sense' of the name, 'Hamlet'—we really refer to an 'abstract entity' or 'set of properties'. I see three immediate difficulties with this argument.

First, consider some of the 'properties' of which Fanny Price is the 'set': e.g. 'loves Edmund Bertram', 'has a brother in the navy', 'disapproves of family theatricals'. It is not clear to me how Lamarque could permit the existence of these properties without allowing their bearer to slip into the same arena of discourse which permits them to be properties. Yet the only kind of entity which could fill this bill is a person. Since *ex hypothesi* Fanny Price is only a person within the 'internal perspective' it seems that these properties could only be properties from the 'internal perspective'.

Second, if a character is a set of properties then any true statement about a fictional character is analytic or necessarily true: 'If a fictional character is constituted by a set of properties then any change in the membership of the set will produce a different character. A character possesses its constituent properties essentially.'[28]

This 'essentialist' approach to character—which I regard as

[28] Ibid. 65.

incompatible with our experience of fiction, and which I shall discuss in Chapter 4—generates the third problem that when we as critical readers disagree about the nature of a particular character there might be cases in which we are forced to conclude that we are not arguing about the same character.

It might be that a character under different interpretations is assigned radically different, even incompatible, properties. If the fiction can support both interpretations we might have to concede that it projects two different characters under a single proper name. In such a case a character will acquire an identity only *relative to an interpretation*.[29]

I take it that 'if the fiction can support' really means 'if the rival interpretations are well justified or well supported in their reference to the text'. Given that, let us suppose that *Mansfield Park* 'supports' two rival interpretations of the personality of Fanny Price. Faced, say, with Trilling's view of Fanny Price as a character who is too righteous by half against Tony Tanner's argument that she is an attractively stable and quiet being, uncorrupted by the corrupt and corrupting forces around her, are we forced to conclude that there are two Fanny Prices: Trilling's Price and Tanner's Price? Are we to conclude that there are two Cordelias since on one interpretation she is a meek saint and on another the proud and obstinate daughter of a proud and obstinate man? Such disputes would make little sense unless they were disputes about the same character. Certainly two different readings of the same work might generate two very different views of the character (personality) of the character named X. But this distinction between 'character of' and 'character named' is not permitted in Lamarque's argument—the reason being that our references from the 'external perspective' do not pick out individuals but concepts.

Lamarque is led into these difficulties because he sees the following dilemma: fictional characters, being fictional, do not exist; yet they cannot be nothing. This dilemma is misleading since it suggests that we need to find a way for fictional characters to exist outside the stories or plays in which they are found. Once on this road, it might look tempting to accept the suggestion that 'in the real world' they exist as abstract entities. My objection is not simply that this leads to unacceptable consequences, but that it is

---

[29] Ibid. 69 (emphasis orig.).

generated out of a false sense of the problem. Mr Micawber is rescued from being nothing, not by being turned into an abstract entity and therefore existing as a general term (in the 'real world'), but by having his complete non-existence outside *David Copper-field* reconciled with his fully-fledged existence within it (an exist-ence that therefore permits him to have the freedom that Lamarque's confused treatment denies). To term Mr Micawber fictional is not to say that he has some kind of existence, but to say that in one sense he exists and in another sense he does not. To say that Mr Micawber exists as an abstract entity is no more a way for that character to avoid 'being nothing' than it would be to say that the character exists as a word.[30] One difficulty for my own argument of course is that in the sense that Mr Micawber exists he does not exist as a fictional character but as a real person. 'Mr Micawber is a fictional character' thus appears to belong to the external convention whereas 'Mr Micawber is impecunious' belongs to the internal convention. Whereas Ryle would insist that statements cannot be about Mr Micawber, for Lamarque the problem is supposed to be solved by treating 'Mr Micawber' as an existent entity: the Micawber-character. Unfortunately this has the disadvantage of turning 'Mr Micawber is a fictional character' into a tautology.

How then do we deal with this difficulty? Consider a rather limited analogy. Within the game of *Cluedo* Mrs Peacock and Professor Plum are people, such that when I speculate (1) 'Mrs Peacock was shot by Professor Plum in the study' this is not, and cannot be, equivalent to (2) 'the blue piece of wood was shot by the purple piece of wood with a miniature wooden gun'. Let statement (1) belong to the internal convention. From the external convention there is no person called Mrs Peacock, no killing, no gun, no study. The two conventions are linked in the sense that the external convention confirms that no murder took place and that *Cluedo* is in progress, while the 'internal' utterances depend for their sense not only on the rules of the game but on the sense such utterances would have in the investigation of an actual murder. Statement (2) is absurd and belongs neither to the external nor to

[30] Which is why the following is absurd: 'we . . . queue up patiently to see Prince Hamlet . . . thrust his sword through a curtain, fold it once again into Polonius, that foolish old garrulous proper noun', William H. Gass, *Fiction and the Figures of Life* (New York, 1972), 37.

the internal convention. However, what kind of utterance is 'Professor Plum is a piece of wood'? Outside the game there is no Professor Plum (unless *per accidens*). Within the game Professor Plum is not a piece of wood but a suspected killer. Nevertheless 'Professor Plum is a piece of wood' is not absurd in the way that (2) is. (Compare 'Micawber is a fictional character' with 'a non-existent being went to debtor's prison'.) In a sense it is true that Professor Plum is a piece of wood. Yet (*pace* Lamarque's approach) this does not mean that Professor Plum exists as a piece of wood. In the sense that Professor Plum exists he is capable of forming intentions to kill, wielding a gun, and remaining silent about the deed (these presuppositions are legitimate even though the deed is never enacted within the game). In the sense that Professor Plum does not exist—i.e. outside the internal convention appropriate to playing *Cluedo*—we cannot compensate for his non-existence by insisting that he exists in some other sense (e.g. a woody sense or as a wooden entity). After the game we are left with a purple piece of wood in our hands, much in the same way that after the film we are left with a blank screen, a projector, and a roll of celluloid. The fact we can say that 'Professor Plum is a piece of wood' no more shifts the reference from Professor Plum the suspected killer to Professor Plum the wooden being than the fact that we can say 'Micawber is a fiction' shifts the reference from a bald-headed friend of David Copperfield to a Micawber-character existing as an abstract entity.

There are of course some difficulties with this analogy. Professor Plum is a piece of wood in the same way that, discussing a road accident at breakfast, I throw a matchbox on to the table and say, 'this is the lorry'. In both cases an object is transformed by 'patterns gone with the game'.[31] In the case of fictional characters there is no entity to which we can point and say, 'let this be Mr Scrooge'. Lamarque, however, seems to need the analogue of a piece of wood in his hands so that he can say: this is what Mr Scrooge really is (a bundle of Scroogean qualities). Since on my view we are left empty-handed—for in the actual world Mr Scrooge is nothing—'Mr Scrooge' must be uttered from the internal convention and 'is a fictional character' from the external convention, such that the

[31] A phrase from Ted Hughes, 'Dick Straightup', in F. E. S. Finn (ed.), *Poets of Our Time: An Anthology* (London, 1965), 70.

statement as a whole has the force of commenting on one mode of discourse in relation to another. The absurdity is only apparent. Compare a situation in the theatre when we point to a pantomime dame and say 'she is a man'. 'She' has internal reference to, say, Widow Twankey; 'a man' switches to the external convention and refers to the actor.[32] Taken out of context, the statement is odd, if not contradictory. Yet, in the context in which the statement is likely to be uttered, the context provides a bridge between the internal and external convention such that the change in 'categories' is expressed within a type of meta-discourse.

POSSIBLE WORLDS

The above is no more than a suggestion of how an account might be developed to rescue us from the obligation to find something in the 'real' world to which our statements about fictional characters must correspond. One of the advantages Lamarque aims to procure is to relieve us of the 'problems' incurred by taking fictional characters to be individuals (according to him they are types). My argument insists that in the sense they exist, they exist as individuals, and—a point I have yet to develop—that our responses to literature are founded upon this presupposition. Another avenue to explore now is whether it is profitable to consider a fictional character as an individual in a possible world. (Lamarque's treatment is one he deliberately employs as an alternative to 'possible worlds' semantics.) As will be seen, perhaps the most that can be said for the application of 'possible worlds' semantics to literary theory is that it is fashionable—at least for those who have no qualms about purging art of aesthetic considerations. Umberto Eco, for instance, in the final essay of his collection *The Role of the Reader*, adds to the already obfuscating repertoire of the professional semiotician a clumsy attempt to apply the latest developments in modal logic.[33] A more modest attempt, along 'humane' lines, has been undertaken by Doreen Maitre, but even here there

---

[32] Thus the 'is' is not the 'is' of identity but perhaps what Arthur Danto has called the 'is' of 'artistic identification'.

[33] See Roger Scruton, *The Politics of Culture: And Other Essays* (Manchester, 1981), 40–3.

is little or no attempt to question the very premises of this enterprise.[34]

My task at this point is not an easy one, because modal logicians are not exactly in agreement about what 'possible worlds' are. So how might we go about developing the argument that fictional characters are individuals in possible worlds? First, it might be said, since a fictional character is not an actual person in the actual world, a fictional character is at least a possible person. Forget for the moment how this might be interpreted by the naïve and common reader in his search for 'believable creations'. 'Possible' here means 'not necessarily not'; and since 'necessarily' means 'true in all possible worlds', it is not true in all possible worlds that Fanny Price does not exist: there is a possible world in which Fanny Price exists. So far this clarifies little. The committed modal logician would no doubt object to anything so vulgar as a translation into 'ordinary language', but if the insights of modal theory are worth sharing we ought to be able to ask which of the following, in plain English, comes closest to expressing the thought:

(P1) There is a world other than our own in which Fanny Price exists.

(P2) There might have been a world other than the actual world in which Fanny Price exists.

(P3) Fanny Price might have existed in our world.

(P2) is ambiguous and is pulled either in the direction of (P1) or (P3) depending on which view of 'possible worlds' is adopted. According to the 'modal realism' of David Lewis, possible worlds really are 'other worlds' which, we are to understand, exist without actually existing. Some out of this infinity of 'other worlds may contain entities familiar to us, but they are 'counterparts', since no individual can occupy different possible worlds. Now this view, in so far as I understand it, throws up a number of problems which are not for examination here. My question is: what implications would this bear for treatment of fictions? Lewis himself is of little assistance here. The only reference I can find to this matter consists in his dismissal of the idea that possible worlds have anything to do with stories, or vice versa.[35] It must be immediately conceded that even if novels were treated as depicting possible worlds, this

---

[34] *Literature and Possible Worlds* (London, 1983).
[35] David Lewis, *On the Plurality of Worlds* (Oxford, 1986), 7 n.

treatment could not apply to all novels or plays since some contain impossibilities (e.g. Pirandello's *Six Characters in Search of an Author*). Indeed Aristotle remarked in the *Poetics* that it is not a fault in dramatic representation to present us with 'probable impossibilities', whereas it is a failing to present us with improbable possibilities. In her London Notebook, Simone Weil makes a similar point when she says, 'where Dickens rings most false is in the passages in which he has described the humble people of England just as they are. Why is it that reality, when set down untransposed in a book, sounds false?'[36] This, to my mind, is a crucial objection to construing literature in terms of 'possible worlds', but even if we ignore it there are still more problems, as I shall show. First, let us consider counterpart theory. On the Lewisian view of worlds (though I do not implicate Lewis in applying it to fictions) there would be a non-actual world containing a Fanny Price.

But if Fanny Price is a resident in a world other than our own (call it W2) there is immediately a problem of trans-world identification. Since, *ex hypothesi*, there is no trans-world identity, the question arises whether the Fanny Price of W2 is qualitatively indistinguishable from the Fanny Price we know to have been lifted from her humble origins in Portsmouth, later to become the mistress of Mansfield Park, and so on. Here it is already tempting to speak of Fanny Price in W2 as a counterpart of Fanny Price in our world. Yet if there were a Fanny Price in our world we would have no need of the recourse to 'possible worlds' as an explanation of her existence. Nor will it do to say that Fanny Price (W2) is a counterpart of a fictional Fanny Price in W1, since this counterpart would be another fictional Fanny Price in W2. Given that Fanny Price (W2) cannot be a counterpart of a 'worldmate' in W1, then who is this Fanny Price in W2? Presumably W2 could be a world in which a Lieutenant and Mrs Price had a child named Fanny, whose brother, William, gained promotion in the navy with the help of a Henry Crawford. Then in W3 there will be another Fanny Price who abandoned her principles and enjoyed a life of cheerful debauchery, and yet other worlds in whch she was drowned in the sea at the age of 2, or did not get born since her parents remained childless. The Fanny Price we are interested in will be one of which

---

[36] *First and Last Notebooks*, trans. Richard Rees (Oxford, 1968), 183.

everything that is true of her in *Mansfield Park* is true of her in W2. In other words, a description of W2 would consist of nothing less than a retelling of the novel. It is no more enough that there is a 'world' containing a Fanny Price in similar circumstances to those described or portrayed in the novel than it would be enough in order to justify the claim that Jane Austen's Fanny Price is a real person to indicate that there happens to be an actual person who moved from Portsmouth to Mansfield Park, Northamptonshire, had an uncle Thomas Bertram, and cousins named Edmund, Tom, Julia, and Maria. Literary narration is not reportage. If Jane Austen writes, 'Fanny always wore a yellow dress', it is not in virtue of the descriptive content of the sentence that one decides whether the sentence refers to an actual person in the actual world; rather it has to do with the intention of the work. And this intention is not a diagnosed mental state of the writer but a presupposition belonging to the institution of story-telling or novel writing. I shall come back to 'intention' later, but let us settle for now with Peter Jones's observation that the 'purposiveness' of a text 'is treated as a property of the form of the text or utterance, not as their cause or causal accompaniment; in this context, intentions and purposes are generally not taken to be the speaker's antecedent plans, inner psychological states or prior musings.'[37] Even if there is in the actual world a Fanny Price who always wears yellow dresses, the sentence 'Fanny wears yellow dresses', if it is a sentence in fiction, does not refer to a Fanny Price outside the novel; though it presumably must be the case that 'yellow dress' must mean the same as when I say 'my sister wears a yellow dress'. And, unless the novel gives us a reason for believing otherwise, place names such as 'Portsmouth', 'London', etc. must be taken in the way we would normally take them. If the Crawfords live in London we would not expect that to be a place north of Manchester (even if the novel never mentions Manchester), nor would we expect it not to have a Trafalgar Square—despite the facetious musings of William Gass in our epigraph. Equally we do not have to be told that when Fanny is out walking she has legs to walk with and lungs with which to breathe. William Gass's 'empty canvas' is a misnomer: it is already filled with our common expectations.[38]

[37] *Philosophy and the Novel* (Oxford, 1975), 183.
[38] I do not mean to suggest that there are no 'expectations' which are inappropriate. See Chs. 4 and 5.

It is of course the case that some novelists may deliberately frustrate these common expectations. But they can only do this against a background of assumptions which are normally legitimate. We can only understand or appreciate 'impossible' fictions in so far as we have some grasp of the concepts which are being violated—and perhaps some idea of the larger purpose of the work which violates them. The fact that there are different levels of meaning to be assigned to many novels and plays already casts some doubt on the value of the 'possible worlds' analysis which sticks with the surface features of story-telling in terms of mere 'events' (not that these are totally unimportant, for the 'deeper' meanings could not be reached without an elementary grasp of the events in the narrative—a matter I discuss in Chapter 6). The question is how a possible world analysis helps even at this level.

We would not even begin to understand a novel—even at the level of mere 'events'—without the common assumptions or pre-suppositions I have mentioned. It follows that these common assumptions must be written into our understanding of a possible world (if stories describe possible worlds). But these assumptions belong to our experience of the actual world. So one might as well consider the 'world' of *Mansfield Park* or of *Hard Times*, not as a self-contained cosmos belonging to another dimension, but as a realm of possibility within the actual world. The question to consider, then, is whether a different view of possible worlds—Kripke's say—can accommodate the existence of fictional characters as possible persons in alternative 'states of affairs'. In his 'Semantical Considerations on Modal Logic', Kripke himself gave a hint that it might. '[Sherlock] Holmes does not exist, but in other states of affairs he would have existed.'[39]

Presumably this suggestion means something like the following: since none of us exists as a matter of logical necessity, the world might have been peopled differently. The children I now have might not have been conceived, my wife might have given birth to different individuals, and so on. Kripke, however, has since detected a problem. In the concluding Addenda to his revised *Naming and Necessity*, he now explicitly rejects the idea that fictional characters can be included on such a 'list' of the contingently unborn. The reasons for this rejection, however, were

---

[39] In L. Linsky (ed.), *Reference and Modality* (Oxford, 1971), 65.

already implicit in the original version of his monograph. Against Lewis, Kripke maintained that statements such as 'Nixon might not have won the election' are made with reference to the actual Nixon, not to a duplicate Nixon (who did not win the election) existing in another world. If proper names are rigid designators (thus denoting the same individual in each possible world) to say that Nixon might not have existed is to say in respect of the actual Nixon that, given other states of affairs, the world would not have contained *him*. But had the world been different in that and any other consequent respect, Nixon would no more have existed as an unactualized possible individual than, things being as they are, I can now name an individual who does not exist but might have done. I might conjure up a huge list of names for the alternative children who might have been conceived at the moment of my daughter's conception, but, unless we wildly suppose that these possible children are ready-made and waiting in the wings for their appearance on the great stage of Being, there is no sense to be attached to the supposition that I would be referring to 'them'. But consider what Kripke now says with regard to his earlier comment on Sherlock Holmes:

granted that there is no Sherlock Holmes, one cannot say of any particular person that he *would have been* Sherlock Holmes, had he existed. Several distinct possible people, and even actual ones such as Darwin or Jack the Ripper might have performed the exploits of Holmes, but there is none of whom we can say that he would have *been* Holmes had he performed these exploits.[40]

If my remarks on unactualized possibles capture the spirit of Kripke's caution with the over-generous ontologies generated by talk of 'possible worlds', then some sympathy extends to the above passage. But I have the feeling that the issue he presents here is rather different. It seems as though he is trying to persuade us that Sherlock Holmes could not have existed on the grounds that some other person could not have been Sherlock Holmes. But, *ex hypothesi*, we do not gaze at possible worlds 'through a telescope' to decide questions of identity: possible worlds are stipulated. We do not therefore contemplate alternative goings-on and then try to decide whether the Holmes-like deeds are performed by Holmes.

---

[40] Saul A. Kripke, *Naming and Necessity* (Oxford, 1981), 158.

'Sherlock Holmes might have existed' must, on the Kripkean view, be treated as a matter of first stipulating that we are talking about *him* (Sherlock Holmes) and then considering ways in which the world might have been different in consequence of this—e.g. that Baker Street would have contained Holmes's residence, that there would have been a companion known as Dr Watson, and so on. This avoids the view of Holmes as an empty cloak into which different possible individuals might have fitted.

'Sherlock Holmes' is not the name of an individual who would have existed had he existed. Part of the trouble is created when Kripke begins: 'granted that there is no Sherlock Holmes'. This is not at all like 'granted that there is no Joshua Palmer' (absurdly said of a particular child who was never conceived). To speak of Sherlock Holmes is not like speaking of the contingently unborn. I can know nothing about any one of the children I might have had because there is nothing to be known. Yet I know a good many things about Holmes, including whose existence is denied by saying 'granted there is no Sherlock Holmes'. The name enjoys such wide currency because Conan Doyle's stories are well known, and not because we are all engaged in speaking of a contingently unborn man. Indeed it is difficult to avoid the temptation to say that if we acknowledge Holmes to be a character in fiction it belongs to our idea of Holmes that he could not be a person in the actual world (Kripke makes a similar point about unicorns). The temptation would have to be resisted if that meant that Holmes is a necessary non-existent; for that would be like saying that no one like Holmes could have existed. Sherlock Holmes is not an impossible object— like a round square. Yet by the routes so far considered, one cannot give an account of his existence in terms of possible worlds.

The source of all these difficulties lies in the endeavour to apply a 'possible worlds' analysis to particular characters, as though we could wrench them from the fictions in which they appear. To go too far down that road even generates the conclusion that there is a possible world in which I can coexist with Polonius, Oliver Twist, or Lady Bracknell—or another in which those three characters could sit down to supper at the same table.[41] This would be as absurd as saying that I might have existed as a fictional

---

[41] Cp. Don Mannison, 'On Being Moved by Fiction', *Philosophy*, 60/231 (Jan. 1985), 71–87.

character. (Although I might not have existed at all, I can make no sense of the supposition that I might have been merely a character in a novel.) Apart from these exotic problems, the main objection to treating fictional characters in this way is that it presupposes that we are already quite clear about what it means to pick out character X and say '*he* or someone like *him* . . .' (is a person in W2, might have existed in the actual world, would have existed if . . . , and so on) when that is precisely the problem a possible worlds analysis is supposed to solve.

FICTIONAL WORLDS

Since we cannot therefore account for the ontology of fictional characters in terms of possible worlds, and since we need to avoid the implication that characters exist, or could have existed, independently of the novel or play in which they figure, we are driven to change the focus of the problem and shift it from the existence of particular characters to the existence of the fictional world containing them. Micawber exists only in so far as there is a 'fictional world' of *David Copperfield*. The temptation to say that Micawber exists and that he does not exist can now be more properly diagnosed not as a type of semantic schizophrenia about characters but as some kind of ambivalence about the existence of fictional worlds. Since we know that *David Copperfield* is a novel we know that the 'world' of *David Copperfield* does not exist. Yet, on the other hand, it is precisely because there is such a novel by Charles Dickens, and because there is a surrounding institution of literary fiction, that we can engage with and discuss what happens in that 'world', without, for that reason alone, being mistaken or deluded. In understanding or articulating the contents of that 'world', the external convention which correctly entitles us to say that Micawber does not exist is now inappropriate, since a non-existent being cannot go to debtors' prison any more than Barkis can marry a non-existent woman.

The emphasis I have so far placed upon the idea of an 'internal convention' may misleadingly give the impression that fictional existence is merely a linguistic matter. That would be a mistake. Although I have described the internal convention as a mode of discourse, it does not follow that fictional persons only exist because, or in so far as, we can speak as if they do. What makes such talk legitimate or intelligible is our shared experience of fictional worlds. That does not mean that we have to be experiencing, or even that we have at any time experienced, the fictional world of *David Copperfield* in order to utilize the internal convention with respect to the characters. Someone who has never read the novel can still employ perfectly intelligible utterances like 'My uncle is more obsequious than Uriah Heep' or 'I am more often in debt than Mr Micawber was'. But the naturalness and legitimacy of this convention derives from the fact that in understanding literary fiction, readers do not merely understand words, any more than one who appreciates a representational painting merely perceives patches of colour. A fictional world is not a collection of words or sentences, any more than a scene in a landscape or a face in a portrait consists of daubs on canvas.

Another way of putting this is to say that a fictional world is 'transcendental'—if this word can now be rescued from the unfortunate connotation of mescaline parties and hippie fantasies of the 'swinging sixties'. Though our experience of the fictional world of a novel or play is mediated through the author's 'verbal arrangements', and if it is not mere fantasy it will be disciplined by close attention to them, the experience leads beyond 'the words on the page' such that we do not merely have an intellectual grasp of linguistic constructions but are able to 'feel into' and 'live into' the scenes, places, people, and events as they are now brought into focus. Here it may be heplful to recall Arthur Danto's point that the distinction between the work of art and its 'material substrate' is analogous in its intricacy to that between mind and body;[42] or his other analogy: that the difference between a 'basic action' and a mere bodily movement is akin to the difference between an artwork and a mere thing.[43] Though of course there is more to a work of literature than mere representation of events, places, and people—which is to say that there is more to understanding a novel or play as a work of art than simply being able to enter into an imaginative grasp of a fictional world—nevertheless that grasp of the fictional world 'transcends' the sort of experience we would have if we regarded the text just as a 'linguistic object'. Indeed it

---

[42] *The Transfiguration of the Commonplace: A Philosophy of Art* (Cambridge, Mass., 1981), 104.
[43] Ibid. 51.

will be my task in later sections of this work to indicate that there is much to our understanding of literature that is not simply verbal or propositional. What I hope will also emerge later is that the distinction between the 'material substrate' and the representational content is not properly grasped unless one appreciates that what we understand and respond to in a work of art is neither found in, nor indeed *imposed* upon, the 'material substrate'. Our negotiation is with the meaning of a representation within a particular medium. In the case of a painting that medium is not mere paint (a mistake contained in the very notion of abstract painting) any more than in the case of a novel, play, or poem the medium is mere verbal arrangements or in a musical composition the medium is mere sound. To put it roughly, a medium is already a shared understanding and a public orbit of interest without which the object of aesthetic response could have no means of speaking to us as a work of art. Time and time again I shall be driven to protest against the self-defeating absurdity of first describing works of art in a way that renders them meaningless and then trying to deal with the pseudo-puzzle of how it is possible to find them interesting or meaningful.

Yet, for all that, there is something genuinely puzzling about the idea of 'fictional worlds'. Surely, it might be said, our interest in and ability to understand fiction would be difficult to explain if the actions and events represented are to be thought of as taking place in other worlds. Yet, against this, we are tempted by phrases like 'the world of *King Lear*' for many reasons, one of which is that the goings-on in *Lear* do not belong to our historical past; they do not take place in 'our' world. This separateness from our world is reflected for instance in our puzzlement about the temporal relations between ourselves and a fictional world. It seems to be no accident that we use the present tense when speaking about the existence of fictional characters ('Hamlet is a man who . . .'). Unless the question about the existence of a fictional character is taken to be an enquiry as to whether there is, or was, an actual person upon whom the fiction is based, the language in which we dispute the existence of fictional characters is again in the present tense: we argue about whether or not Hamlet exists, not about whether or not he existed. Similarly, Wittgenstein asked: 'Can I say that a play has a time of its own, which is not a segment of historical time? i.e. I can distinguish earlier and later within it but there is *no sense* to the question whether the events in it took place, say, before or after Caesar's death.'[44]

If we choose to ignore what lies behind the question, the answer will be 'no'. The events in J. B. Priestley's *An Inspector Calls* clearly take place after Caesar's death just as clearly as they take place before the sinking of the *Titanic*. Yet it cannot be said that they *took* place after the death of Caesar or before the 1914–18 War. These events are neither of our historical past, nor of our present. Yet the curtains open, the year is 1912 in the year of our Lord, and the events are happening now—not here in the Haymarket Theatre, but 'here' in the North Midlands, neither as they were then nor as they are now, but as they are in the 'now' of the performance. The characters are neither here in the theatre, nor could they be reached by catching a train (or a time-travel machine) to Brumley. I do not mean to be whimsical. These curious anomalies seem to reside in our very experience of watching a play, and they have been far more eloquently captured by Stanley Cavell in his discussion of the 'presentness' of a fictional world. Cavell finds it plausible to say of our experience of fictional characters that they and we occupy the same time but not the same space. We do not occupy the same space in the sense that we cannot reach out and touch them: not because the distance is too great, but because 'there is no distance between us, as there is none between me and my image in a mirror'. How then could it be that we occupy the same time? The reason he gives is that we make the present of the characters our present (without making our present theirs):

And the time is always now; time is measured solely in terms of what is happening to them, for what they are doing now is all that is happening. The time is not necessarily *the* present—that is up to the playwright. But the time presented, whether the present or the past, is this moment at which an arrival is awaited, in which a decision is made or left unmade, at which the past erupts into the present, in which reason or emotion fail . . . [45]

Those remarks preface a discussion on precisely what kind of absurdity it would be were we to try to intervene in the fates of dramatis personae. But the conclusion he reaches, relevant to our

---

[44] Ludwig Wittgenstein, *Culture and Value*, ed. G. H. von Wright in collaboration with Heikki Nyman, trans. Peter Winch (Oxford, 1980), 10e.

[45] 'The Avoidance of Love', in Stanley Cavell, *Must We Mean What We Say? A Book of Essays* (New York, 1969), 334.

discussion, is that we are 'present at what is happening' (present but without a position). Since what *they* are doing is *all* that is happening, we are not there: 'the only difference between them and me is that they are there and I am not'.[46] On the face of it those remarks might look absurd, since they might be taken to suggest that fictional characters exist and we do not. But taken as a phenomenological observation on our experience of a fictional world it is difficult to beat. For the 'common sense' that raises an eyebrow to this might as well be the 'common sense' that equally dictates that the Turner landscape before me is nothing but splodges on canvas, or that the dying cadence of Mimi is nothing but a matter of wave-disturbance. Just as I cannot stroll across the grass or cross the river in Constable's *Dedham* because I am not there,[47] so I cannot rush on to the heath to reason with Lear—not because he does not exist, but because as far as the play is concerned *I* do not, and indeed cannot, if I am to understand it.

The point of this argument is not to do with the 'kind' of world a fictional world is, but with our relation to it. It is another way of explicating the fact that we cannot occupy the same possible world as a fictional character—for otherwise we should be led into the oddity of saying that it is possible for fictional characters not to be fictional or that it is possible for us to be fictional (two sides of the same false coin). Once we shift the question in the direction of our experience of fiction, it should be seen that the 'separation' between ourselves and a fictional world is not the issue if we are to give an account of the properties of such a world. I mentioned earlier that just as we are tempted by the expression 'the world of . . .', we are equally puzzled or even repelled by the idea that what the novel or play depicts is a 'world' other than our own, for this suggests that it is remote or inaccessible (in which case how should we even begin to understand a 'fictional world' and why should it be of any concern to us, morally or otherwise?). The only possible way to reconcile these seemingly opposed doubts is to insist that a fictional world is not a type of world differing from the actual world, any more than Constable's river is a different type of river from an actual one. The 'world' of *Mansfield Park* differs from our world,

[46] Ibid. 339.

[47] Nor could I cross it even if I travelled to Dedham, Essex, and crossed the river there—though there must be some connection between Dedham, Essex, and Constable's *Dedham*. (I owe this point to Anthony O'Hear.)

not in the sense that it contains different sorts of creatures from actual persons, but in the sense that we cannot be a party to anything that happens in it. Exactly what implications this has for our responses to fictional persons and fictional events will be examined later; but it is a prerequisite for our contemplation of a fictional world that we are entitled to the defeasible assumption that the persons in it are the same kind of creatures we are, and that the tears they weep, the blood they shed when pricked, will not be substantially different from our own.

2

Fiction Versus Fantasy, Pretence, and Make-Believe

It does seem that philosophers who are fond of invoking pretending have exaggerated its scope and distorted its meaning. (J. L. Austin, 'Pretending'[1])

GAMES AND LANGUAGE-GAMES

Talk of fictional worlds is not a matter of positing 'other worlds' existing within or beyond the actual world, but a reflection of the shared currency of our experience of literary representation. Although such experience involves the reader's imagination, and not just some linguistic faculty, a particular fictional world is neither a mere figment of the imagination nor a property of verbal arrangements, but the result of a collusion between the work and those who have the capacities to respond to it. Interaction between the work and reader/spectator is itself only possible against the conventions and traditions of artistic representation, which is to say that the 'ontology' of fictional worlds is not a matter of logic and metaphysics but of shared participation in the public institutions of literary practice, which bears all sorts of relations to other forms of artistic practice.

While therefore it is appropriate to adopt a 'language-game' approach, it should be remembered that Wittgenstein's coinage of this metaphor was meant to point, among other things, to the connection between uses of language and human activity, such that what belongs to a particular language-game can only be understood against the part it plays in human life, i.e. in particular activities, ceremonies, and practices, or in particular ways of life. There is thus an implied connection between the idea of a language-game and a 'form of life'. To say for instance that religious utterance belongs to a language-game means neither that it is a sort of word-

---

[1] In Donald F. Gustafson (ed.), *Essays in Philosophical Psychology* (London, 1967), 116.

game nor that the practice of religion is itself a game. But—and here is the point of the analogy—just as there is no common essence to everything we call games, so it can be misleading to model our understanding of a 'move' within a particular language-game on what seems to be a similar 'move' within another. In the case where we are concerned literally with games, the point can be illustrated as follows. 'But what if one man says that handling the ball is a foul and another says that handling the ball is not a foul? Are they contradicting each other? Surely they only are doing so if they are playing the same game, referring to the same rules.'[2]

The point of this illustration arises where D. Z. Phillips is considering, as regards religious belief, whether it makes sense to say that the non-believer 'contradicts' the believer when he says that he does not believe what the believer believes. My purpose in mentioning this is not to launch into a discussion of religious belief, but to refer to it as providing an example where utterances such as 'thanks be to God' cannot be analysed apart from their surrounding context in human life. The force of this particular utterance cannot be divorced from the part it plays in religious practice and in the life of the religious believer. Thanking God is not to be thought of in the same terms as thanking an uncle for the new bicycle or thanking the waiter when he brings the soup; nor for that matter is it like the 'thank God' said in response to winning the football pools. Thanking God is not an expression of gratitude for favours conferred or the polite acknowledgement of goods received, nor is it an exclamation. It is not said in response to particular events, but is an expression of unconditional Devotion, involving acceptance of the will of God, and this involves a religious attitude to the whole of life and a religious conception of the world. To say that such utterances cannot be understood apart from the language-game of religion is not to say that religious discourse is a sort of exclusive code sealed off from ordinary discourse. For what we might like to call 'ordinary discourse' is not something apart from the language-games that comprise it; rather, it is to say that misunderstanding results from thinking of religious statements on the model of, say, empirical claims, scientific hypotheses, or metaphysical speculations.

The reason for invoking a language-game approach to deal with

[2] D. Z. Phillips, *Faith and Philosophical Enquiry* (London, 1970), 85.

the problem of our discourse about and experience of literary fiction is not to suggest that there is a single form of discourse to be identified and described here (an approach I have resisted), but to indicate the absurdities involved in trying to give an account of the 'status' of 'statements within or about the novel' by recourse to the wrong models—and, what is part of the same mistake, by failing to take account of what distinguishes our dealings with works of literary fiction as works of art from our dealings with other uses of language involving fictitious or non-existent objects. I wish to bring out the importance of this by considering what I regard as Kendall Walton's misguided assimilation of fictional discourse and of our experience of literature to 'games of make-believe'.[3]

Whereas on my view we can refer to and make true or false statements about fictional persons, for Walton 'it is true that Crusoe survived a shipwreck' really means 'it is fictional that Crusoe survived . . .'. The reason that we usually drop the intensional operator 'it is fictional that', according to Walton, is that assertions like 'Crusoe survived' are a matter of pretence. That is, the speaker pretends to assert that Crusoe survived a shipwreck or, what for Walton amounts to the same thing, he makes it fictional of himself that he is actually asserting something. This 'pretence' makes him an 'actor in a game of make-believe'. The speaker, that is, belongs to 'the world of a game of make-believe which he plays with the novel, a game in which the novel serves as a prop'.[4] Furthermore, one does not have to make such utterances in order to be playing a game of make-believe with the novel, for just to read a novel in the spirit of novel-reading is itself to play a game of make-believe in which the reader 'pretends to believe' that, for instance, Tom Sawyer attended his own funeral.

This analysis, which I do not find convincing, may be prompted by some observations on our experience of literary fiction which overlap with my own position.

It seems to me that Walton makes a shrewd and important point by saying that as appreciators of literary fiction we do not promote

---

[3] Walton has written a series of articles, but quotations are taken from 'How Remote are Fictional Worlds from the Real World?', *Journal of Aesthetics and Art Criticism*, 37/1 (Autumn 1978), 11–24, and 'Fearing Fictions', *Journal of Philosophy*, 73/1 (Jan. 1978), 5–27. His book *Mimesis as Make-Believe: On the Foundations of the Representational Arts* (Harvard University Press) was published too late for me to take account of it here.

[4] 'How Remote are Fictional Worlds?', 21.

fictions to the level of reality but, instead, we descend to the level of the fiction. Thus we have a 'dual standpoint':

We, as it were, see Tom Sawyer both from inside his world and from outside of it. And we do so simultaneously. The reader is such that, fictionally, he knows that Tom attends his own funeral and he is such that, fictionally, he worries about Tom and Becky in the cave. At the same time the reader knows that no such persons as Tom and Becky ever existed. There is no inconsistency here, and nothing very mysterious. But this dual standpoint which appreciators take is, I believe, one of the most important functions of the human institution of fiction ... Theorists have long floundered in the gap between our two perspectives, trying doggedly to merge them into one (for example, our perspective is sometimes thought of as a unitary one which is some kind of compromise between 'under-distancing' and 'over-distancing'). But once the duality of our standpoint is recognized, things begin to fall into place.[5]

If things fall into the place carved out by this correct identification of a common source of confusion one should be less inclined I think to accept Walton's analysis of fictional discourse. His hint of 'two perspectives' seems to confirm my argument about two different modes of discourse rather than justifying his belief that statements about fictional persons are pretended assertions. In fact, contrary to his own warning, his theory of fictional discourse does suffer from the temptation to merge these two perspectives into one. From my argument that 'Hamlet does not exist' and 'Hamlet thought that *P*' do not contradict one another, I claimed in the previous chapter, *pace* Anthony Kenny, that to say 'Hamlet's thoughts are imaginary like his existence' is a needless and illicit compromise. Walton's translation of 'Crusoe survived' into 'it is fictional that Crusoe survived' seems to point to a similar mistake. Where Kenny relies on the word 'imaginary' to adjudicate between what he has assumed to be two rival statements, Walton relies on the *deus ex machina* of the fictional operator. Yet the operator explains nothing. It does not confer intelligibility upon an other-wise unintelligible sentence, since we must already understand that sentence in order to understand it when prefixed by an operator. Walton realizes of course that someone who says 'Crusoe survived a shipwreck' is not necessarily meaning to assert 'it is fictional that . . .', which is why on his account 'Crusoe survived' then becomes

[5] Ibid. 21–2.

an 'assertion'—i.e. a pretended or make-believe assertion. He is driven in this direction partly because his treatment of discourse about fictional persons is never sufficiently emancipated from the bogus need to show how they can be accommodated within what Wittgenstein called 'the language-game of giving information'. If you take that for your model of all intelligible utterance then other forms of discourse have to be explained (where they are not simply dismissed) in terms of how they do or do not measure up to it.

While there is something true and important about saying that as appreciators we 'descend to the level of the fiction', that descent is only a descent into pretence if the fiction itself is to be regarded as a matter of pretence. Gareth Evans, who incorporates Walton's starting-point into his own analysis of fictional discourse, claims with a confidence I cannot share that 'it is fairly easy to see that a story-teller is pretending to have knowledge of things and episodes. But we must realize that audiences of novels, plays, films etc. are also drawn into a pretence.'[6] By 'story-teller' Evans seems to mean the person who gives an oral delivery to an audience, and this effectively ignores the problems which arise when we consider, as we shortly shall, precisely who is supposed to be doing the pretending in a story-book or novel. But even in the former case, things are not as simple as they appear. There are two distinct ways of referring to 'the story-teller'. There is the actual man, Karl Deepvoice, who happens to be here doing the job, and there is 'the story-teller' as a role the man occupies. If someone were to say of the actual man, Karl Deepvoice, that he is 'pretending to have knowledge of things and episodes' (that he 'pretends to be informa-tionally-related . . . to the events he relates'[7]), he would surely be demonstrating his ignorance or misunderstanding. Either he does not know that Deepvoice is telling a story, or, like Thomas Gradgrind, he simply does not understand or appreciate the kind of activity telling a story is (he does not know the difference between telling stories and telling lies). If, on the other hand, we refer to the story-teller as a role (as in football we refer to 'the centre-forward' as a position), then it is still not clear how the concept of pretence gets application here: for it is a role *within* the

---

[6] Gareth Evans, *The Varieties of Reference*, ed. John McDowell (Oxford, 1982), 353.

[7] Ibid. 359 n. 31.

fiction (as 'centre-forward' is a role or playing position within the game of football). And it belongs to our understanding of that role, at least as traditionally conceived, that the teller does not pretend to have knowledge, but actually does have knowledge of the persons and events he describes.

The teller, as a role, is 'internally related' to the characters and their circumstances, much as the centre-forward (or perhaps a better analogy: the referee) is 'internally related' to the other playing positions, or 'roles', on the field. In other words Deepvoice is not speaking as Deepvoice but as a teller-within-a-fiction. He reports, describes, and perhaps—using a suitable range of accents or dialects—even mimics the characters (who to him are not fictional). The pretence theorist will now be itching to say that on this view it follows that Deepvoice pretends to be the teller, and, accordingly, that we pretend he is. But if speaking from within a role has to be construed as pretence simply because that role does not exist outside the institution of story-telling, then should we not also say that Jimmy Toeboot pretends to be centre-forward, and that we pretend he is, simply because without the institution of football there would be no centre-forwards? Does Charles Dutoit pretend to conduct and we pretend that he does, while also 'pretending' of course that the sounds the orchestra make are melodies?

A similar objection can be raised against the idea of a novel 'giving information' within 'the scope of a pretence'. Who is supposed to be giving such information, the narrator or the author? If the former, then, as I shall argue in Chapter 5, the narrator is as fictional as the persons and events in the novel. The narrator no more pretends to have knowledge of 'things and episodes' than David Copperfield pretends to run away to Dover. Of course if the narrator is ironic, or deliberately insincere, the narrator may pretend various things, but that is precisely the kind of distinction a pretence theory would have trouble with. To say on the other hand that it is the author who is pretending to have knowledge of this or that, invites the riposte (not as circular as it looks): 'no he isn't, he's writing a novel'. Given that the intention of novel writing is not to give information, the novelist is not inviting the readers' collusion in a falsehood. The tacit existential disclaimer that prefaces and accompanies our experience of fiction entails not that the statements describing the persons and events are thereby false (thus requiring a pretence that they are true) but that it would be an *ignoratio elenchi* to consider them to be false. The non-existence of fictional characters no more requires a pretence that they exist than the non-existence of Neptune requires us, in looking at a painting of Neptune, to make-believe that it is a photograph.[8]

By fixing the analysis on 'assertions', 'statements', or 'propositions' in fiction, the search is then on for some strategy of making sense of them that has little to do with our engagement with works of art, as such.[9] It is then made to sound as if the solution lies in assigning such 'statements' to a general class of utterances which give information (or, in the jargon, serve as 'informational props') within the scope of a pretence. The use of proper names in fiction, for instance, then becomes a matter of 'empty singular terms used connivingly in a linguistic game of make-believe'.[10] And since the emphasis is on the logical status of statements, assertions, or propositions, our commerce with literary fiction finds itself in the same rag-bag as the 'let's pretend' of children playing mummies and daddies, cowboys and Indians, or games with mud pies, all of which are cited by Walton as examples of fictional worlds: 'There is roughly a distinct fictional world corresponding to each novel, play, game of make-believe, dream or daydream.'[11]

Walton accomplishes this by defining a fictional world as a 'collection of fictional truths': fictional truths in turn are 'fictionally true propositions'. There is, however, a further distinction drawn between fictional truths and make-believe truths. The latter are a species of fictional truths which are governed by the participants' agreement in principles regulating a game of make-believe, as when children agree to let globs of mud be pies. The principles then may generate further truths which can be discovered to be make-believedly the case as the game proceeds.

An immediate question that arises, even taking this analysis on its own terms, is precisely how we are to extrapolate from the 'let's

---

[8] Walton, however, does take the view that we make-believe that we see e.g. a man in a painting of a man. (See 'Pictures and Make-Believe', *Philosophical Review*, 82/3 (July 1973), 283–319, 'Are Representation Symbols?', *Monist*, 58/2 (Apr. 1974), 285–93, and 'Points of View in Narrative and Depictive Representation', *Noûs*, 10/1 (Mar. 1976), 49–61.)

[9] For further exploration of this criticism see Colin Falk, 'Fictions and Reality', *Philosophy*, 63/245 (July 1988), 363–71.

[10] Evans, *The Varieties of Reference*, 353.

[11] 'Fearing Fictions', 12.

pretend' that broomsticks are horses and that globs of mud are pies, to the pretence alleged to be involved in literary fiction. There is no entity in the actual world that entitles the aspiring make-believer to say 'X = Nicholas Nickleby'. In the case of a play in performance there are of course actors, such that Sylvester Lightfoot 'is' Laertes and Sir Anthony Treadboard 'is' Hamlet. But if the idea of pretence here is invoked to explain how it is possible for the audience to understand what is happening in the fictional world it fails lamentably, since the audience must already know they are in the presence of a fictional world, and understand something of what is going on in that world, in order to understand the alleged pretence: for the pretence is not that Laertes kills Hamlet but that Sylvester Lightfoot kills Sir Anthony Treadboard. It is because I know that in the fictional world Laertes is attacking Hamlet that I know the actors are 'pretending' to fight. Here it should be remembered that if we have need to tell a young child that a stage fight is 'pretend', this is likely to be because the child thinks that one actor is attacking another actor. The child has not yet acquired the distinction between actor and character (which itself is part of understanding what it is for those events to be taking place in a fictional world).

Our reassuring murmur to the child is therefore just that: reassurance. It has neither the aim nor the function of anything that might be called aesthetic education. All we have done is to tell the child what is *not* happening (in the material world of the stage). But the understanding we want him to acquire of what *is* happening in the fictional world cannot be acquired through thinking of fiction in terms of pretence. For there is no way of 'tunnelling out' from the material elements of a representation. To invite him to 'pretend' (i.e. 'make-believe') that the pretence is not a pretence only to invite him to make-believe that one actor is attacking the other actor, which is not the kind of thing we are doing at all in attending to the content of the representation. The 'pretended actions' of the actors are the material elements of the representation as the streaks of paint on the scenery are material elements of the representation of Elsinore Castle. But it is our perception of what is represented that informs our perception of the material elements of its composition, not the other way round. We can no more tunnel out from the latter to the former than we can proceed from a microscopic examination of bodily movements to a conception of those movements as human acts or actions.

I have used inverted commas round 'pretended actions' to distance myself from the hypothesis I have been examining, since I am not happy even to grant that 'pretended actions' is a correct description of the actor's actions *qua* material elements of the representation, any more than I would grant that the colours and shapes painted on the scenery pretend to be Elsinore Castle. Though it will take the rest of this chapter to elicit the real source of what I can only call the philistinism of the approach I am criticizing, I must add a further comment about acting as pretence.

What may divert critical attention away from the vulgarity of that conception is that the very word 'pretence' (as Austin points out in our epigraph) has been grossly overworked. By being stretched to cover quite different phenomena, it has blurred important distinctions between, say, an impersonation, a leg-pull, an affectation, a pose, an act of mimicry, and the art of mime. Even outside the context of art, there is a limit to what can properly be regarded as pretence. A characteristically witty example given by Austin: 'To pretend to be a bear is one thing, to roam the mountain valleys inside a bearskin rather another.'[12] Austin concedes that a pretence can be 'elaborate', but there are cases which would be more accurately termed ones of 'impersonation', 'imposture', or 'disguise'. Though distinguishable from pretence, these cases bear some relation to it, and that fact itself suggests the inappropriateness of its use to describe our commerce with fiction in art.

If someone insists that Sir Laurence pretends to be Richard III, even to describe the 'pretence' as 'elaborate' would be stretching things a bit far (and it would be near insanity to call it a case of impersonation, imposture, or disguise). 'Let's-pretending' of course is not a case of pretence (proper) but it is derivative, or, as Austin calls it, a parasitic case.[13] So unless the word 'pretend' in the 'let's pretend' case is a mere pun, there must be *some* connection with the ordinary idea of pretence. And if that is the case we should perhaps ask ourselves why it would sound so obviously absurd, if not downright insulting, if a drama critic were to write, 'Sir John

[12] 'Pretending', in Gustafson, *Essays*, 113.
[13] Ibid. 113 n. As Austin also points out, 'pretending to be' in the 'let's pretend, make-believe, party-forfeit way, is a very recent usage, perhaps no older than Lewis Carroll' (ibid. 111).

Gielgud's pretence at the Old Vic last night was really superb', or 'Redgrave pretended to be Lear really well'. (Indeed it would be just as misguided to use such terminology even to commend the performance of a mime artist, or, for that matter, a mimic.)

The predictable objection will be that 'pretence' here is a logical matter and nothing to do with what the actor does well or badly. But, as has been seen, I do not accept it as a logical description either of the idea of the actor 'being' the character or of what the actor is doing during the execution of his role.

MAKE-BELIEVE AS FANTASY

So far, my remarks have been concerned with difficulties internal to the pretence/make-believe approach. More needs to be said about what is wrong with the approach itself. What I first wish to show is that the pretence/make-believe view involves a different notion of a fictional world from my own. Before that, it should be noted that the role of make-believe is not entirely clear in Walton's treatment since at times it seems that make-believe is simply the mental analogue of pretence (which of course is itself a perform-ance) such that if X pretends that P, Y in colluding with the pretence make-believes (i.e. 'pretends to believe') that P.[14] At other times 'make-believe' is given a wider extension, as when we are told that the participants 'belong to a world of make-believe [distinct from the fictional world of the novel] . . . in which the novel serves as a prop'.[15] Though the second formulation leads more abruptly to a view of novel-reading as fantasy-engagement, it will be seen, I think, that the seeds of fantasy are already sown with the first formulation. However, to avoid possible misunder-standing I shall refer to make-believe (1) and make-believe (2).

The view of fictional worlds as collections of fictional truths is tailor-made for the cognitive attitude of make-believe (1). The propositional attitude we have towards what we regard as true statements is that of belief. The construal of 'statements' in fiction on the model of information-giving statements therefore requires the reader's adoption of an attitude which serves as a surrogate for

---

[14] 'Readers pretend to *believe* that Tom attended his own funeral . . . the reader is such that fictionally he believes this.' ('How Remote are Fictional Worlds?' 21.)
[15] Ibid.

belief, since he knows such statements to be literally false. Make-believe (1) seems to be intended to serve as a surrogate, not in its being a kind of belief (akin to Price's 'half-belief'[16]) but in its being some kind of mental pretence that what we read describes what is in fact the case. But this is as far removed from engaging with a fictional world as in my previous example of make-believing that the actors in a play are not pretending. All the reader is then doing is to enter into a fantasy that false statements are true, just as children enter into a fantasy, collective or private, that broomsticks are horses or that mud pats are pies. That is not to say that fantasy is delusion. The children are not deluding themselves that one thing is another. But what they are doing is neither a response to, nor an attempt to understand, an imagined situation. Their make-believe serves no purpose other than the sheer enjoyment of make-believe, which necessarily oversimplifies or blots out the constraints of reality. In fact it hardly seems appropriate to refer to the intentionality of make-believe in terms of 'fictional worlds'. For, though all fiction is to some degree logically indeterminate (we do not ask what the Mona Lisa's legs look like: though of course that does not mean she is legless), the child's interest and attention is purely centred on the thought *that* the broomstick is a horse and *that* he is riding it, and the intentional context in which the thought is regarded as true is so vague and schematic as to be opaque to the legitimate expectations and quests of the imagination in 'realizing' the thought. By contrast consider the following passage taken from an undistinguished novel I have purloined from my young daughter's bookshelf:

The pony was surprised and laid back his ears warningly. Patsy spoke to him and, holding on tightly, she kicked him on.

He trotted forward eagerly, and Patsy marvelled at his bouncy action and clung on for dear life. He soon broke into a canter and his stride was long and smooth. His ears went forward and the canter soon became a gallop.

Patsy clutched at his mane and pressed her knees firmly into the pony's flanks. The wind fanned her cheeks and blew back her hair. She leant forward and patted him encouragingly.

Round and round the field they galloped. Patsy began to enjoy the sensation and found it surprisingly easy to stay on his smooth back. As for

---

[16] H. H. Price, *Belief* (London, 1969), 302–14. (Walton explicitly denies that make-belief is half-belief: 'Fearing Fictions', 7.)

the pony, he seemed to be enjoying it too for his ears were forward and he tossed his head from time to time.

Patsy felt like giving a loud 'Tally ho' but restrained herself. She could hear nothing except the wind rushing past her ears and the thunder of the pony's hooves. She could not have stopped him even if she had wanted to and he kept on lengthening his stride till he was rushing round as if chased by a wild bull.[17]

Clearly this is not written by any 'Shakespeare of the novel'. But, trite and commonplace though the writing may be, with the usual trail of clichés ('clinging on for dear life', 'fanned her cheeks', 'the thunder of the pony's hooves'), even this extract shows a level of realization we would not expect to be present in the 'gaming' case. The reader is at least given some insight into the demeanour of the pony and the feelings, sensations, thoughts, and emotions of the rider as she enters into a relationship with a wilful creature that is not as predictable or obedient as a stick of wood. The broomstick rider, though in for an easy ride, could hardly find it 'surprisingly easy to stay on his smooth back' (and even from this small extract you may be sufficiently interested to know that the girl gets thrown off!).

Now of course in playing games of make-believe, whether of cowboys and Indians, mummies and daddies, riding broomstick-horses, or playing with mud pies, children may develop the scenario in such a way that it takes on sufficient richness and emotional complexity to be called a fictional world, but here surely they leave the province of make-believe and enter into drama. Though it may not be easy to know the precise point at which play ends and drama begins, that does not mean that there isn't a real distinction. But if we must use the term 'world' to cover what is thought to be the case within the scope of a game of make-believe, or even within, as Walton claims, 'dreams and daydreams', then this fails to provide a distinction between fictional worlds and fantasy worlds. Indeed his use of make-believe (2) collapses straight into fantasy. If the reader belongs to 'the *world* of a game of make-believe he plays with the novel' (my emphasis), then the novel is merely subservient to the game of fantasy, or fantasy world of the reader. It becomes, in Walton's own words, 'a prop'. This is an infelicitous though instructive metaphor. A theatrical prop, like the

[17] Joan Hallett, *The Bucking Chestnut* (London, 1950), 28.

other accoutrements of the actor's trade, belongs to the 'material world' of the stage, which is not the intentional object of perception in so far as we are attending to the play. However, props are also used by stage magicians; and there is much in the make-believe view to suggest that reading a novel is like performing a conjuring trick.

IMAGINATION

I have discussed the price we pay for ignoring the aesthetic context which distinguishes our experience of works of art from our participation in games of 'let's pretend'. More now needs to be said about that context. The invitation extended to us by a work of art is addressed to the imagination rather than to our capacity for make-believe. The most important aspects of that contention, for our purposes, will be seen to lie in the moral implications it generates. But for now some epistemological groundwork is necessary.

Imagination, like make-believe, is distinct from belief, but in a different way. Imagination takes the form of thinking *of* P rather than thinking *that* P. Even when imagining takes the construction 'imagining that' it does not follow that imagining that P is the same as, or entails, thinking that P.[18] I can imagine that it is snowing without thinking that it is, or imagine that I am in Switzerland without thinking that I am there. The contrast here seems to be between what Roger Scruton has call 'unasserted' and 'asserted' thought[19]—which is essentially a distinction between entertaining the thought that P and judging ('inwardly asserting') that P. The terminology of 'asserted' and 'unasserted' originally derives from Frege's well-known argument that a particular sentence can have either an asserted or unasserted occurrence in what someone says without the meaning of the sentence being different in each case. The sentence 'it is raining' means the same whether I use it to assert that it is raining or whether the sentence occurs 'unasserted' in 'Harold believes that it is raining' or 'if it is raining

---

[18] A recent discussion of distinctions between imagination and belief and between imagining, pretending, and supposing can be found in Alan White, *The Language of Imagination* (Oxford, 1990).

[19] Roger Scruton, *Art and Imagination: A Study in the Philosophy of Mind* (London, 1982), 84–106.

then I am a monkey's uncle'. Just as Frege concluded that assertedness is not part of the meaning of a sentence, so Scruton argues, via an analogy between mental judgement and the overt act of speech, that the content of a proposition must be the same whether judged to be true or whether simply entertained. In other words, what is 'before the mind' in entertaining *P* is the same as what is 'before the mind' in believing *P* (otherwise it would be impossible to judge that a proposition being entertained is true).

Though this does not yet elicit the real point of my journey, when we apply this distinction to the problem of fiction the bare fact that we neither believe, nor are required to believe, that fictional occurrences are actual occurrences constitutes no impediment to our ability to understand them (though of course there is the problem of emotional response, to be taken up in Chapters 4 and 5). Since it is literally inconceivable that a non-existent man should perform the deeds of Hamlet, in attending to the play we think *of* Hamlet as an existent man without thinking *that* there is any such person. Not only therefore do we not need the concept of make-believe or pretence to substitute for, or compensate for, the absence of belief involved in the imaginative grasp of fictional worlds, the former misconceives the nature of literary fiction and, accordingly, disfigures our experience of it.

In being directed to the imagination, a genuine work of art calls upon capacities for understanding which are not concerned with the literal truth or literal falsity of what is represented. Imagination, as Kant put it, is indifferent to existence. And here, as later, I stand firmly within the Kantian tradition that regards 'disinterestedness' as a distinguishing feature of the aesthetic attitude, such that the understanding we have of works of art arises from contemplation purged of practical or appetitive interests. This entails neither 'aestheticism' nor the denial that our experience of art makes a difference to our practical and moral engagement with the world. But that is not a matter for this chapter. What it does mean is that in our engagement with a work of art we are left free to contemplate objects and occurrences and explore their meanings and significances, as represented, to a degree and in a manner neither possible nor appropriate (nor in some cases morally justifiable) were the objects or occurrences actual.

This liberation from the constraints of literal truth, or truth as correspondence, is not a freedom from truth to life or truth to experience, which is another reason for distinguishing imagination from the fantasy of make-believe (as Collingwood did in his argument that make-believe belongs neither to genuine nor to serious art, but to 'amusement-art' *à la* Hollywood).[20] Moon-eyed romances, blood-and-guts thrillers, or political dramas with a tub-thumping message may be only too 'true to life' if some sort of literal 'realism' is taken as the criterion, and if it does not matter that by oversimplifying emotion they cater to and gratify the crudest levels of feeling or sentiment compatible only with the barest minimum of thought. The 'worlds' presented are recognized at a glance—either because, like chocolate-box lids and picture postcards, they strive for 'accuracy' and resemblance to the actual world in the most superficial of respects, or because, like mono-chrome strip-cartoons and cardboard cut-outs, they reduce the world to the perception of the simpleton, allowing the reader/spectator like a child in kindergarten to paint on them the colours of his fancy.

The essence of my dispute with the pretence theorists comes down in the end to a matter of how we are to describe the kind of relationship that must exist between the reader and the work for real understanding to be possible. In games of pretence the scope of thought is narrowed to the scope of the pretence, and this makes a difference to the kind of thought involved. In the first place, pretence is a quite different kind of concept from that of imagination. As Alan White puts it, 'Pretence shows an ability to perform, whereas imagination shows an ability to conceive.'[21] Not only is it possible to pretend without imagining and imagine without pretending, but even where a pretence may be informed or assisted by the 'performer's' capacity for imagining for instance that the broomstick he is 'riding' is a horse, the thought is nevertheless 'blinkered' to wider considerations that would or might inhibit the pretence. The broomstick-horse rider may in some sense imagine that he is galloping through Sherwood Forest or that he is racing in the Grand National, but he is not required, indeed it might be counter-productive, to imagine what it really would be like to do these things. Both for onlooker and participant, the thought of the 'rider's' being in such-and-such a set of circumstances is bought on the cheap. The rallying cry of 'let's pretend' is not an invitation to participate in a fictional world where actions and consequences and the circumstances in which they arise demand some sort of emotional credibility. Instead, it is more like a password that entitles the participants to bypass what in literature or painting would have to be shown.

What I mean by 'showing' will be made clearer in Chapter 8. But now is as good a time as any to stake the claim that 'showing' does not necessarily mean 'describing'. To be shown something by or through a work of art, while not involving belief in the actual existence of what is represented, nevertheless requires that we can find in the representation something that compels a certain kind of assent. In the vernacular this assent is sometimes described as 'credibility' or 'plausibility', though these words in connoting 'believability' can for that reason be misleading, if, that is, we take them to be the same sort of 'believability' that applies in the case of, say, a statement made to the police. The duty officer's concern with believability is a concern with the literal truth of statements purporting to give information about some matter of fact or empirical state of affairs. In art, assent neither contradicts nor conflicts with the disbelief that Coleridge wrongly thought we have to suspend, since it is not a matter of assenting to the truth of a proposition we believe to be false.

In W. H. Auden's poem, 'Victor: A Ballad', there is a quality and power that sustains our attention and thought, without the thought, or the pretended thought, that the persons or events are actual.

> He stood there above the body,
>   He stood there holding the knife;
> And the blood ran down the stairs and sang,
>   'I'm the Resurrection and the Life.'[22]

By the time we have reached this stanza the tension has been so great, partly because of the rhythm in which the thoughts are conveyed and partly because what seemed to start off in the spirit of comedy takes on a darker aspect in the ten stanzas preceding the realization of the deed, that our horror is strangely combined with relief. Victor, driven to religious obsession through his upbringing

---

[22] *W. H. Auden: A Selection by the Author* (Harmondsworth, 1958), 51.

at the hands of a cold, religious fanatic, has carried out 'divine' punishment against his wife Anna, who has behaved like Jezebel. Yet it is not our awareness of these circumstances alone (which we know not to be 'real') that compels assent to what seems to be the inevitability of the killing (in 'reality' she might have escaped). Rather, it has to do with the way that the feeling of inevitability is contained in the music and imagery of the verse.

When therefore we reach '. . . the blood ran down the stairs and sang, | "I'm the Resurrection and the Life" ', the terrible beauty of these lines strikes us not only as metaphor but, in the same instant, as a 'literal' perception (perhaps seen through Victor's eyes). Our pity for the victim, now combined with fear and disgust at the sickening vividness of the 'literal' perception of the singing blood, thus coexists with our pity for the killer, a pity brought to resolution in the next stanza:

> They tapped Victor on the shoulder,
> They took him away in a van;
> He sat as quiet as a lump of moss
> Saying, 'I am the Son of Man.'

Since in the earlier part of the poem Victor is a figure of fun, both for his associates and for ourselves, it is as though we have some complicity with the way things turn out. The price of our new understanding of Victor is a sense of guilt at the earlier conception it forces us to abandon. Indeed at a 'live' poetry reading, there is a point at which the laughter of the audience turns to embarrassment.

The understanding we have here, though it is not and cannot be totally unconnected with an awareness of the events and occurrences which might be described in paraphrase, has nothing whatever to do with believing or being tempted to believe, nor therefore with 'pretending to believe', what such so-called fictional propositions or fictional statements would assert. What we find convincing, and do not pretend to find convincing unless we have failed abysmally to understand it, is—as Leavis would surely put it—the way the poem works as a poem. And it is through the medium of poetry, not by 'information' given in a pretence, that we are led to feeling and discovery.

Similarly, what we are given in a novel or a play is an experience; and what we seek in the attempt to understand the work is something which will give unity and coherence to our experience of it. Faced with a difficult or complex work, our immediate task may even be to make enough sense of it to feel that we are in the presence of something intelligible enough to be called a fictional world. And, except in cases where our access to the work is marred by the sort of linguistic difficulty some pupils have in reading Shakespeare, the 'intelligibility' here is not simply an intellectual, but an emotional, and perhaps moral, matter.

One of the reasons for calling a fictional world a world is not simply that it provides an intentional context in which this or that can be said to be true, but that we are led through a writer's handling of his chosen medium to experience characters and their circumstances within some sort of *Gestalt*. In order to accept the invitation to the imagination we therefore must be prepared to enter into a relationship with the work, such that our understanding of the characters needs to be as genuine and convincing as our understanding of actual people. This is not to say that our understanding of fictional characters is in all respects like our understanding of actual people, though I shall pursue that *caveat* in later chapters. What I want to draw attention to here is that the 'make-believe' view cannot give an adequate picture of the reader's relationship to the work; for that relationship cannot be understood in isolation from the traditions and practices that make it possible.

The pretence/make-believe view seems to pose the problem in this way: think first of the huge gulf between the 'reality' on the one hand, and the appearance, the illusion of fiction, on the other. The reader's apparently intelligible commerce with that illusion must therefore be explained, and explained in such a way that his dealings with it can be brought down from the clouds and accounted for in terms of his commerce with reality. Thus we must interpose between the real world of the reader and the fictional world of the text a set of conventions for converting apparently illusory 'information' into information which he regards as true— not within some gaseous or ghostly 'realm',[23] but within a game which, at bottom, is no different from other games of pretence.

The huge paradox here, as I have tried to show, is that such an attempt to bring fiction down to earth actually turns it into fantasy.

---

[23] 'The fictional world is not to be construed as a realm in which it is *true* that Crusoe survived' ('How Remote are Fictional Worlds?', 16, emphasis orig.).

And the reason for this is that it has a myopic view of what does interpose between the reader and the text—or since 'interpose' suggests a model I wish to reject entirely, better to say that this type of theory (not a million miles away from the semiotic view) overlooks the cultural context of our experience and understanding of works of art. What the reader is immersed in is not a set of conventions regulating the catch-all category of games of 'let's pretend', but a community of feeling, thought, and sensibility that sustains and is sustained by the creation of, and response to, works that are only intelligible to beings who are initiated into that community. What Walton narrowly calls 'the human institution of fiction' (though in the sense that he uses 'fiction' to cover practically anything that is strictly speaking not a matter of fact, it is also too wide) would be better termed 'the human institution(s) of art'. Our understanding of the existential status of literary fictions does not take place in what Evans describes as a *'linguistic* game of make-believe', but within a language-game in the Wittgensteinian sense. And if we want to know how our dealings with literary fictions are tied to the real world, we should do better to look there rather than to the barrenness of the mere application of logical theory. For novels, plays, and poems (as well as musical compositions, operas, sculptures, and ballets) do indeed exist, and so do the traditions and practices within which they have their life.[24]

The reader who reads with understanding does not belong to 'the world of a game of make-believe' but to a community of readers who seek meaning and truth in fictional representations. It is such a concern for meaning and truth that is the basis of criticism, which, despite some present fashions, is neither a personal whim nor an abstract exercise feeding on a remoteness from the common reader. Literary criticism is intersubjective and testable—testable not in accordance with some in-theory of criticism, but in virtue of how it enables the common reader to experience and re-experience a fictional world with greater understanding. It will be my task to show how such understanding is not only compatible with, but necessitates, moral understanding. But such a view cannot be derived from the positions so far rejected.

[24] I shall say more about the import of regarding art as a 'form of life' in Ch. 8.

3
The Moral Attitudes

The idea of a blame-free world does not seem to make sense.
(Mary Midgley, 'The Flight from Blame'[1])

DEEDS AND DOERS

In Chapter 4 I will argue in more detail that in responding to
literary fiction we do and must have moral responses to fictional
characters. It is unintelligible to suppose that we could gain access
to understanding representations of human action by thinking of
such action in a way which is radically different from the way we
perceive and understand the actions of human beings. Despite their
differences the literary theories discussed in Chapter 1 require the
reader to think of the actions of fictional characters in terms of
their function either in a 'sign system', a metaphorical labyrinth, or
in an interweaving texture of symbolic or poetic ideas.

But unless they are understood as actions how can they have any
'textual' or literary function? What sense could we make of *King
Lear* without understanding that Edmund deceives his father and
his brother? Precisely what sense could we make of such 'deception'
if it were not to be thought of as a human act? To be sure, the
deception Edmund engages in is 'thematically related' to other acts
of deception in the play: the deception of Lear by Goneril and
Regan, Lear's own self-deception, and the benign 'deception' we
witness as Edgar prevents his father from committing suicide. But
these thematic relations can only be appreciated if we know what
we are relating to what.

The idea we shall encounter in the next chapter is that our
understanding of the actions of fictional characters is understanding minus our moral attitudes: we cannot intelligibly engage in
moral approval or disapproval of fictional characters. There is a
very deep confusion here which goes far beyond any problems to
do with literary fiction: it is I think a misconception about what

---

[1] *Philosophy*, 62/241 (July 1987), 287.

actions are and how we interpret and understand them; in short, a misconception about the very nature of human life.

MORAL ATTITUDES AS MERE FEELINGS

To penetrate the source of this confusion, the rest of this chapter is a philosophical digression into a discussion of the moral attitudes and their involvement in interpersonal understanding. Indeed it seems reasonable to think that one of the reasons that such confusions about fiction rarely get challenged is that there is a general tendency, even among some philosophers (or should one say especially among some philosophers), to think that moral 'evaluation' is in one way or another distinct from our perception and understanding of human conduct. 'Blaming' for instance has been treated as though it were some sort of added extra, and has been wrongly equated with hatred or punishment. The philosophical root of the problem has a lot to do with a particularly vulgar conception of the fact–value distinction which in various ways has bedevilled modern moral philosophy. There is for example a Humean tendency to think of moral approval and disapproval as mere feelings or sentiments, while on the other hand there is the tendency, derivable from a certain strain in utilitarianism, to think that blame, like punishment, is a sort of strategy or policy governed by practical interests and purposes.

While the first stresses the non-rationality of moral attitudes, the second has an inflated and distorted conception of their 'rationality', turning it into a species of calculation. I shall have more to say about both of those tendencies later, but it seems that neither can give an adequate picture of the nature of human action and how we understand it. Utilitarianism in particular effectively severs a man from his acts. 'Morality' is a kind of policy or instrument: the moral agent is a centre of practical reason for whom morality is a means to a further end and for whom altruism stands in need of an 'external' (empirically describable) pay-off. 'Good' means expediency and 'harm' means frustration: and such a thought lies at the heart of the empiricist ethic of consequentialism, which can never fully allow us to belong to what we do. In locating goodness and badness solely in the effects or consequences of our actions, it implies a severance between the doer and the deed.

Human acts and actions are not mere observable changes in the environment. We do not and cannot (except in idle theoretical speculation) regard people's actions as if they were parcels dropped from mail trains. We see people as being 'in' their actions, such that what they do expresses what they are and how they see things. If we seriously believed that our identification of acts and actions were simply a matter of attending to observable or measurable changes in the world we would have no means of distinguishing between two acts which, though outwardly similar, are quite different. The man who sends flowers to his mother in order to comfort her is *doing* something different from the man who sends flowers just to get into her good books and perhaps receive a greater slice in her will. Once we allow that there is more to interpreting actions than simply noting their surface features (and noting their surface features still involves seeing them as human actions and not mere bodily movements) there is room for dispute about the description we would accept as truly or *fairly* representing their nature or quality. This consideration I think already undermines the idea that our approval or disapproval of what a person has done is an emotive or practical accretion upon his action 'neutrally' conceived. This point, however, requires considerable explanation, for the legacy of the fact–value 'dichotomy' provides constant temptation. I am not concerned to argue that there is no distinction between fact and value, but to question some of its dubious applications. I shall begin by considering some implications of Strawson's distinction between 'reactive' and 'objective' attitudes.

In his lecture 'Freedom and Resentment'[2] Strawson argued that no theoretical conviction (such as a belief in determinism) would enable us to discard those feelings and attitudes involved in our perception of human beings as morally responsible for their actions. Those philosophers who think otherwise, Strawson claimed, are seduced by the powers of theoretical abstraction into a failure to remember how deeply embedded these reactive attitudes are in the nature of our dealings with one another. Although we may question, or seek justification for, many of our social practices, there are some beliefs and attitudes for which no external justification can be sought—without, that is, attempting in effect to stand

[2] In P. F. Strawson (ed.), *Studies in the Philosophy of Thought and Action* (Oxford, 1968), 71–96.

outside the actual framework of human experience and ask whether it is rational to be human (a pointless question since we cannot choose to be other than human). The fact that we can and do, in certain cases, suspend many of the reactive attitudes—e.g. in the way we regard the mentally subnormal or the insane—is no proof, he argues, that we could suspend them indefinitely. As far as the insane are concerned we are able to adopt something like an 'objective attitude' towards them by divorcing ourselves from the resentment and indignation which would normally be occasioned by breaches of 'good will', and by seeing such people as not free, responsible agents, but as objects of social policy or treatment.

There is something inherently self-defeating about trying to contemplate the existence of a society in which what Strawson calls 'objective attitudes' flourished on a grand scale. We are not entitled to suppose that these attitudes would be our 'objective attitudes' writ large; for such attitudes reside *within* a framework of reactive attitudes, such that the latter have an important bearing on the attitudes which contrast with them. No matter that we see some people as not fitting recipients of the reactive attitudes, our 'detachment' in such cases is not an attitude of indifference, nor is it merely inspired by the consideration that it would be pointless to blame or punish them. Our willingness in such cases to try to suspend the reactive attitudes of resentment and censure is itself a moral attitude. Since we see them as exceptions, we could consider it inhumane or unjust to blame or punish these people. This is not an attitude which would be possible in a human society without reactive attitudes (even if we could make sense of such a supposition).

These observations, far from weakening Strawson's thesis about the irremovability of moral attitudes, actually strengthen it. But a matter that does not seem to receive much consideration in his treatment is the extent to which our suspension of blame is tied up with a correlative inclination to change the description under which particular acts or actions are subsumed. Declining to blame is not merely a matter of withdrawing sentiments. Surely we would regard the insane man who sets fire to a public building because his 'voices' are telling him to do so as not *doing* the same sort of thing as the lout who does it for fun or the ruthless terrorist who does it for a political objective?

The point I wish to make is more general than that example

suggests. Suppose that I discover a friend has betrayed a confidence. I may be indignant and resentful, or I may not. But in either case the judgement 'he betrayed a confidence' is unaffected. Suppose I now discover circumstances which suggest he is not the rogue I thought he was. The words slipped out while he was drunk, or he was talking in his sleep, or perhaps his wife was depressed and, in a desperate attempt to get her to see things in perspective, he found himself revealing my long battle against alcoholism or the brave face I had been putting on a terminal illness. Discovering this, I may feel inclined to say that I no longer blame him. But this lessens my inclination to say that he 'betrayed' a confidence. Perhaps the changed description is 'he revealed my secret'. At any rate I shall be seeing his act under some different description. I shall have a different conception of what he has done.

The cost of overlooking this would be to encourage the idea that blame is merely a subjective reaction, like a feeling: on the one hand we have the 'reality'—X did Y—and the only difference between A who blames X and B who does not is that A has a feeling of disapproval. Hume paved the way for this type of crude Emotivism by conceiving of approval and disapproval as feelings. Since for Hume what we approve or disapprove of cannot be located 'out there' in the properties of objects, approval and disapproval are 'sentiments' rooted in the mind: i.e. they are psychological tendencies, such that when we are presented with 'certain characters or dispositions' we are compelled by a kind of psychological necessity to 'feel the sentiment of approbation or blame'.[3]

Even if blame were to be thought of as a feeling or emotion, that would not render it impervious to the questions we can ask of any emotion: why are we feeling it in these circumstances, and is it justified? Hume could not permit such questions. Not only did he posit a gulf between Reason and Passion, but he thought that such sentiments could never be justified in the sense of being called rational since it is not possible to derive judgements of value from judgements about what is the case. Given this chasm between fact and value, and given the view that a man can only be moved by that which already touches his inclinations, morality is a matter of inclination and not of reason.

[3] David Hume, *Enquiry Concerning the Human Understanding*, ed., L. A. Selby-Bigge (Oxford, 1962), 102.

To discuss Hume any further would be an unnecessary digression. Given all the work done by philosophers on the nature of emotion I take it that it is not controversial to maintain that emotion *per se* is not 'opposed' to reason; that our emotions in particular cases are amenable to rational assessment; that our capacity for emotion is an essential ingredient in the rationality we do have (not only is it rational to fear fire, it would be irrational not to fear it). But in order to regard blame as an emotion it would not be enough to regard it as answerable to the sorts of questions mentioned above. All that is established by the applicability of such questions is that emotions are connected to beliefs and desires. (I can only feel jealous of Matthew if I believe that he is getting or is likely to get something I want.)

But suppose that in applying for a job my rival candidates are Sid and Dick. It does not seem absurd to suggest that if Sid wins I shall be jealous whereas if Dick wins I shall merely be disappointed (I will not begrudge him his success). Although exceptions can always be found, in general it seems that emotions have particular rather than general objects. If my fiancée deserts me for Rodney I might well be angry, sorrowful, or bitter, without experiencing the jealousy I would feel if she deserted me for Bruce. While it is of course true that some people might feel jealous of anyone at all who stood in the way of their own projects or fulfilments, that is a matter for individual psychology rather than being a point about the grammar of jealousy. Possibly the man who is susceptible to such indiscriminate jealousy is one who for that reason we would regard as obsessed (like the Duke in Browning's 'My Last Duchess', who was jealous of all other men his wife 'looked on').

The distinction between emotions and attitudes is a difficult one because they are importantly connected, but I find myself in agreement with Roger Scruton's argument that while some emotions such as love, hatred, anger, and depression are 'particular in respect of their objects', others, such as despite, are universal, or have a universal element involving 'some element of consistency'. 'If I despise a man it must be on account of some quality such that I would despise anyone who was similar in that respect.'[4] My love

---

[4] Roger Scruton, 'Attitudes, Beliefs and Reasons', in John Casey (ed.), *Morality and Moral Reasoning* (London, 1966), 41.

for Mary may not be independent of my perception that she has particular qualities. But the love is not grounded in these qualities such that if Gladys exhibits them I must love her as well. On the other hand, if I admire Cuthbert's integrity my admiration is directed to the quality he exemplifies, such that if Rupert has that quality I shall also admire him (or, perhaps more accurately, admire his integrity: for there may be other factors inhibiting me from admiring *him*).

Perhaps this is another consideration for distinguishing the two types of case. For, strictly speaking, it is not Mary's qualities I love; I love *her*. But my admiration 'for' Bill is not necessarily admiration 'of' him. I may continue to love Mary despite the loss of the qualities I once celebrated (and it would be a shallow kind of love that was merely conditional upon their persistence) while it makes no sense to say that I could continue to admire Bill despite the cessation of his admirable qualities. One should be cautious, however, about making the distinction purely on that basis. As an emotion, love is a special case. There might be other emotions which are equally 'particular' without being restricted in the same way to the uniqueness of their objects. Take anger. It is significant that 'anger' cannot be used as an active verb in quite the same way that 'love' can. 'I anger John' is not a grammatical equivalent of 'I love Mary'. If I am talking about my anger, and not John's, I can only be 'angry with'. But the presence of reasons for anger does not preclude the 'particularity' of the emotion. While my anger may be rendered intelligible to someone by saying 'he called me a fat fool', it would not be wrong to think that I might not have been angry at this remark, even though I can see that it is offensive (being offended by it is another matter). To see it as an insult, however, would be different. Seeing something as an insult necessarily involves indignation, though not necessarily anger.

I therefore wish to distinguish anger from attitudes of disapproval. I may perceive a situation as 'anger-worthy' (to recall a coinage of Bantock's) without being angry. In this sense the anger is something 'over and above' the perceived situation that gives rise to it, even when the anger is justified (either in the sense of being intelligible or in the sense that I have a right to be angry). Further, when a person is angry the anger can be explained by pointing to a particular set of circumstances. Disapproval differs in both respects. I cannot perceive something to be worthy of disapproval without in some sense disapproving of it; and any attempt to explain my disapproval cannot rest merely with the unique particulars of a situation but can only be seen to be reasonable or justified by its implied reference to something more general which the particular case exemplifies. To say that I disapprove of Tom and Elizabeth leaving their young children unattended while they go out enjoying themselves is not the same as saying I do not like it (indeed I may not like it without disapproving of it). For it to be disapproval I must see their behaviour in such a light that I would not condone it in anyone else: 'no one should go off and leave their children like that'. And no doubt I would expect others to agree with me. To say that I disapprove of X is not merely to point to something about me, but about X: namely that it should be disapproved of.

It is time to apply this insight (if that is what it is) to the discussion of blame. The key point here concerns the 'universal element'. Since disapproval is an attitude, and since blame must include disapproval, it looks as if we ought to describe blame as an attitude. But here we must ask why it seems less natural to speak of an attitude of blame than it does to speak of an attitude of disapproval. One reason for this may have something to do with the fact that I can speak of disapproving of an act, or a practice, of Xing where Xing is described in neutral terms. 'I disapprove of meat-eating and fox-hunting while he approves of meat-eating and fox-hunting.' We do not have a similar use for 'I blame'—except perhaps when we use 'blame' in a responsibility-ascribing sense: 'I blame *you* for that', or '*he's* the one to blame for the road accident'. In the latter sense of blame we are concerned with a state of affairs which is held to be consequential upon the activity, or non-activity, of a particular person, such that his contribution to the state of affairs is held to be more prominent or significant than any other contributing factors.

Blame in that sense is often rather like finding the culprit. In some cases it is likely to involve a practical interest and is usually expressed in the form of a speech act. My present concern is with the idea of blame that does not operate like an accusatory searchlight. We may know full well that Smithers is the one who is responsible for the consternation in the staff meeting last night, but there is the further question of whether we blame him for what he did. As it stands this question is rather ambiguous, as is the example. For we must distinguish between the case of a man who we are agreed has performed an undesirable deed, yet might not be fully 'to blame' for what he did (i.e. there are excuses) and the case of the man who was fully 'in' his action yet we disagree about whether what he did was wrong.

Therefore let us expand the example. Suppose that Curriculum Committee meetings at Turncoat Comprehensive are usually quiet and peaceful (if not boring) events. On this occasion, Smithers, a history teacher, objects to a proposed curriculum 'initiative' on the grounds that it is fashionable rather than educational. The fact that he stands his ground causes consternation among the senior management. They tell him he is being negative and standing in the way of progress. Eventually there is uproar. Smithers wins one or two allies but this serves to exacerbate the conflict and the meeting ends, unresolved, on an unpleasant note.

In the common room, opinion is divided between those who blame Smithers for his performance last night and those who do not. Let us exclude from consideration those who might think that it is always wrong to do something which might upset a meeting. Now it would be simple-minded to represent the ensuing disagreement in terms which just imply a clash between 'pro' and 'con' attitudes (as in 'I am for vanilla' versus 'I am for strawberry'). For the deeper dispute would be very much tied up with the kind of importance one is inclined to place on the issues at stake in the meeting itself. Person A considers the affair to be a storm in a teacup: Smithers is to be blamed because he was getting steamed up over a triviality. Person B, a 'progressivist', blames Smithers for his stick-in-the-mud and arrogant challenge to Progress. C declines to blame him since he deplores the railroading tactics of curriculum directors and perhaps sees Smithers's protest as a small voice of integrity in a cheapening world.

In each case there is an intimate relationship between how the action is to be seen and described and whether or not it is felt to be blameworthy. We begin with as neutral a description as can be found in the circumstances, and one to which Smithers himself would assent: 'Smithers upset the meeting' (call this description X). What this formulation conceals is that, at least as far as B and C are concerned, the dispute is not really about Xing as such. B and C have different attitudes towards the fact that Smithers Xed, but only because they would give completely different accounts of what he was doing *in* Xing. For *B* it is a kind of sabotage; for *C* a righteous and justified protest.

BLAME AS ACCOUNTANCY OR RECORD-KEEPING

At the opposite extreme from the Humean tendency to regard blame as a feeling is the belief that it is more like a deliberate policy governed by various practical interests and purposes. Whereas for Hume blaming is essentially passive, on the latter view blaming is essentially active. It is a policy or strategy, fleshed out with metaphors drawn from accountancy: debit and credit sheets, record cards, and, no doubt, filing systems. This is utilitarianism with a vengeance. And one of its most characteristic exponents is Joel Feinberg. Feinberg distinguishes between those ascriptions of responsibility which function as if in answer to the question 'who did it?' or 'who is responsibile?' and what he calls 'strong ascriptions', which hold the offender to be responsible in the sense of being 'to blame' for his 'defective or faulty performance'. Ascriptions of blame in the latter sense can be 'charged to one's account', 'entered on one's record', or—outside 'institutional contexts'—made part of one's 'reputation' (a reputation being an informal analogue of the formal notion of a record). 'There is', we are told, 'something "quasi-judicial" or "quasi-official" about defeasible ascriptions of blame' even in informal contexts. As to the formal features of records, 'they are found in such places as offices of employment, schools, banks, and police dossiers and they are full of grades and averages, marks and points, merits and demerits, debits, charges, credits and registered instances of fault'.[5] But even outside institutional contexts, the way we view the actions of people involves a sort of record-keeping in that when we hold them to blame for particular acts or omissions we are in effect saying that the 'fault' is registrable upon their reputation. Our interest in the accuracy of registering faults on a reputation is a practical one, bearing on practical decisions to be made about that person in the future. Even more strongly, Feinberg contends that what we are to *count* as defective performance is itself largely governed by practical considerations: 'In general, I should think, a person's faulty act

---

[5] Joel Feinberg, 'Action and Responsibility', in Alan White (ed.), *The Philosophy of Action* (Oxford, 1970), 100.

is registrable only if it reveals what sort of person he is in some respect about which others have a practical interest in being informed.'[6]

DIFFICULTIES WITH THIS ARGUMENT

Perhaps 'difficulties' is too euphemistic to convey the depth of my disagreement. Feinberg's analysis of blame makes it sound far too calculating. It does not and cannot reflect the nature and quality of the moral attitudes, and it involves a debilitated view of the kind of values that enter into our critical appraisal (he would call it 'assessment') of human conduct. It is revealing that Feinberg's examples are almost exclusively cases of minor incompetence: cases where someone botches, flubs, flounders, flunks, or fails. Once or twice we find a fleeting reference to something slightly more serious (e.g. killing Cock Robin or cheating at cards) but we are soon back to cases of stammering, absent-mindedness, miscalculation, ineptitude at baseball, and the breaking of windows. My objection is not simply that it is not clear how one can extrapolate from this 'one-sided diet' to general conclusions about blame. It is also that his arguments are dubious even with these examples.

He restricts the discussion unnecessarily by considering examples of the kind of 'fault' in which people do as a matter of fact have a practical interest; and this interest, admittedly, feeds back into what we would be likely to count as instances of defective performance, fault, omission, and so on. The police officer who, in attempting to stop a fleeing mugger, accidentally breaks a window in the process is not necessarily guilty of clumsiness or ineptitude for the breakage. One must concede to Feinberg that what we are prepared to count as an act of clumsiness or incompetence depends upon the situation (or role) we consider the agent to be in. In many cases this judgement is not just made possible by a number of social conventions, customs, and practices, but is a reflection of them. We do not abstract actions from the particulars of bodily movements (i.e. bodily movements are not 'components' of actions). Rather, the concepts through which we view actions are in an important sense given to us through the interests, purposes, and values enshrined in a publicly shared language. We do not

[6] Ibid. 102.

'work out' that the man who pulls the trigger has a lot to do with the bullet that enters his victim's heart. The gunman's responsibility for the death is already presupposed in the given coinage of 'gunman', 'shooting', 'victim', 'killing', or 'murder'. Given that our interests and priorities are reflected in language, it is not merely a linguistic quirk that we can tread 'inadvertently' on a snail but not on a baby (to use Austin's well-known example). In this limited sense our very perception of human action is, to use an overworked phrase, 'socially determined'. And where we do dispute and disagree about the description that should be assigned to a particular action (about, that is, the limits of a person's responsibility and about what are direct consequences of his actions) we can do so only against a wider background against which much is agreed and taken for granted (though not necessarily as a result of deliberate consensus).

But this point in the end actually tells against Feinberg; for we can grant all of the following: that as human beings we have practical purposes and interests, and that these purposes and interests will be reflected in the judgements and expectations that govern our imputations of fault, ascriptions of responsibility, deficiencies in skill, and so on. But that is not the whole story. That we have an interest in people and their achievements that extends far beyond the practical has an important bearing even on our 'practical assessments'. That we do not expect window cleaners to break the windows they are employed to clean is one of the many tacit presuppositions that would inspire us to attribute clumsiness or incompetence to window cleaners who break them; and since we have a practical interest in keeping our windows intact we shall no doubt avoid window cleaners who are clumsy in this respect. But this little piece of common sense hardly entitles Feinberg to his 'quasi-official' view of blaming. For even in this case we do not blame the window cleaner *in order* to serve our practical interests. And, conversely, if the defeasible ascription of blame were defeated by excuse or justification we should not withdraw the blame solely on the grounds that no practical purpose would be served by blaming.

If we discover that the window cleaner was in the first stage of a heart-attack and, losing his balance, put his foot through the window, we would relinquish the blame because we would 'see' the action differently: though still accidental, it would no longer be an act of clumsiness. Ceasing to blame here is not just a matter of 'withdrawal', but of coming to see something. The blame disappears with the changed perception, much as the belief that P disappears when we realize that P is false. One must make this partial concession to Hume; that in the sense I have discussed there is an involuntary aspect to blame, just as there is to belief. Whereas praising is always an act, blaming need not be. It becomes an act when it is communicated to someone. But it is nonetheless blame when we are silently struck by the adverse complexion of the act in question, through seeing it as an instance of fault, failure, omission, and so on.

Feinberg seems to overlook this involuntary aspect of blame, partly because he does not draw a clear distinction between blame as a kind of perception and blame as an act (or at least he equivocates by using, on occasion, unexplained terms like 'overt blame' which seems to function as a near synonym for 'punishment'). But even if we are to understand 'overt blame' as 'any sort of outwardly manifested disapproval of a person for his defective performance'[7] it is strange to suggest as he does that whether or not we (outwardly) blame someone will be governed by considerations of 'practical utility'. If someone says 'stop blaming me' this is less like a request for silence than an entreaty for the accuser to reconsider his perception of what has or has not been done (e.g. 'I didn't insult him, he took offence at an innocent remark'). If in reconsidering we do see the matter differently we discover at the same time that the accused man should not be blamed—not because it would be pointless, but because it would be wrong (both in the sense of being inappropriate and in the sense of being unjust). Even though we might have had good reasons for thinking him to blame, our discovery that he is not inclines us towards an apology—a tendency which shows that we have an interest in the truth that transcends a merely practical interest.

Though Feinberg is right to say that not all cases of blame are cases of moral blame (p. 96) he overlooks the ethical dimension that attaches even to cases where the 'fault' is not thought to be a moral fault. Not only do we have a duty to be as fair and just as possible in our appraisal of a man's performance, but, given that we are not merely practical creatures, some of the values that reside

---

[7] Ibid. 103.

even within our perception of faulty or defective performance at the practical level are not exclusively utilitarian. Our response to the fruits of great skill or craftsmanship, smooth efficiency, intelligent planning, careful execution of a task, involves not just the narrow satisfaction that is associated with instrumentality (seeing these things as means to 'useful' ends), it involves an admiration and approval which is aesthetic. Such achievements are also valued as ends in themselves: they are seen under the aspect of beauty. To appreciate the skill involved requires discrimination or taste, or in some cases what Michael Polanyi has called 'connoisseurship'.[8] We speak of a secretary's 'impeccable' organization, an executive's 'immaculate' planning, and we can find in the dying art of the tailor, or of the carpenter, an excellence that is sustained by love.

> I remember my father's hands,
> For they were supple and strong
> With fingers that were lovers—
> Sensuous strokers of wood.[9]

When we are alive to excellence in its various forms, the aesthetic elements of our appreciation seem also to touch our moral sensibilities. Our perception of a fine achievement is not fully separate from our perception of the care that is presupposed in the relationship between the man and the task. And this dedication itself may require qualities of character that it is tempting to call moral qualities: self-effacement, humility, a concern for perfection rather than mere expediency. As Wittgenstein wrote of Bach: 'Bach said that his achievements were simply the fruits of industry. But industry like that requires humility and an endless capacity for suffering, hence strength.'[10]

Why, then, should our disapproval of incompetence, dullness, carelessness, shoddiness, clumsiness, not be seen against the fullness of our appreciation for their opposites? If that appreciation goes beyond practical concerns, why should it not be that our disapproval of 'faulty or defective performance' also goes beyond considerations of practical utility? What Feinberg seems to miss is

[8] Michael Polanyi, *Personal Knowledge: Towards a Post-Critical Philosophy* (London, 1973), ch. 4.

[9] Clifford Dyment, 'The Carpenter', in F. E. S. Finn (ed.), *Poets of Our Time: An Anthology* (London, 1965), 52.

[10] *Culture and Value*, ed. G. H. von Wright and H. Nyman, trans. P. Winch (Oxford, 1980), 71e.

that the spirit of blame also has a disinterested quality. We have a propensity to blame people for their clumsiness in a way that is 'over and above' matters of simple efficiency. If we see various types of accomplishment under the aspect of beauty, we see clumsiness under the aspect of ugliness. Even when clumsiness does not stand in the way of a desired objective, it is intrinsically undesirable. The window cleaner who keeps backing into his bucket and knocking it over may nevertheless complete the job satisfactorily and without undue time-loss. On the utility view this ought to mean that we have nothing to blame him for; yet to see him as clumsy is to blame him. We do not expect or require him to have the grace of a ballet dancer, but neither do we expect clumsiness; for it is associated with the lumbering of elephants and the stupidity of bulls in china shops. It has an 'inappropriateness' about it: an incongruity. We may be a little lower than the angels, but since we are not so low as the apes we are not merely repulsed by clumsiness of movement but by the verbal or emotional clumsiness known as tactlessness. And unless we regard language merely as a tool for 'getting the message across' we are also repulsed by the sheer ugliness of inelegant, ungrammatical speech and writing.

FACTS AND VALUES

I have pointed to an involuntary aspect of blame and to the spirit of disinterestedness that is associated with it. These two aspects of blame take on an even greater significance in cases where blame involves moral disapproval. Moral blame is unlike reproach and reprimand which are 'forward looking'[11] in having a restorative purpose. It is more akin to a type of understanding. To blame is to have drawn a conclusion, even though no explicit process of reasoning may have preceded it. I see a father taunting and embarrassing his young child in public. I do not 'work out' that this is an act of cruelty. I instantly see that he is being cruel to his son. Thus I do not have the 'optional extra' of blaming. 'Cruelty' is an evaluative term, having its life in a language which reflects and shapes our dealings with one another.

My argument therefore needs to be distinguished from intuition-

---

[11] J. E. J. Altham, 'Reproach', *Proceedings of the Aristotelian Society*, 74 (1973/4), 263–72.

ism. I am not arguing that we 'intuit' the external 'properties' of an action in the way we see that Deirdre's dress is yellow. Neither am I committing myself to what Hare dubbed ethical 'descriptivism'. The latter view of ethics is exemplified in Philippa Foot's article 'Moral Beliefs'.[12] Mrs Foot maintained that disputes about human harm can be settled by pointing to the facts: for not just anything can count as human harm. Her rendition of 'moral objectivity', however, relies too heavily upon the alleged similarity between harm and injury. Whether or not someone is injured is a purely factual question, and any dispute about the matter can be settled by well-attested procedures. We do not in general dispute what it is for the body to be intact, in proper working order and functioning properly, any more than we have grave doubts about what it is for goods we have purchased to be damaged. But damage is only one species of human harm. Not only is it possible to harm someone without damaging them (e.g. by lying to them) but in some cases it is possible to say that one has been damaged though not harmed. You slip in the corridor and push me against the wall. 'No harm done,' I say, clutching my bruised arm. I do not just mean that the damage is slight. I mean also perhaps that I realize you didn't do it on purpose. On the other hand if my trusted colleague lies to me, he may not *cause* me harm (I may be unaware of the lie) but I am harmed in the sense that I have been deceived— not accorded the respect upon which trust is based.

Though it might be right that 'not just anything' can count as human harm, it does not follow that we are always forced to agree about what does. The idea of harm carries an implicit evaluation about the proper condition of man or about what is good for the soul. And though there might be a consensus of agreement about what constitutes a healthy or wholesome state of mind, it is only too evident, particularly these days, that such judgements by no means carry universal assent.

Consider those who think we ought to regale schoolchildren with sexually explicit 'gay' novels. Do those of us who object do so simply on the grounds that such people have got their facts wrong? And might we not enter into a moral dispute with someone who says that this is simply a dispute about the facts? For that view itself involves a disputable attitude towards the nature of

---

[12] In Philippa Foot (ed.), *Theories of Ethics* (Oxford, 1967), 83–100.

human experience: it presupposes for instance that the 'harm'
being objected to is something which is empirically observable, like
the effects of food-poisoning. Surely we may protest that we are
not merely concerned with the probable or likely effects of the
practice but with the values implicit within the practice itself—e.g.
it is corrupt, whether or not it also corrupts. Perhaps an even
clearer example is the outrage at the judge presiding over the
Ealing Vicarage rape case who tried to justify his lenient sentencing
on the grounds that the woman in question had not been harmed
by the experience. The 'harm' here was made to sound like a
matter of observable consequences, whereas it could be objected
that she suffered harm simply by being the victim.

This argument about human harm applies *mutatis mutandis* to
Geoffrey Warnock's discussion of human needs.[13] Warnock's
attempt to 'objectify' moral judgement relies too much on the idea
that what we are to count as human needs is a factual matter.
While it would be unnecessarily drastic to deny that there is such a
thing as human nature, it is not possible to reach a value-free
conception of it. For any attempt to describe what man is must
involve judgements and presuppositions about what man should
or ought to be, and what is likely to militate against his 'flourish-
ing'. Compare Goneril's 'O the difference of man and man', or
Macbeth's

> Aye, in the catalogue ye go for men;
> As hounds, and greyhounds, mongrels, spaniels, curs,
> Shoughs, water-rugs, and demi-wolves, are clept
> All by the name of dogs. The valued file
> Distinguishes the swift, the slow, the subtle,
> The house-keeper, the hunter, every one
> According to the gift which bounteous nature
> Hath in him clos'd; whereby he does receive
> Particular addition, from the bill
> That writes them all alike; and so of men.

Warnock's talk about human needs belongs not to the 'catalogue',
but to the 'valued file'.

If I have rejected the neo-naturalist position, why do I say that
blaming does not involve a 'leap'—e.g. from the domain of facts
to the domain of values? The quick answer to this is that I have

---

[13] G. J. Warnock, *The Object of Morality* (London, 1971).

not posited two such 'domains'. It would be misleading to say: here are the facts of what X has done, now I shall leap to an evaluation that goes beyond the facts; for the evaluation may be implicit in what one takes the facts to be. To recall my earlier example of Smithers, the history teacher: the difference between those who blame Smithers and those who do not is reflected in what they take Smithers to be doing *in* Xing; in other words they would see the Xing under some description that is already evaluative. But that two people may reach different evaluations does not mean that values are totally independent of facts.

If I learn that a historic building is to be demolished to make way for a new bingo hall, my disapproval has a great deal to do with the facts: e.g. (1) H is a historical building, (2) H is to be demolished, and (3) the local council value H less than they do a bingo hall. Tomkins, however, approves, while conceding (1), (2), and (3) to be facts. On Emotivist theories of the 'booh-hurrah' type, the difference between Tomkins and me would consist in nothing more than two opposed subjective mental states. But to construe 'mental states' in this way is tantamount to denying that there can be real disagreement about values, or indeed agreement (for on this depleted view the moral 'agreement' of two or more people could only amount to a coincidence). We can only understand mental states, *a fortiori* opposed mental states, in terms of their objects. Tomkins and I have a different understanding of the situation and one that is based on reasons. On the surface I may be said to disapprove of the demolition, but in another sense that is only a surface description of what I am reacting to, as it is equally a surface description of what the other man is approving of. Given that we have reasons for our disapproval, these reasons take account of facts but our responses to these facts are informed (or misinformed) by certain presuppositions of value. I am not reacting just to a demolition: the demolition is directed only to layers of bricks. What I regard as being destroyed is not just a building but a historical legacy. To Tomkins, however, what they are doing is improving the local amenities: a useless object is being removed to make way for something more useful. This does not mean that our perception of value is identical with our perception of the facts, but it does suggest that our view of the facts is coloured by what in life we regard as being important. Tomkins and I agree that H is a historic building. But while to him the force of the word 'historic' suggests nothing more than *H* is old, to me it means that it has historical significance. While to him the bingo hall will replace the historic building, I shall regard it as irreplaceable.

Something else this example is intended to illustrate is that what is at stake in speaking of 'what is done *in* doing *X*' may not be just to do with the question of consequences. Clearly there are cases in which to speak of 'what is done in doing *X*' has the function of including the actual or probable consequences of an action within a description of that action. 'In pouring radioactive waste into that river they are killing the wildlife, damaging the health of innocent people, and so on.' But if I say 'in demolishing *H* the council are destroying the past' the destruction I conceive of is not a consequence of the demolition in the way that falling bricks are a consequence of the swinging hammer. The destruction lies *in* the act of demolition: it is an assault. Similarly in lying to my friend I can be said to deceive him, whether or not he is taken in as a result. I do not deceive him just by lying to him but also in lying to him. Here, as with the previous example, it is not that values are in some way added to the facts as icing is added to the cake; but rather that our values are reflected in the significance we assign to the facts.

Nothing in this chapter, then, should be taken to imply that there is no distinction between fact and value. On the contrary, two extreme positions need to be rejected. The first is that there is an unbridgeable gulf between fact and value: a view much encouraged by the 'Naturalistic Fallacy' which, in one of its formulations, insists on the 'gulf' on the grounds that the relation between statements of fact and normative or evaluative conclusions can never be strictly deductive. (It does not follow from this, however, that moral opinions or value-judgements are totally independent of facts.) At the other extreme there is the view that all statements of fact are really value-judgements in disguise. A staunch advocate of this view might for instance adopt some variant of the Protagorean theme that man is the measure of all things. Hence he might argue that the concepts through which our understanding of the world is mediated reflect human interests and purposes; that without these interests and purposes we would not make the distinctions we do, nor see the world as divided up into certain kinds of stuff. He might then go on to say that everything is 'relative' or 'culturally determined'. Provided he does not get too carried away, there is some truth in what he says. We are not passive receptors of 'reality'. 'Reality' is the fruit of interaction between ourselves and what is not ourselves. Had we not seen fit to pick out something called the teenage years there would have been no teenagers (though Johnny, who is a teenager, would still have existed). Further, as Mary Midgley has pointed out in her book *Wickedness*, as far as the universe is concerned there is no 'up' or 'down'; but for all kinds of reasons to do with the kind of creatures we are, the idea of up and down is such a key concept that it enters into our very understanding of social practices, achievements, and failings. Yet however 'decision-laden' or 'interest-ridden' statements of fact might be, they are none the less factual for that. It is no less a fact that certain sales figures have gone 'up' or that yonder cliff is a dangerous 'drop' for its being the case that human interests, values, and purposes lie behind these classifications. Perhaps all statements of fact are to some extent decision-laden, but that does not cancel out their fact-stating function. It does not prove that what we take to be facts are really values in disguise.

Where then is the distinction to be drawn? There is no simple answer to this, since the question is too wide. As that question concerns us here I can only answer it by saying that values characteristically reside in attitudes towards the facts, without committing myself to the idea that these attitudes are mere feelings or that they are in some way superimposed on a factual base. This is the real point lying behind my discussion of 'what is done *in* doing *X*'.

Understanding what is wrong with a person's deeds is not merely a matter of making a cognitive judgement. To understand a wicked act is to condemn it: for it is to link the quality of the deed with the bad intentions that are involved in its execution. Given this close relation between the doer and the deed, between a man and his acts, to condemn the act is to condemn the man. But what of the saying 'hate the sin but not the sinner'? Much of course depends on what the saying means. What it cannot (logically) mean is blame the sin but not the sinner. We do not blame sins, we blame the people who commit them. Indeed to refer to a man's act and endorse the description 'sin' is already to blame him. However, though we may detest what he has done and though we may feel revulsed by his actions, it does not follow that we are hating him, even though we understand why some people may hate him. Unlike anger (which, as Aquinas argued, can be a moral emotion), hatred does not aim at good or truth. Hatred seems to have an interest in falsifying its object to keep it hateful. As Dilman has, I think rightly, argued: while genuine love and friendliness have their interest centred in the other person—such that the genuine love can coexist with recognition of the other's faults—hate has an interest in blinding one to the qualities of the other that might not be hateful; hence there is in this sense an asymmetry between love and hate.[14] That some people hate the sin *and* the sinner is undoubtedly true; but the condemnation involved in blame is unlike hatred in its being compatible with a concern for truth and justice.

THE HUMAN WORLD

The moral attitudes of blame and disapproval are neither merely feelings nor utilitarian strategies, but are deeply and essentially involved in the way we conceive of human action. The concept of a person is itself partly a moral concept. From the standpoint of a scientific view of the world (in so far as it would not distinguish persons from the rest of nature) the world does not contain persons as we conceive of them. The way that we think of persons is predicated on a distinction between persons and things. As persons—even on the inadequate world-view that treats us as little more than 'centres from which behaviour is directed'—we are, in Charles Taylor's words, 'loci of responsibility'.[15] The responsibility we ascribe to persons is different from the 'responsibility' we ascribe to the causal processes of inanimate things, or even from the 'responsibility' we ascribe to the lower animals, since it is indissolubly linked with such concepts as intention, freedom, and the will.

The rock that falls and crushes my toe may be 'responsible' for my injury, but only in the sense that it is the cause of it. Since any estimation of the rock's 'activity' can only be logically given in terms of causal laws, it would be mere superstition to regard the rock as answerable for its 'action'. Neither could it be excused on the grounds that it fell accidentally (since there is no contrary

---

[14] Ilham Dilman, *Love and Human Separateness* (Oxford, 1987), 126.
[15] Charles Taylor, *The Explanation of Behaviour* (London, 1964).

possibility that it fell deliberately). There are philosophers of course who aspire to explaining human behaviour in terms of causes—a complicated problem into which I cannot enter here—but unless these 'explanations' are mechanistic explanations (thus divorcing our understanding of action from its cultural surrounds by thinking of it in terms of bodily movements) the concept of 'cause' is never entirely perspicuous. Even if mechanistic explanations are in a sense conceivable, they could not explain action as we conceive it. And in any case, given that the human acts and actions portrayed in literary art are actions in the 'common sense' meaning of the term, it would be irrelevant to pursue the question of scientific explanation any further here. To understand human action within the 'common sense' frame of reference is to make sense of it within the 'human world', or the *Lebenswelt*. To understand or explain a human action or a pattern of conduct is not to be concerned with general laws, but with reasons, intentions, beliefs, desires, and purposes.

In explaining why a given action was performed we are likely to be concerned with the reason for its performance, a concept which is different from that of cause. The link between purposive explanation and our understanding of persons is this: that it involves intentionality. My understanding of the rock's falling does not involve intentionality for it would be bizarre to enquire into what the rock thought itself to be doing. The behaviour of the rock is not 'goal-directed'. Nor, in the narrow sense of the term, is human behaviour. We have a conception of the ends we are prepared to aim at and pursue them in the light of that conception. This alone would be enough to distinguish our behaviour from that of the animals who, being denied language, cannot represent the environment to themselves in such a way. But the distinction between human beings and animals is deeper than that. Animals have no means of escaping from the present and are confined to a life of immediacy. Yet it is this liberation from the present which informs what we mean by purposive behaviour. The very idea of a purpose involves a conception of a future state and of oneself as playing an active and determining part in that future state. My having a particular purpose therefore involves a conception of the world as not only persisting through time, but of a world which is in some way amenable to my projects and plans, and therefore susceptible to my influence. However, as rational, feeling creatures we are moved by reason and compassion and conceive of limits to the ends we are prepared to aim at and of the means we are prepared to embrace in pursuit of the 'goals' we do have. That some people seem to breach this condition is not to the point, since it is no accident that we call them ruthless and unscrupulous—terms which cannot, without absurdity, apply to inanimate objects or to the behaviour of the lower animals.

To understand human behaviour, even from a distance as it were, therefore involves some understanding of the ends towards which those persons aspire and of the conception they have of their circumstances. To understand such things is already to have one's perception guided and shaped by values, given that values, in R. F. Holland's slogan, 'rest on differences'.[16] In other words, to understand human behaviour is to see it against a background of better and worse possibilities. Given that we as knowing subjects do not, and cannot, stand outside the human community of thought and feeling, our understanding will not be 'value-neutral', but will call upon our capacities for moral understanding, for we shall regard some acts and practices with approval and others with disapproval.

Any attempt to understand ways of acting, thinking, and feeling is at the same time an attempt to understand the world-view implicit in them: and here we might just as easily be morally repulsed by what we find as we might be inclined to attitudes of admiration or respect. Understanding human action is not merely a cognitive exercise, we see the actions of people with the eyes of evaluation, and this will be reflected in the way that we describe what lies before us. This is not to commit us to descriptivism; it is to say that moral attitudes and presuppositions of value are written into the descriptions that are available to us. We may of course 'choose' some descriptions rather than others, but this itself reflects the way that moral attitudes are contained in the descriptions. If we are misguided enough to approve of a terrorist we shall not agree with the moral attitude implicit in describing what he does as murder (indeed given that the very word 'terrorist' is itself pejorative it is not surprising to witness the attempts of some pro-terrorist supporters to discredit words like 'terrorist', calling such terms 'emotive').

---

[16] R. F. Holland, *Against Empiricism: On Education, Epistemology and Value* (Oxford, 1980), 55.

There is a distinction that needs to be drawn here, however, for it will be crucial in later chapters. Much of what I have said in this section is concerned with the way that moral concepts and moral attitudes are involved in our conception of human agency, because human agents are persons. We take it as read that if X is a human action it is an action performed by a person and therefore is amenable to moral understanding and moral judgement. But clearly we do have moral responses to people that arise not simply because they are persons but because of a particular moral opinion we may hold, and which we realize may not be held by others (e.g. that rapists should be castrated or that abortion is always necessarily an evil, and so on). This distinction will be important for my discussion of fictional characters and much confusion would result from not drawing it. It is fairly predictable that I shall go on to say that fictional characters, within the 'internal convention', are persons and therefore fitting recipients of moral attitudes. But there are two caveats here. The first is that since we do not and cannot interact with fictional characters we cannot logically experience or manifest the reactive emotions of, say, gratitude, forgiveness, or resentment any more than we can punish, chide, censure, or reproach them. The second is that the moral expectations which do enter into our understanding of them must be distinguished from those expectations which come not from their simply being persons, but from particular moral opinions which, for the purposes of the work, we may suspend. Indeed in this sense I shall argue in Chapter 7 that agreement with the moral opinions expressed in or by a particular literary work is neither a necessary nor sufficient condition of perceiving its literary merit.

This leaves us with a problem to be taken up in the course of the next two chapters, and one that has to do with our mode of access to fictional characters. For in our understanding of, and responses to, actual people there is room for an element of discretion in the way we subsume their actions under particular concepts or particular descriptions, whereas the controlling voice or controlling intelligence of the work has already subsumed the actions of the characters under particular descriptions, not only stipulating the focus of our concern with those characters but also inviting us to adopt particular attitudes towards them. In what sense can those attitudes be ours?

4

Moral Responses to Fictional Characters

> ... the image in contemplation is neither pleasurable nor painful; and it does not attract to itself either moral approval or disapproval. (Michael Oakeshott, 'The Voice of Poetry in the Conversation of Mankind'.[1])

Given that we lay claim to understand situations portrayed in novels and plays, how does this understanding differ, if at all, from our understanding of the human beings and circumstances that surround us in the actual world? To what extent do moral beliefs and moral attitudes legitimately enter into our response to fictional characters and their circumstances? Fictional characters do not belong to the actual world. They do not join in our interpersonal relationships; their actions and decisions no more aid or impair our aims and activities than ours do theirs. Indeed if they are merely constructions, servants to the artistic purpose of an author, could it not be said that they lack the necessary condition of personhood: responsibility for their actions? Since, like puppets, they do no other than their role dictates is it not profoundly mistaken to blame them or approve of them for what they do? And is it not still more mistaken to feel sad for them, to be gladdened by their achievements or satisfied by the resolution of their conflicts?

No satisfactory answer to those questions can be attempted without considering the nature and importance of our interest in literature, and a fresh impetus to this enquiry was provoked by the Radford/Weston debate in 1975.[2]

[1] In Michael Oakeshott, *Rationalism in Politics: And Other Essays* (London, 1962), 218.
[2] Colin Radford and Michael Weston, 'How can we be Moved by the Fate of Anna Karenina?', *Proceedings of the Aristotelian Society*, suppl. vol., 69 (July 1975), 67–93.

RADFORD'S ARGUMENT

Though Radford thinks that it is remarkable that we are the kind of creatures who are moved by the suffering of our fellows (because it is not logically odd to suppose we might not have been like this) we should not deduce from that, he says, that there is something odd about the emotions themselves. They are intelligible and rational only in so far as they are connected with belief in the existence of their presumed objects. In being moved by X we believe X to exist (or to be likely or probable). And if we discover that this belief is mistaken, or in some way unwarranted, then we either give up the emotion or, in the light of its undue persistence, can be legitimately accused of irrationality in that respect. We are 'moved' (made sad, frightened, etc.) by the exploits, fortunes, plights of fictional persons.

If we do not believe them to exist, how can we be moved? Radford does not deny that we are, or that he is. The question is, how can this not be regarded as incoherent or irrational? Hence, Radford concludes, after considering and rejecting various 'solutions', our emotional responses to fiction, brute and unavoidable though they are, rest upon a mistake.

Radford begins his discussion by treating 'being moved' as if it were a kind of gratuitous sentiment, or overflow of feeling, but one we may grudgingly call rational when it is tied down to belief in the existence of what we are moved by. It is noticeable that his examples of 'being moved', where they are not examples of near histrionics, concentrate on such things as weeping, tension in the breast, and lumps in the throat. But the more significant sign is the ease with which he contemplates the prospect that we might well have been creatures who are not moved by what happens to others, i.e. almost totally indifferent to our fellows. It is not clear what this supposition amounts to. We all might have been, he tells us, 'as some men are, viz. devoid of any feeling for anyone but themselves; whereas we cannot conceive that all men might have been chronic liars' (p. 67). The reason we cannot conceive that all men might have been chronic liars is that the act of lying presupposes a background against which it is at least possible to be honest. This background could not exist if there were no honest people. But just because this example is obviously absurd, it does not follow that the previous example is perspicuous.

What entitles us to suppose that Radford's Alternative Man would be like the 'some men' in his example? Clearly some men are selfish, callous, cold, insensitive, and so on. But these epithets resound with moral overtones. We do not just see such men as being different, but see the respect in which they are different as a failing. We regard such indifference not as a neutral condition visited upon will-less victims but as an attitude or disposition for which they can be blamed. If Radford's counter-factual supposition only amounts to the suggestion that instead of men there might have been creatures resembling animals or robots then nothing significant follows from this about our involvement with fiction. But what is revealing is that Radford here seems to imply that our capacities for caring about one another are just feelings which are added to our lives, such that we can contemplate what our lives might be like without them. 'Men might have been different in this respect' (p. 67) as though they would have been the same in all other respects.

For Radford there is no problem imagining how parents might experience the loss of a child in much the same way that a car-owner experiences the loss, theft, or destruction of his car (p. 67). He even oversimplifies what is involved in the reaction of the car-owner. We do not just *happen* to feel put out when our property is stolen or wilfully destroyed: we regard the matter as an intrusion, an affront on our liberty, or as the violation of a right. We experience not merely the inconvenience of losing an object we would rather not be without, but feel we have been wronged. We may take up a variety of attitudes to what we regard as the wrong done to us, but each of these possible attitudes exists against a background of values, themselves made possible by a network of human relations in which people do care about one another. It is only against such a background that the loss of a valued material object can have the significance it does for us.

Radford's oversimplification of what it is to 'be moved' in actual cases leads to an oversimplification of our responses to fiction. He makes it sound as though emotion were a kind of inexplicable discharge or effusion, but one which we can just about make sense of provided it is tied to belief. But in many cases emotion is so much more like a mode of apprehension. Indeed were I not stricken by grief upon the death of a loved one you could rightly accuse me either of not really loving the person concerned or not really grasping the fact of his or her death. In the latter case the presence of the requisite emotion seems to act as a criterion for having the requisite belief. The matching of emotion to belief here has to do with the idea of appropriateness within a particular context. It is therefore significant that we are not, or at least not if we are sensible, sane, and balanced people, absolutely heartbroken in responding to literary tragedy. My sadness at the death of Cordelia is simply not of the same order as even my sadness at the death of a mere associate, not because, as followers of Hume would insist, we delight in the former spectacle, but because it is something more than feeling, just as it is something more than feeling to perceive, and therefore be in some measure affected by, the monstrous cruelty of Regan.

Radford, however, does have a genuine problem to confront us with in pointing out that in our experience of fiction we lack the belief attaching to actual cases. Thus there is something to explain, rather than to brush aside as Weston and others have done. For Radford may well concede that such responses are not mere feelings but still insist upon asking how any form of feeling is possible, given that we do not believe the objects of our imagined acquaintance to be actual. Here it is necessary to bring in the distinction discussed in the previous chapter between emotions which have particular objects and emotions which have universal objects. Feelings or emotions directed to particular objects are a puzzle in the fictional case, and I shall try to deal with that problem in the next chapter. Emotions having universal objects, however, can surely be accommodated here. Given that we do not just happen to be nauseated by Regan and Goneril, our moral condemnation is not 'incoherent' even though we do not believe Regan and Goneril to exist: for it is rooted in an objection to qualities of character we should condemn in anyone, living or dead, actual or imagined. If our moral condemnation of Hitler is genuine, we should condemn anyone similarly placed who did what Hitler did. And surely the same is true *mutatis mutandis* of Iago, Bill Sykes, or Miss Bingley. Wickedness can be every bit as much an attribute of a fictional character as, say, being bald or fair-haired is. And how do we understand wickedness except by condemning it, even in fictional cases?[3]

---

[3] If this remark seems unconvincing, please note I return to the matter in Ch. 5.

WESTON'S ARGUMENT

For Weston, however, the above argument would not do at all. He slides out of the difficulty by arguing that in responding to character X one is responding not to X but to the literary work. Weston is correct to insist that our response to fictional characters must be understood in the context of our response to art, and equally correct to accuse Radford of overlooking this point. What is problematic is the way he develops the argument. So impressed is he by the difference it makes to us that characters in literature are fictional that he supposes they have a different 'kind of reality' (p. 84). According to this argument, Mercutio, for example, is very different from a real person. 'He' is part of a work of art, hence it is neither to Mercutio nor to his deeds or his fate that we respond: what we respond to in fiction are episodes or themes in their relation to the significance of the work as a whole. Since the significance of literature lies in the 'conception of life it provides' it is to a particular vision of life that we respond, not to individual characters or their circumstances.

The trouble with this is that it is difficult to see how literature could 'illuminate our lives' in the way he suggests if we are to believe that the kind of engagement most of us do have with fictional characters is inappropriate as a response to a work of art. When we experience a novel or a play for the first time we are not merely searching for thematic connections, relations between images, and other refinements which occupy the literary critic; if the writer has done his job well we are engaged by the plot and are interested in what happens to the characters. And no amount of literary criticism will deepen our understanding of the work if we do not feel what I shall here call 'primary engagement'.[4] (And it would be a strange kind of literary criticism that always made us less interested in the characters, except of course in cases where they turn out to be less interesting than they seem.) The problem arises in trying to give an intellectually respectable account of this interest. But Weston's reductionist move fails to tackle this problem since, it seems, we have no such interest to explain: our interest lies elsewhere. I say 'reductionist' because, for Weston, literary works

---

[4] If I may be permitted this term without immediately spelling out what a 'secondary engagement' might be (see Ch. 6).

are 'essentially objects of discussion and interpretation'. Without the 'primary engagement' I do not see what would be left to discuss or interpret. And I do not see how this primary engagement is possible if it excludes a moral interest. Since Weston firmly excludes moral response to fictional characters, it is worth considering this aspect of his argument in more detail.

There are two principal reasons why Weston claims that we cannot, logically, experience a moral response to fictional characters. The first has to do with the kind of relation (or, rather, lack of it) between fictional characters and ourselves. The second is that fictional characters are never free to do other than they are portrayed as doing (a very confused argument). Though these reasons overlap, I shall take them in turn. Consider first the following statement: 'We are not engaged with characters in our capacity as moral agents: we do not blame or praise characters for their actions, for there is no sense in which they can be said to be responsible for them.' (p. 92)

One certainly does want to give some account of the difference between our engagement with characters and our engagement with actual people in terms of the possibilities of our interaction with them, and as Weston rightly says, 'we cannot interact with *dramatis personae*' (p. 91). The conclusion he draws from this is that 'we cannot respond to characters as agents', and by this I take him to mean either that any response on our part to a character must be governed by the consideration that a character is not an agent or that we cannot respond to characters as agents who act upon us and with whom we interact. The second interpretation is uncontroversial enough. But the first is riddled with misapprehensions, and since there is enough in his article to suggest both interpretations the first needs teasing out a little.

Of the relation between fictional characters and ourselves, Weston says: 'We can neither grow and develop together; nor help nor impede one another's plans and activities' (p. 91). A correct inference from this would be that the relation between ourselves and a fictional character can never be that of one agent to another, hence we can never respond to a fictional character as one who stands in such a relation to ourselves. But the inference he seems to make is that a character is not an agent. I realize that Weston has other reasons (which we shall shortly consider), but as far as this argument is concerned, the conclusion does not follow from the true claim about the impossibility of interaction between fictional characters and readers or audiences.[5] Whether or not fictional characters are (moral) agents is a question which is not to be settled by attending to the relations which can or cannot exist between us and them, but by attending to the relations which can and do exist between one fictional character and another. Within the same fictional world, fictional characters can grow and develop together and can help or impede one another's plans and activities. Within the terms of the 'internal convention' discussed in the first chapter, they are no less capable of moral agency than we are.

In responding to the next stage of Weston's argument I shall at the same time have to confront a problem created by juxtaposing two of my own major conclusions. I have argued that moral concepts are essentially involved in our understanding of persons. And while I have suggested that fictional characters are persons within the internal convention, I also concluded that we are 'distanced' from a fictional world, such that we cannot be a party to anything that happens in it. This places a limit on the moral responses we can have to fictional characters, i.e. it rules out those moral attitudes we have to people simply because they are in the world, or because of the possibility of our interaction with them. Weston's failure to draw this distinction leads him to believe that *all* moral attitudes must be excluded from our responses to literary characters. The argument I shall henceforth develop is that some moral responses are appropriate to, and some inappropriate to, our understanding of characters and their circumstances.

A number of moral concepts are intimately bound up with the way that we can, in principle, affect others and they can affect us. For this reason it would be nonsense to say that we could be indignant, resentful, proud, or jealous in responding to a fictional character. Nor, I think, could we forgive one (or at least I am not sure what forgiveness would amount to in this case). But in so far as we respond to a literary work with an interest in the kinds of people it depicts, with an interest in what happens to them, what they will do and suffer, and how they will respond to their circumstances, we will inevitably be involved in blame and approval. In reading the text of a play we will 'place' the characters

---

[5] There is of course a sense in which fictional characters act upon us, though not in the way that we, as non-fictional agents, act upon one another.

in such a way that even when no explicit directions are given by the playwright we will be sensitive to the tone of their voices, and the attitudes, beliefs, and intentions governing the tone.

When we are confronted with the dialogue and the stage directions, we make sense of the words on the page, not as the code-breaker interprets signs, digits, or noises, but more as the lover sees the spirit that shines through a pair of eyes. We share with the actor who considers his script for the first time, a need to make sense of a speech, an action, a gesture, not by seeing these as disembodied abstractions to be pieced together but as embodied expressions of a human spirit. The plot is not a mechanical chart of comings and goings, but can only be grasped with the kind of understanding appropriate to human relations. There is no more a set of skills or techniques for understanding fictional characters than there is for understanding our fellow men. The words on the page are not understood in the same way we understand a physics textbook or a book on computer programming; they are servants to our capacity for seeing beyond the words the emergent properties appropriate to literature. In the case of a novel or a play we see not words but deeds; we see relationships, promises, betrayals, hopes, disappointments, and jealousies; we see ambition, greed, resentment, reconciliation, self-sacrifice, or the fulfilment of an evil project. And the deeper our understanding of actual persons, the deeper our understanding will be of fictional persons. The greater our insights into human nature, the greater our ability to appreciate or criticize the genuine or superficial insights into human nature that the novelist or playwright is expressing. If we are not prepared to admit to ourselves that evil is seductive we shall not understand Macbeth. If we are not able to grasp that love cannot be weighed and priced we shall not understand Cordelia, nor shall we understand why France married her. If we do not see for ourselves what is ridiculous about pomposity we shall not find Polonius a comic figure.

In the light of such considerations, it seems absurd to suggest, as Weston does, that we do not blame fictional characters for what they do. And where he speaks of praise, there would be less confusion if he referred to the attitude of which praise is the outward expression. Praising certainly does seem to require the possibility of interaction; or, since we may praise historical figures, let us say that praise requires a shared ontic domain. Though the admiration or approval which underlies praise is not straight-forwardly 'chosen', we can choose to praise—and a consideration inhibiting this performance may lie in the envisaged consequences of so doing. More crucially, praise can be capricious or insincere yet still be praise (consider educationists who advocate that all pupils should be praised in order to reinforce a 'positive self-image'). In other words, although the attitudes which underlie outward expression of blame and sincere praise may be polar opposites, praise and blame are not, since the latter does not lose its status as blame when it is not outwardly expressed. To clarify: I do not see how I could appreciate (in *King Lear*) Kent's sense of justice without having the attitude that underlies sincere praise. But that is not to praise him. In order to praise him I should have to say something like 'well done Kent', or 'Kent is a good chap'. The first is logically inappropriate since I cannot speak to him. The second looks like praise, but here I must agree with Weston that praising does seem to be an activity which only makes sense against a background of expectations that we may, at least in principle, change people's attitudes or persuade them to act differently (though this is by no means a concession to utilitarian theories which hold that praise and blame are undertaken for a practical purpose).

In this sense, and in this sense alone, there is something of importance to be extracted from Weston's claim that 'we are not engaged with characters in our capacity as moral agents'. Though it would hardly be commendable, my interest in another person may be a purely practical one. I may wish to know what makes him 'tick' in order to manipulate him to get what I want (it is said that Senator McCarthy was highly proficient in this corrupt sense). On the other hand I may have a purely moral interest. I may wish to understand Hitler's life to find out whether my moral beliefs about him are justified. Our interest in a fictional character cannot be a practical interest, since a fictional character has no existence in the actual world. And it cannot be purely a moral interest. It makes no difference to Jimmy Porter whether or not my beliefs about him are true or false, or whether I approve or disapprove of him. This is not simply because he cannot be hurt by what he does not know (for I may indeed do someone an injustice without him knowing). It is rather that our interest in Jimmy Porter is not totally independent of our interest in *Look Back in Anger*. Our interest in the play is not exclusively moral: or, if it is, then we are reading it in the spirit inappropriate to literature (using it simply as a vehicle for the exercise of our moral judgements) or we are assuming that the value of literature lies exclusively in its moral purpose—in which case we have not distinguished art from propaganda.

None of this, however, implies that we have no moral interest in fiction. I think we must have such an interest if we are to make sense of novels and plays. We must for instance regard Claudio's gullability (his willingness to believe the lies about Hero) as a failing, as a shallowness or immaturity of character, or perceive Iago's scheme as a betrayal of trust, a sordid enterprise. And why must 'blame' be over and above these judgements and perceptions? Confronted with such perceptions of our fellow men we are presented with all sorts of other questions which do not arise in the fictional case. If I am aware that my friend's wife is seducing the milkman, I am confronted with the necessity for judgement and decision about what, if anything, I am to do about it. And my propensity to act, or feel obliged to act, in one way rather than another may itself be fed back into my perception of what has been happening. Blame has many nuances, and in the course of our lives the form it takes may well be tied up with our tendencies towards indignation, resentment, and anger, or generosity, humility, and forgiveness, or insecurity, indecision, and paranoia. The fact that these conditions are missing from, or must be suspended from, the blame we attach to fictional characters does not rob it of its status as blame. What we have here seems to be blame in a 'pure state', as it were: unalloyed with some of the confederate emotions that attend our experience of the actual world (and there are those who locate the educative power of fiction precisely in that detachment). But we are not so detached from a fictional world that we do not condemn the atrocities we may witness, feel uplifted by the goodness that rises above it, or saddened by the virtue that is trampled into the dust. And in this I am placed at odds with Michael Oakeshott's argument that literature, belonging as it does to the 'idiom of poetry', and therefore consisting in 'images of contemplation and delight', is so far removed from 'desire and aversion', 'approval and disapproval', that we cannot regard Othello as a murderer, and that we must say of all fictional characters that moral approval or disapproval are alike inapplicable to these images; they are not people who inhabit or who have ever inhabited the practical world of desire and enterprise, and consequently their 'conduct' cannot be either 'right' or 'wrong' nor their dispositions 'good' or 'bad'.[6]

The similarity between Oakeshott's remarks and Weston's argument seems strong. Both share this confusion: that because novels and plays are art forms which therefore differ from, say, scientific and historical discourse, fictional characters are nothing like real people. 'Hamlet never went to bed.'[7] One can agree with Oakeshott that in our engagement with images in literature we '[move] about among them in a manner appropriate to their character' (p. 261). But that does not mean that it is inappropriate within what I have called the 'internal convention' to repudiate Weston's view of characters as mere devices or Oakeshott's view of them as 'phantoms'. The fictional world that contains them *is* a 'practical world of desire and enterprise'. That cannot be, of course, if Weston is right that literary characters have no freedom. And I have the feeling that even if we were to confront him with my 'internal convention' he would go on to deny that characters are responsible for their actions even within the internal convention.

I now must therefore take up the necessity/contingency issue shelved in Chapter 1. Lamarque's 'essentialist' doctrine of fictional characters insisted that they are only free to do other than what they are portrayed as doing in the sense that the author could have written a different work.[8] Weston seems to share Lamarque's 'essentialist' leanings but, unlike Lamarque, sees no possible difficulty in the conclusion that fictional characters necessarily do what they do. In fact for Weston it is not a conclusion but rather a premiss towards the further conclusion that we do not respond morally when reading fiction:

In the world of our everyday lives we can feel for people in the situations they find themselves in, and this is possible because people and their situations are to some extent separable, for things might have gone differently for them. But in fiction this isn't so. Whereas my son might not

---

[6] 'The Voice of Poetry in the Conversation of Mankind', in *Rationalism in Politics*, 227.

[7] Ibid. 226.

[8] 'What might have been different is not Tom Jones but *Tom Jones*' ('Fiction and Reality', in Peter Lamarque (ed.), *Philosophy and Fiction: Essays in Literary Aesthetics* (Aberdeen, 1983), 56).

have been killed in a car crash, Mercutio must die in the way he does. And this 'must' has nothing to do with a causal nexus but indicates that Mercutio is part of a work of fiction: if a character in a play does not die in that way then either he is not Mercutio or it is not a performance of Shakespeare's 'Romeo and Juliet'. (p. 85)

This is a bad argument. To explain why, it is necessary to distinguish what is true and what is false about those remarks. The fate and fortune of not just Mercutio but every other character in the play is inscribed on the pages of Shakespeare's manuscript. What is written dictates to the actor playing Mercutio that he must 'die' in a certain way and that the actor playing Tybalt must bring about Mercutio's death according to the stage direction: 'Tybalt under Romeo's arm thrusts Mercutio'. But the 'must' in 'Tybalt must thrust Mercutio and Mercutio must die' is one which is operative on the actors, not on the characters. The reason why the actor playing Tybalt must thrust Mercutio is not that Tybalt 'must' do what he does, but rather that at this point in the action that is what Tybalt does do. The character, Tybalt, has a freedom which the actor playing him cannot share. It is true that Shakespeare does not present an account of a situation, he stipulates what happens; but he stipulates what Tybalt freely and intentionally does, not what he is constrained to do.

A thoroughgoing Westonian would be committed in the end to regarding characters as bundles of abstract properties (a view which I have already argued is incoherent). I cannot imagine Weston being satisfied with a view that robs a fictional character of all that is of interest to us about human beings, yet that is where his argument ultimately leads. Possibly he is seduced to wrong conclusions by the kind of thought expressed in the following remarks by Rush Rhees:

When we think of some life in a novel going as it does and ending as it does, this belongs to the way we think of that character. It would not be the Anna Karenina we know if her life had gone differently. If someone tries to re-write the novel with a different ending, he will show how little he has understood.[9]

Rhees goes on to contrast our understanding of a fictional character with the kind of understanding we can have of an actual person.

[9] 'Art and Philosophy', in Rush Rhees, *Without Answers*, ed. D. Z. Phillips (London, 1949), 148.

And here his point seems to be that in the latter case there are a greater range of possibilities about what may or may not be true of that person. 'It is always possible that I shall learn of events and circumstances I had not supposed—that his life was not all I had supposed it was' (ibid.). Rhees points to an important difference here, because in fiction we do often have access to a complete life, or to understanding what a particular life may mean. But it would be wrong to suggest that we are never to be faced with considerations that may lead us to revise our estimate or impression of a particular fictional character, or of the significance of that life. Surely that is one of the things that literary criticism is, or should be, about. (Indeed the interpretation I discuss of Fanny Price's character in Chapters 6 and 7 is a completely different picture of Fanny Price from the one I had at the age of 17.) The limitation—and this is what Rhees is stressing (so too is Oakeshott, though it leads him to wrong conclusions)—is that there are forms of speculation which, though they might be appropriate in thinking about actual persons, are inappropriate to fictional ones. But that does not mean that we cannot or should not raise *any* questions which are not explicitly 'answered' in the text. Such speculative questions are only pointless and absurd where they do not bear upon the meaning of the play. Though it might be futile and absurd to raise an enquiry into the number of children born to Lady Macbeth, it is illuminating for instance to consider what quality of relationship might have existed between Othello and Desdemona had Iago not interfered (indeed the play seems to provoke such a question). And it is a mark of our interest in *King Lear* that we are inclined to wonder what became of the fool. The legitimacy of such questions (leading us back to the work and perhaps to a greater understanding of it) counts against the interpretation that someone like Weston might put upon Rhees's remarks. To take those remarks as support for the 'essentialist' or 'non-contingency' view would be unwarranted. Of course, 'it would not be the Anna Karenina we know if her life had gone differently'; but it would not be the Florence Nightingale we know if *her* life had gone differently. And 'it belongs to the way we think of' Alexander Pope that he was a hunchback, lived in Twickenham, and wrote satirical poetry. Though there are of course differences between actual and fictional cases, how could we deny to fictional characters the contingency of circumstances pertaining to any life, yet go on to suppose that the actions attributed to a particular character are portrayed as expressions of that life?

How could any novel or play provide a 'conception of life' if our perception and understanding of the characters are devoid of the moral presuppositions and moral modalities which are essentially involved in our conception of persons?

If we leave this matter aside, there is still Weston's further point to be considered that we do not judge fictional characters by our own moral standards but by the 'conception of life' the play provides. Without careful qualification, that view would lead to a type of moral relativism which is fundamentally incoherent, and it would not be rendered less incoherent by hiding itself behind the aura of a literary theory. The most radical interpretation of this thesis would have to be firmly resisted if it were to imply that a fictional world is a self-contained cosmos with moral premisses entirely different from our own (Weston in any case repudiates the idea that art is a self-contained game). However, the importance lying behind Weston's point can be brought out in a different way via a distinction between moral expectations and moral opinion. By moral expectations I do not mean expectations which are grounded in other things but ones which provide the grounds for our understanding of persons.

Whereas it is possible for people to disagree over matters of moral opinion, moral principle, or moral codes of conduct, such agreement or disagreement is itself only possible against a shared background which is so fundamental to anything we could recognize as human life that even the word 'expectations' seems inadequate to describe it, and any attempt to articulate it can sound banal or even bizarre. And certainly 'expectations' here does not mean inductive generalizations or theoretical beliefs.

We regard the actions of human beings in a wholly different way from the way we regard the 'actions' of robots, and this lies at the basis of our moral sense. But the way we conceive of, and react to, other human beings and what they do is not based on something like an intellectual belief or theory that they are human. We do not first observe their 'behaviour' and then infer, or reach the 'opinion', that it is the behaviour of a human being (as though such things need to be put to the test). Our attitude towards another person, as Wittgenstein reminds us, is 'an attitude to a soul'.[10] The soul is

---

[10] *Philosophical Investigations*, trans. G. E. M. Anscombe (Oxford, 1967) II. iv. 178e.

not a puff of gas; nor a spiritual substance, as Descartes thought. To say that my attitude to another person is an attitude to a soul, is to say that it is an attitude to *him*, both as an individual and as a fellow human being. But that is not to have an 'opinion' that he is a human being (who 'therefore' is capable of joy and suffering, laughter and sadness, pleasure and pain, etc.). As Peter Winch puts it:

Our characteristic reactions towards other people are not based on any theory we have about them, whether it is a theory about their states of consciousness, their likely future behaviour, or their inner constitution. We may well, of course, have our ideas about all these matters. We may for instance notice at once that someone in the street is joyful or distressed; and we have our expectations concerning their likely behaviour, at least to the extent that many things would astonish us. We should be aghast if someone were deliberately to approach a stranger and gouge out his eye. But such recognitions and expectations, together with our own reactions to other people, are on the same level, equally primitive. That is not to deny that often our reactions *are* based on reflections about others' states of mind, or probable future behaviour. The point is, first, that it is not always so; and second, that our *un*reflective reactions are part of the primitive material out of which our concept of a human person is formed and which makes such more sophisticated reflections possible.[11]

By calling our characteristic reactions to other people unreflective and primitive, Winch is not suggesting that our life in human society has no part to play in our expectation, say, of how a man will react to being given terrible news, such as the death of a loved one. What he does deny, and I think rightly, is that such expectations, or reactions to things like the joy or suffering of another person are derived from intellectual beliefs or theories: 'Yes, the life I have lived with other human beings is responsible for my reaction [e.g. of fear that a man being given tragic news will suffer] but not by way of any general theoretical beliefs it has led me to hold—though it may of course be that I do hold such beliefs.'[12] One's 'attitude' to a human being as to a soul is not one we could simply 'decide' to adopt or not to adopt.

Several years ago Wilfred Beckerman, in an article in *The Times*, claimed that it is irrational to 'pass moral judgement' on people for

---

[11] '*Eine Einstellung zur Seele*', in Peter Winch, *Trying to Make Sense* (Oxford, 1987), 147 (emphasis orig.).
[12] Ibid. 152.

anything they do, including even acts of extreme violence or cruelty, since we are, he said, causally determined by genetic and environmental factors. 'It is undignified, I suppose, to admit that we are just a form of infinitely variable robot; but, sadly, that is the fact of the matter.'[13] Ignoring the truth or falsity of that particular claim, what Beckerman advocates (and it is significantly contradictory that he does advocate how we *ought* to respond to 'wrongdoing') is not really coherent. He contends that while we should lock dangerous people up, 'there should be nothing personal about it': 'We need to be able to say, "we are sorry about this, it is not your fault that you are a monster. But society cannot tolerate such revolting behaviour, and we have to prevent you from giving free reign to the 'bad' sides of your nature with which you have been inflicted".' What Beckerman recommends is in effect that we should stop regarding one another as human beings. Though to advocate this with his high moral tone already shows the impossibility of the project: if we are robots, why should he try to persuade us to act or think differently? But that is not my real point. What is of more interest is contained here:

None of this means, however, that behaviour which sickens us most has to be tolerated. This dangerous deduction is usually the result of a failure to distinguish between passing moral judgements on people and passing judgements on acts that people carry out. That we cannot say that people are 'bad' in a moral sense does not preclude our saying that certain acts are 'bad' in the sense that they inflict suffering on other people.

Beckerman speaks of 'passing moral judgement' as though this were optional, like a little court scene in our heads which can be vetoed, and yet we are allowed to see such things as 'cruelty to children' as 'indescribably revolting'. That perception is to remain unchanged even though our perception of 'action' can apparently be divorced from the surrounding human context in which we view any human action. He even says that people can only be 'bad' in the sense that an apple is 'bad' if it makes you ill ('One would not dream of passing moral judgements on the apple for being what it is'). But apples do not 'inflict' suffering. They are not capable of acts of 'cruelty'. And the 'suffering' that people 'inflict' upon one another is not, and cannot be regarded, simply as a bodily state brought about through an impersonal, causal process in nature.

[13] Wilfred Beckerman, 'The Problem of Judging Evil', *The Times*, 17 Dec. 1986.

Even in cases of deliberate physical injury, our sense of the harm inflicted cannot be separated from the knowledge or thought that one person has done this to another. If a child falls on the ground and breaks his arm, our sense, and the child's sense, of the suffering and the harm is of a wholly different order from the suffering and harm inflicted if a parent, or even a total stranger, had broken the child's arm. Our conception of the suffering that one human being can inflict upon another goes far beyond ideas of physical injury, or indeed of any separately identifiable state towards which the action of another person could be considered merely a means. We can wound and insult people with words, or simply by ignoring them, and this hurt only has the force it does within our sense of relation to one another, not as 'infinitely variable robots' but as human beings.

The application of this argument to fiction is that in so far as we are to regard fictional characters as *doing* things, as engaging in acts and actions, we cannot have a non-moral or non-human perspective on their 'actions'. Our moral expectations are built into our very conception of what they are doing, e.g. when they tell lies, commit acts of cruelty, disregard bonds of friendship, mistreat their fathers, mothers, brothers, sisters, or when they are kind and generous, loyal and faithful, honest and true, self-sacrificing, brave, principled, or fair-minded. Whatever further significance we see in their actions, or however much we may enter into further debate about the nature and quality of their deeds and of their significance for the meaning of the literary work, our conception of a character as a human being has the mark of an 'attitude to a soul'.

The question of moral opinion, however, is different. I do not suggest that moral opinions can be taken up or discarded at will either, but there is surely a difference between the common moral expectations that are involved in seeing people as human beings (which is not something we have an 'opinion' about) and having an opinion about a particular moral issue, or a belief or commitment to a particular moral code. Here we can be presented with a problem when questions of morality and questions of literary criticism diverge. In this sense Weston would be quite right to object that it would be inappropriate or misguided if we expected a literary work to obey the dictates of our own personal opinions or moral convictions, and if we judged the merits of the work on such criteria. (Though one needs to point this out quite forcibly to those misguided people who write to the *Radio Times* praising a play for 'raising important issues' or complaining that such and such a fictional detective sets a bad example by smoking or by forgetting to lock his car door.)

It also makes a difference that we cannot interact with fictional characters. Confronted with an actual person whose actions or attitudes we find morally nauseating, it might be, at least in some circumstances, a perfectly reasonable or proper response to turn aside, dismiss him from our thoughts and focus our attention on other things. Such a response to a fictional character, except in unusual circumstances, would be bizarre. In life we might avoid a Jimmy Porter like the plague. Yet someone who says 'I shall neither read nor see the rest of the play because Jimmy Porter is a brash young man who gives me the shivers' would be demonstrating a signal failure to understand the institution of art. It does not follow from the fact that Jimmy Porter is nauseating that the play itself is nauseating, any more than it follows from the fact that a novel portrays boredom that it is a boring novel. Or as R. S. Thomas writes of the painting by Degas, *Women Ironing*:

> this is art
> overcoming permanently
> the temptation to answer
> a yawn with a yawn.[14]

Moreover, in many cases it is highly unlikely that the response we would have to particular fictional characters incarnated as actual persons would be like the response we have to them as fictional persons. If we could be confronted by an actual Fanny Price, it is by no means obvious that our feelings towards her would be like the ones Jane Austen's novel entreats us to have. I am reminded here of a drama critic who claimed that he adored Jimmy Porter, yet would find him insufferable in real life. The serious point lying behind this otherwise absurd speculation is that it does indeed make a huge difference to the kind of understanding we have of fictional characters that we are not engaged with them in the way we can be engaged with actual persons. If we tried to understand our fellow human beings exactly in the way we understand fictional characters we would be placed at a stage of

[14] 'Women Ironing', in R. S. Thomas, *Between Here and Now: Poems by R. S. Thomas* (London, 1981), 53.

remove inappropriate to interpersonal understanding. For, as David Hamlyn has argued, it is criterial of the kind of understanding we have of human beings that we are able to engage in relationships with them.[15] And in our relationships with others it is not unintelligible to speak of 'groundless' responses exemplified for instance in some kinds of hate or aversion.[16] We can in some circumstances hate or feel revulsed by another without having a reason. A 'groundless' response of *that* kind to a fictional character would lack sense. And it is always incumbent upon us to justify whatever feelings we do have about particular characters not only by giving reasons, but reasons which are appropriate as an interpretation of the literary work in question. Further, it is not a limitation upon our capacity to understand fictional characters that we cannot enter into relationships with them. What I here concede to Weston must carry the rider that it would be a limitation upon our understanding of fictional characters if we did not conceive of them as persons whose qualitites are revealed in *their* relationships with other (fictional) persons—a point which Weston's argument seems to overlook.

This chapter has raised more questions than it has settled about the relation between morality and literature, and these must be taken up in later chapters. What I have tried to establish so far is a rather rough-and-ready distinction between moral responses which do seem inappropriate as responses to literature and those moral responses which need to be rescued from Weston's rather rigid exclusion. This is to be explained by saying that since, as Weston quite rightly says, novels and plays characteristically present us with a conception or 'vision' of life, with various perspectives on human experience (though not simply as a means towards them) then if we are to understand such works we cannot divest ourselves of the moral presuppositions that enter into our understanding of persons. The former category of responses are inappropriate in so far as they intrude upon our willingness to submit ourselves to the work itself. As I shall later argue, in attending to a literary work we are responding to a human voice that is showing us something. In responding, say, to the character Hamlet, we are as Radford

---

[15] David Hamlyn, 'Person-Perception and our Understanding of Others', in T. Mischel (ed.), *Understanding Other Persons* (Oxford, 1974), 1–36.
[16] David Hamlyn, 'The Phenomena of Love and Hate', *Philosophy*, 53/203 (Jan. 1978), 5–20.

rightly says responding to *him* (Hamlet), but one needs to add 'through our response to Shakespeare's play'. In his analysis of the latter engagement, Weston drops out some of the things, indeed the most central things, that make such an engagement 'coherent'.

5
Readers and Spectators

The ugliness of a human being can repel in a picture, in a painting, as in reality, but so it can too in a description, in words. (Ludwig Wittgenstein, *Zettel*, 226, p. 40)

UNDERSTANDING, EMOTION, AND MORAL RESPONSE

Although what I have called the 'internal convention' provides an intentional context through which we refer to and speak about fictional characters as persons, there is more to the idea of a fictional world than would be suggested by thinking of it as a logical or semantic construct giving sense to an author's or a reader's 'statements' about fictional objects. Fictional worlds are imaginatively engaged with and thus experienced. By calling them worlds we imply that they have, or need to have, sufficient unity and coherence to be intelligible; intelligible, that is, not merely in some abstract or theoretical way (like a theorem in mathematics) but intelligible to our emotions. Fiction may be a man-made contrivance, but, as will be argued in Chapter 6, that does not mean that 'life' in art is a different kind of life. We do not first understand a story and then set about understanding the characters (as though they were mere units in a grand scheme which we can read like a diagram of the underground railway). Understanding the story involves understanding the characters as people. If that is the case, the 'credibility' we seek in a story is inseparable from the 'credible' realization of character.

The latter cannot be provided either by the mere stipulation of a narrator or by the act of make-believe. Here again I am led to anticipate an argument given later in more detail (Chapter 8) that being shown something in art is quite different from merely being given information. Consider for instance a not unfamiliar criticism of Iris Murdoch's novels that, while telling us much about the characters and their 'physical worlds' (often in painstaking detail), they do not lead us to feel or experience what the narrator apparently wishes the reader to accept as truths about them. Ian

Robinson for example remarks: 'Iris Murdoch's characters, to be sure, fall in and out of love with the frequency and nonsensicality with which other people when in a run-down condition catch colds. Some symptoms appear, *A* is said to be in love with *B*, then the symptoms go away again and all is as it was.'[1] If our understanding of a particular narrative requires our understanding of the love between two characters, it is not enough to be told that they are in love. The love must be realized or shown, and in a way which connects with what we can recognize as love between two human beings. But according to another critic, 'we follow her narratives out of curiosity, not concern; we are not usually moved by the fates of her characters, simply startled and intrigued by the unexpected turn of events, as if we were watching a game of snakes and ladders played with human beings for counters'.[2]

For our purposes it would be irrelevant to consider the justice or injustice of these critical accusations against Iris Murdoch. Philosophically, the interest is this, that it is not unreasonable to paraphrase such critics as claiming that her fictional worlds tend to lack a certain kind of emotional intelligibility. And if we agree at least with the principle lying behind such criticism it seems that we should say a reader's emotional engagement with a fictional world is not merely some kind of addition but is a requirement for his understanding, such that we could not question whether it is rational to be 'concerned' or 'moved' (*à la* Radford) without thereby questioning whether it is rational to understand a fictional world.

But if we can enter into perfectly intelligible discussion about fictional persons without the belief that they actually exist, why should we suppose that understanding such persons and their circumstances would be any less intelligible without that existential belief? Within the internal convention we do think of fictional characters as existing persons without thinking *that* they exist; and it is within the internal convention (the language-game of fiction) that we understand them and what they do with the same emotional and moral expectations that are written into our understanding of human beings (how else would fiction be intelligible?). As

---

[1] *The Survival of English* (Doncaster, 1981), 201.
[2] S. W. Dawson, 'Iris Murdoch: The Limits of Contrivance', in Boris Ford (ed.), *The Present: The New Pelican Guide to English Literature*, viii (London, 1983), 230.

far as moral expectations are concerned, Weston, as we have seen, seems to hold the belief that fictional characters cannot be approved or disapproved of since they cannot be extracted from the fiction. But it is precisely because they are located in fictional worlds that we do and must, in understanding such worlds, think of characters and their actions in the way we think of people and their actions.

Since moral attitudes have universal rather than particular objects we could say that the problem of belief is not a difficulty here since I can (rationally) have an attitude to X even though I do not believe X to exist (or perhaps even believe X to be likely or possible). Someone might for instance condemn the very idea of time-travel ('it is not for us to interfere with nature') without believing either that the means for time-travel exist or that time-travel is logically possible. Or, to take another case, in entertaining the hypothesis that all human beings might in principle be prevented from dying (given enormously advanced medical technology) I might have a moral objection to the idea of such an enterprise, thinking for instance that it would be an attempt to rob life of meaning (think of Janáček's *The Makropulos Case*). Indeed if it were not possible to have moral attitudes to states of affairs we do not believe to be actual it is not clear how we could give an adequate explanation of how it is that, for moral reasons, we wish to prevent some states of affairs from actually occurring. Suppose that Hitler had never existed and that we merely read about such exploits in a work of fiction. The genocide perpetrated by a fictional 'Hitler' would be no less blameworthy than it is in the actual case. In the fictional case we would no doubt be less upset. But that is not the point. Within a fictional world, murders must be as terrible as murders really are. Macbeth does not commit a species of lesser sin called fictional murder any more than he stabs Duncan with an imaginary dagger. The word 'fictional' is an existential disclaimer that applies to the fictional world as a whole. In the sense that the fictional world does not exist, neither do the murders. In the sense that it does exist the murders are actual murders which are actually dreadful.

If the intelligibility of a fictional world had nothing to do with our moral emotions then we might as well laugh at *King Lear*. (And it is surely no accident that there is something incomprehensible about such an example: how could such 'laughter' be intelligible?[3]) Someone who does not feel appalled at the goings-on in *King Lear* simply does not understand the play. Our interest in the death of Cordelia is not simply an abstract interest in the function it may have in a symbolic weave or in a narrative scheme. If we have a humane comprehension of the events and the circumstances out of which they arise, we must feel a sense of loss. That sense of loss is not of course like an inference or deduction from a series of fictional propositions: it is created through the medium of poetic drama. But the medium is not a sort of iron curtain sealing off some phantasmic realm from penetration by our moral attitudes. What is revealed to us *through* the medium has to do with the suffering, torment, blindness, and ruthlessness of human beings. We are not, however, overcome by emotion in the way we would be in the case of actual grief. Someone who is saddened by the death of Cordelia does not need 'bereavement counselling' (or if he does, it might be better to send him to a psychiatrist). The medium, and a writer's handling of it, also makes a difference to the way our emotions and attitudes are involved in understanding the representation. For example I think, while feeling little, that Mrs Norris in *Mansfield Park* is an abominable woman. She is smug, self-centred, hypocritical, domineering, cruel, and callous. Do I blame her? How can I say this without blaming her? She is no less to blame because she is fictional. However, for reasons which will be made clear later, that this blame does not amount to the strong sense of outrage or moral revulsion we can feel with some other fictional characters (e.g. Goneril and Regan) can only be explained by considering our mode of access to fictional characters.

FICTIONAL NARRATOR AND IMPLIED READER

Jane Austen has given Mrs Norris the above qualities. But it is a fallacy to think of the relation between an author and his characters in terms of God and His creation. As far as the world in the novel is concerned Jane Austen does not exist. Certainly Jane Austen has written the novel, but in responding to the world she has created we react to its occupants, and Jane Austen is not, and cannot be,

---

[3] Laughing *at* X is not just a matter of making a laughing sound in the presence of X. (See Peter Winch, 'Text and Context', in *Trying to Make Sense* (Oxford, 1987), 29–31.)

one of its occupants any more than we can be. The narrator is a role within the fiction: a fictional voice. 'And what of my poor Fanny?' is not uttered by a narrator who happens to be one of the characters (as is the case with some novels) but neither is the narrator Jane Austen. The 'my' in 'my poor Fanny' is not the 'my' of ownership. It does not mean 'the character I have created': it means 'the person with whom I sympathise'.[4] We know who Jane Austen is, but we do not know who the narrator is. It is an unidentified voice—even when it says 'Let other pens dwell upon guilt and misery'. The 'pen' is as fictional as the characters. It is not Jane Austen's pen. Jane Austen decides what the characters do. The narrator, however, describes and reports. The voice is not 'making up' a story but telling us what happened. In the language-game appropriate to her craft, as soon as she puts pen to paper in writing her novel, Jane Austen ceases to speak as Jane Austen, for it is a different kind of 'speaking'. The medium determining the nature of her utterance turns the use of the first person singular into a 'someone' who knows what has happened and is telling us, without thereby dictating or determining what happens (in the sense that Jane Austen determines the plot and decides on the fate of her characters).

In responding to the fiction, although we know that Jane Austen has written every word, that she is the controlling intelligence behind the *work*, we enter into a kind of 'bargain' with the author, and one that only has the sense it does against the conventions and traditions of story-telling. That 'bargain' transforms the author into a voice calling itself John or Mary or nobody in particular. It is to that voice we respond and through which we experience the characters, though, for reasons given in Chapter 2, this is not a matter of pretence or make-believe. Having made that proviso, I do agree with Walton that as appreciators we 'descend to the level of the fiction'. In attending to the narrator I attend to a fictional voice, and it is tempting to say that strictly speaking it is not *I* who am addressed by the voice, for such modes of address have been suspended. 'An artist works for an audience without speaking to

---

[4] In some novels of course the internal and external conventions can be mixed, such that the narrator plays with the 'fictionality' of the characters. But the impact of 'meta-narrative comment' relies upon the reader's awareness of the absurdity.

anyone.'[5] The assumed self of the narrator addresses an implied reader. Just as the narrator is a role within the fiction, so too is the implied reader. As an appreciator of the fiction I occupy that role, but that does not entail that I imagine myself as someone else: the role of implied reader is not a person but a mode of attention.

In case this argument is beginning to sound distressingly Continental, let me clarify it by saying that, as a point about the intentional objects of perception, we may distinguish the following positions.

1. Outside our engagement with a literary text, the reader may regard the text simply as print. At this level there can be no engagement with meaning—despite the confused pretensions of the psycholinguist, Frank Smith, who has convinced numerous English departments that comprehension equals *imposing* meaning upon 'the meaningless surface-structure of print'.[6] It is a confusion even to call 'print' a surface-structure since, as far as reading is concerned, it seems to lack everything that might be called a structure. And psycholinguists like Smith put it at that level by definition. What they do is select a description of written matter which clearly entails non-engagement with meaning, and then kick the premiss away again by ludicrously insisting that it can be a bearer of meaning, but only if meaning is imposed upon its lack of meaning. 'Surface-structure' entails by definition that it is outside the realm of discourse in which meanings are discussed, and it is therefore quite literally meaningless even to call it 'meaningless'—i.e. that it *fails* to mean. It is not 'up for grabs' at this level. We no more engage with 'print' than we engage with splodges on canvas when attending to a painting. Nor is 'print' what a writer writes or 'splodges' what a painter paints (unless we wish to insult him).

2. We may regard the text simply as words. But since words are only vehicles of meaning on the highways of discourse, this again is a surface description of what the writer writes and of what we attend to. Mere words, or arrangements of words, are not the intentional objects of our attention (although in critical practice we

---

[5] Rush Rhees, *Without Answers*, ed. D. Z. Phillips (London, 1949), 44. Rhees's point here is that the artist does not work to satisfy an existing audience but 'to create an audience through his work'.

[6] This absurd dogma sails through his three books, *Reading* (Cambridge, 1978), *Understanding Reading* (New York, 1982), and *Writing and the Writer* (London, 1982).

may wish to articulate how our impressions are importantly affected, say, by the use of this word rather than that, or this arrangement rather than that arrangement in a particular context). As far as stories are concerned (though the application of this point is wider) we do not first attend to words and then go on to construct ideas. As Wittgenstein put it, 'Certainly I read a story and don't give a hang about any system of language. I simply read, have impressions, see pictures in my mind's eye, etc. I make the story pass before me like pictures, like a cartoon story. (Of course I do not mean by this that every sentence summons up one or more visual images, and that that is, say the purpose of a sentence.)'[7]

3. A reader may regard the text as a piece of discourse of a certain *sort*—e.g. a love-letter, a novel, a play, a sonnet, a lampoon, a philosophical tract, a prayer-book, a suicide note, a business letter, or a set of instructions on the maintenance of gas-fired central heating boilers. At this level he is engaging with a particular type of discourse and thus with the text as a vehicle of communication. Given that we have, within the public context that determines them, a range of different expectations to bear on particular kinds of texts or particular genres, it is only at this level that we can even begin to regard the work as a vehicle of meaning, appropriate to the kind of discourse it is. And this confirms the importance of speaking of the purpose or intention of the work.

4. The reader engages with the 'fictional world' of the novel or play. Given that we can in some sense engage with a novel or play without particularly understanding it or responding to it, we cannot rest with level (3). Since it is part of the intention of a novel to lead the reader into the story it contains, the intentional 'object' of my attention when reading a novel is the fictional world and the persons and circumstances it contains. When my attention is absorbed, and this absorption is justified with sufficient understanding, I seem to enter the fictional world, while remaining outside it. (Indeed it is this phenomenon which produces the involvement-yet-detachment I discuss in Chapter 8.) Perhaps it would be better to distinguish two levels here. In entering the fiction I attend to a narrator's voice. Through my engagement with that voice I am led to attend to what the voice says, such that the

[7] *Zettel*, eds. G. E. M. Anscombe and G. H. von Wright, trans. Anscombe (Oxford, 1981), 243, p. 43.

narrator becomes 'transparent' and almost seems to be bypassed as I 'see' and 'hear' the characters for myself as though I had direct access to them. At other times I am conscious of attending to the narrator. And of course, depending on the way the novel is narrated, this dual attitude—or perhaps oscillation of attention— may be intended in the very presentation of the work. However, this phenomenon takes place *within* the experience of fiction and should not be confused with the 'dual standpoint' mentioned earlier; for the point there was that no matter how deep our involvement in fiction we are still fully aware that it is fiction.

This now leaves us with a different problem to confront. It would be illogical to suppose that we see fictional characters as half-people who perform half-deeds in a half-way house of exist- ence. Within a fictional world the characters are responsible for their actions. They are moral agents. Their sins are no less blameworthy than actual sins. Yet the price of engaging with a fictional world (our 'entrance-fee', as it were) is that we contem- plate that world without being a denizen of that world: we surrender our status as moral agents, but not our capacity for moral attitudes. Although I have said that moral attitudes do not require belief in the actual existence of their objects, that only establishes the possibility of moral attitudes to fictions (or, in the broadest sense, their necessity—given that fictional characters are seen as persons). But there is the further question of the form such attitudes can take. *A* and *B* may morally condemn *C*, yet their attitudes in other respects may be different. *A* may take a more severe view of the matter than *B*, and so on. Yet this depends, among other things, on the character and personality of *B* and *C*. Where is the scope for such 'autonomy' in responding to fiction? I shall try to deal with this general difficulty in the next section.

ACCESS TO CHARACTERS AND THE FORM OF OUR ATTITUDES

In the mode of imagining appropriate to fiction we are 'there' without being a party to anything that happens, but are affected by it. Yet the fact that we cannot intervene means that we are not affected in the same way we would be if we could, in principle, intervene. In the actual world this 'inactivity' would be amenable to moral assessment: e.g. it might be considered prudent or callous.

Our experience of a fictional world is the nearest to being disembodied that we can ever get. Here, in passing, it is as well to note that there is a crucial difference between our experience of a novel and our experience of a play in performance. In the latter case we seem to be really present yet without material existence—or at least we seem to be invisible witnesses. This point occurred to me during a performance of Peter Shaffer's *Amadeus*.

SALIERI [*calling to audience*]. Vi Saluto! Ombri del Futuro! Antonio Salieri—a vostro servizio!
[*A clock outside in the street strikes three*]
I can almost see you in your ranks—waiting for your turn to live. Ghosts of the future! be visible. I beg you. Come to this dusty old room—this time, the smallest hours of dark November 1823—and be my confessors!

(I. ii)

In engaging with the world in the novel I am not so much a witness as a member of an implied audience/readership. The play proceeds as though there were no one watching,[8] whereas the fictional voice of the narrator requires an implied audience to share something.

I shall return to drama later. What I want to explain here is that the implied audience to the narration makes a difference to the nature of our moral response. Whereas Jane Austen is the creator, the voice I attend to may not even share the moral views of the novelist (which is another reason for not assuming that the two voices are one). In attending to the narrator the implied reader is not only invited to take up moral attitudes but they are already given in the narration. In our experience of people in the actual world we are free, within limits, to see their actions under a variety of different descriptions. Human actions do not come to us conveniently packaged with labels on; we often have to decide what it is a person can be said to have done or caused. All this takes place against a background of expectations, assumptions, and presuppositions of value which are not themselves 'chosen'. But within this shared inheritance we form our own views of people.

In certain cases judging the nature and quality of another person's actions cannot be wholly separated from the 'picture' we

---

[8] Except in cases like *Amadeus*. There it seems that as 'ghosts of the future' we too are fictionalized.

have of the other person. Sometimes we will rely on this 'picture' to inform our judgements ('I don't believe he was lying; he's not that sort of chap') and sometimes our judgements change our view of that person's character ('well if he can do *that*, he's not the sort of person I thought he was'). In our experience of a novel we are in a sense confronted with people whose actions have already been interpreted. That does not mean that there is nothing left to understand or that we will always find ourselves in sympathy with the attitudes expressed in the narration. To say that the characters have already been interpreted means that we are presented with *an* understanding of them. We are told or shown what they have done, caused, been responsible for; what they have suffered, what their interests, motives, hopes, beliefs, and perceptions are. We are shown things which in actual life would be a matter of conjecture, assumption, belief, or individual judgement. However incomplete, the rudiments of the 'picture' are given to us through the narration. We do not surmise that Mrs Norris does not really care about her sister, Mrs Price, whom she 'helps'. On the contrary, through the narrator we learn that she never had any intention of inconveniencing herself or of supporting Mrs Price's daughter, Fanny, but that she simply wanted it to seem as if she had taken a leading part in easing Mrs Price's burden and giving the child the benefit of better surroundings. 'Under this infatuating principle, counteracted by no real affection for her sister, it was impossible for her to aim at more than the credit of projecting and arranging so expensive a charity . . .'[9]

Now the seeming paradox is that on the one hand we do blame her: we do see her as a scheming, self-righteous, and hypocritical busybody. But, on the other hand, how is this to be reconciled with the fact that we have, according to the rules of the 'game', suspended the autonomy of judgement that belongs to our understanding of actual people? Given what we have to surrender of ourselves, are these moral responses any the less ours?

First perhaps we should distinguish cases of emotional response involving particular objects from moral responses involving universal objects. Consider the case of a character who is intended to elicit an emotional response—Uriah Heep. In his case we are

---

[9] *Mansfield Park* (New York, 1964), 9. (All references will be to the Signet/New American Library edn.)

invited, and it seems that most of us accept the invitation, not merely to blame him but to feel revulsion towards him, to dislike him intensely. (The case of Mrs Norris is not like this, for reasons I shall later explain.) These feelings or emotions are not entirely independent of our moral perceptions (e.g. that he is a conniving, duplicitous cheat, as well as being an obsequious man) but they are feelings and emotions nevertheless. We do not merely despise what he stands for: we dislike *him*. He has an odious and repulsive manner which is disgusting, like slime. But feelings of disgust and repulsion carry an implicit reference to the person who experiences them. To *find* something disgusting is not merely to point to the quality of a thing but to see it as a quality that affects oneself.[10] Whereas in saying that Henry's behaviour is despicable I am not necessarily saying something about myself but about Henry and his behaviour, in saying that *X* is disgusting I am also saying something about myself in relation to *X*. But how is this relation to *X* possible in the fictional case? I can find no other solution to this difficulty than to take up a hint given in Roger Scruton's argument that our emotions or feelings towards fictions are imagined feelings or emotions. Since emotions directed to particular things presuppose a belief that these things exist, and that belief is missing in the fictional case, what we respond to is an imagined object; and in our attempt to understand it we imagine the emotion that would be appropriate if the object were actual. In contemplating such emotion we form a 'conception of what from the subjective point of view it feels like. Then [we] find [ourselves] drawn into sympathy with [that] emotion.'[11]

In his book, *Feeling and Reason in the Arts*, David Best has treated this argument about imagined objects to a cursory dismissal. Unfortunately one has to diagnose Best's reasons for this, since he does not give them explicitly; but as far as I can see, it is prompted by his failure to distinguish 'imaginary' from 'imagined'. He objects, 'one does not *imagine* that Othello murders Desdemona; Othello *does* murder Desdemona.'[12] But this is no argument for denying that Othello and Desdemona are imagined objects and

---

[10] See David Pole, 'Disgust and Other Forms of Aversion', in Pole, *Aesthetics, Form and Emotion*, ed. G. Roberts (London, 1983), 219–31.

[11] 'Fantasy, Imagination and the Screen', in Roger Scruton, *The Aesthetic Understanding: Essays in the Philosophy of Art and Culture* (London, 1983), 132.

[12] *Feeling and Reason in the Arts* (London, 1985), 178 (emphasis orig.).

that the murder is an imagined murder. It is only possible to say that Othello murders Desdemona from the internal convention. In that sense, and in that sense only, the murder is not an imagined murder. Nevertheless it is an imagined murder if we are speaking from the external convention. From the external convention there is no actual murder. But, for reasons given in Chapter 1, there is a dangerous ambiguity in reaching for the adjective 'imaginary' since it is not clear that it has a home in either the internal or the external convention. Within the internal convention the murder is not imaginary: it actually takes place. But outside the play there is no such murder, not even an imaginary one. In saying that we do not imagine the murder, Best uses the word 'imagine' in a sense that suggests 'fantasize'. Certainly we do not fantasize that Othello kills Desdemona (a word that implies we are either mistaken or that we are entertaining as true what is false). And it is a fallacy to think that the description 'imagined murder' entails that kind of proposition about our mental states. In order to understand the play we are required to imagine everything that happens in that fictional world. But since it is that world as a whole which is an imagined world, it is not made up of a series of individual or episodic acts of imagination. In other words I do not simply imagine Othello murdering Desdemona in the way that I now imagine a twelve-footed canary settling on my typewriter. In imagination I engage with the fictional world of *Othello* of which that murder is only a part.

It might be objected, however, that the argument about imagined emotion makes it sound too much like a deliberative activity. In responding to a fictional object do we really have to 'work out' what would be appropriate as a response if the object were actual? Don't we just respond immediately to the fiction? This tempting objection rests on a couple of misconceptions. Although I have denied that our reference to fictional objects is really a reference to what exists in the 'real' world, that does not mean that we have to deny that our understanding of, or reaction to, a fictional object has some connection with the feelings we would have if that object were actual. We do not therefore 'work out' what it would be appropriate to feel in an actual case, for that is already contained within our understanding of the fictional situation. But since we know it to be fictional, our emotions do not dispose us to the kind of action they would in an actual case.

In the painting *The Beheading of St John the Baptist* by Pierre Cecile Puvis de Chavannes, St John kneels in the foreground while his executioner, rear left, motions to strike. Were we present in reality the horror we should feel might dispose us to do something—rush to stop the hand of the executioner, or run away—or we might remain immobile, transfixed with terror. Since we know this to be a painting, we contemplate what we see; but this 'inactivity' does not correspond even analogously to the inactivity of standing transfixed with horror at an actual scene, for the latter is not a state of contemplation: it is more like a state of paralysis. We have a sense of the horror that would arise in actuality. To that extent we feel it and may even have some bodily feelings, but what we witness in the case of the painting is not just some sort of likeness to an actual scene (representations are not mere imitations): we also experience ideas and thoughts contained within what is depicted. (There is thus a difference between responding to a representation and responding to, say, a photograph of a spider, where the mere likeness causes an involuntary shudder.) In the case of the painting we notice, as we would not in the heat of the actual moment, the blue leaf falling to the ground, and think of this not just as a sort of visual pun against the blue robe of the executioner but as an idea that invites us to consider the beheading in relation to occurrences within nature. We also notice the dark green leaf on the ground and this serves to confirm the thought. This seems to inform our view of the resigned and placid look on St John's face in stark contrast to the face of Salome, which is placid in a different way—expressionless, yet in a way that suggests satisfaction. In contrast again, we view the seated figure of a woman in a green dress, her arms covering her face. That figure, in its colour and its shape, draws us back again to the tree which dominates the background. This seems to remind us that death in nature is all of a piece with rebirth, and St John's eyes are fixed upon the cross, suggesting thoughts of the life to come. His imminent death is as inevitable as the completion of the leaf's fall. Viewed as an event in nature, the beheading has no more significance than the termination of a physical object: yet such a thought is strangely transfigured as we are now invited to share St John's view of his death as the mere destruction of his body. With that thought our original and primitive feeling of horror gives way to a calmer view of his death as something that has meaning and dignity.

Since in understanding a painting we are not responding to a mere likeness, we are invited to see the fictional world of the painting as having a meaning. And though our search for that meaning involves thinking, what we come to understand through the painting cannot be grasped independently of our feelings and emotions. In the case of a novel our access to the fictional world is through the narrator, and we respond to that voice not as though it were a sort of speaking machine that states what is the case, but as a living voice with which we have some relationship, a voice that expresses a human perspective on what is taking place in the fictional world. I do not have to believe that Mrs Norris exists in order to blame her for her actions: it is enough that I understand the story. When the narrator in Jane Austen's novel reflects on the selfishness of the amateur actors in their rehearsals for a perform-ance of *Lover's Vows* we cannot accept that they behaved selfishly and not blame them; for to concur in this judgement is a way of blaming. The narrator does not, however, merely express an opinion, but shows the selfishness and egoism in, for instance, Rushworth's incessant bragging about his 'two-and-forty speeches'.

Whether or not I disapprove of Mrs Norris or any other character will therefore depend on whether or not I trust the narrator. Since, logically, the author cannot be the narrator, even in cases where we might expect them to be at one in their attitudes, it is not absurd to disagree with some of the attitudes the narrator expresses or reveals (though there is an important qualification to this, as will be seen later). The independence of author and narrator is also demonstrated by the fact that there are some novels in which the narrator turns out to be insane. However, it is also important to remember that Jane Austen's novels belong to a genre. This affects the 'bargain' between author and reader. In regarding her novel as 'naturalistic' I am therefore prepared to assume that the narrator is one I am to trust, and therefore if I find myself at odds with the narration this will reflect either a failure of my understand-ing or the need for me to justify this disagreement (a point to which I return in Chapter 7).

However, in so far as I do 'go along' with the narrator I am not subjected in *Mansfield Park* to long passages which 'moralize' about the characters (such as one finds in Dickens). At times I am given Mrs Norris's exact words and form a conception of her through them. At other times I am shown the effects she has upon other people. In life such judgements would by no means be so certain or straightforward, and may often be a matter for moral dispute. In the novel the matter has already been decided. Here we must consider how a literary work determines the form our attitudes can take. I am invited to share the narrator's attitudes not just by being told what Mrs Norris did, what she caused, what really motivated her and so on, but through the tone and style of the narration itself. Confronted with an actual Mrs Norris I might be unable to control my temper. I might wish for her early demise, or hope that she marries a foreigner and emigrates. Not only is it the case that I cannot wish such things of a fictional character, but in any case the tone and style of the narration disposes me to find Mrs Norris's obnoxiousness amusing: 'Sir Thomas sent friendly advice and professions, Lady Bertram dispatched the money and baby-linen, and Mrs Norris wrote the letters' (p. 7). Here, Mrs Norris, the infuriating busybody, is rendered harmless by the bathos. To feel outraged by the lady would be a failing in sensitivity, a failure to appreciate the mood of the narrator (if the narrator can get the woman into perspective, why can't we?). Consider the situation in actual life when a friend describes his familial conflicts. If the way he describes these conflicts is serious and severe we might be prepared to consider that his mother-in-law is a force to be reckoned with. If, however, he puts her down in a joke or with winning cynicism, we shall perhaps feel inclined to consider these faults as foibles.

The narrator leaves us in no doubt that Mrs Norris is to blame for a number of things. To this extent our moral attitudes are engaged: we quite rightly condemn the way she behaves. Yet partly because of the style of narration, and partly because the world this voice describes seems riddled with minor forms of vice and folly, we are led by the nose to offset the blame against the realization that there is something intriguing and amusing about human failings, that these failings are not the exclusive property of one or two individuals, but well-nigh universal. Mrs Norris's brand of villainy is only made possible because of Lady Bertram's couch-reclining indolence, Sir Thomas's pompous blindness, the unwisdom of a sister who opted for a disastrous marriage to a drunk, teemed with more children than she could cope with, and so on. The 'cushioned ease' of Mansfield Park, the over-activity of the London-based Crawfords, the disorder of the Portsmouth family—

none passes without implied censure. Yet the censure of all three
lessens the impact of the censure of any single environment. Each
environment produces a soil in which some kind of vice may
flourish. This has an effect upon our attitudes to the characters as
individuals. Evil is not seen as a force originating in the individual,
but as a kind of seduction away from the true spirit (the order and
decorum) of Mansfield Park. The characters in this sense are
victims without being one jot less responsible for the vices which
the environment provides the opportunity to exercise.

If we understand this story we therefore must blame the characters for their shortcomings. But this blame is not separable from
understanding what happens, understanding the interplay of different forces and what they represent. Someone who read the novel
and found it possible to blame *only* Mrs Norris or Lady Bertram
would not understand the story. To fix on Lady Bertram's indolence and not to see the opposite danger of incessant activity (the
noisy, bustling chaos in Portsmouth, the mischievous energy of the
Crawfords, the 'improving' zeal of Mr Rushworth, the busybodydom of Mrs Norris) would also fail to appreciate why we are asked
to approve of, and admire, Fanny Price. For she has a quiet repose
without being lazy, and an active moral sensibility without the self-
righteousness of Mrs Norris or the unseeing pomp of Sir Thomas
Bertram.

Though, then, we do morally approve or disapprove of fictional
characters, we do so not by singling out particular characters from
the work, but by coming to see what the work is about. If we find
ourselves drawn in by the narration, the attitudes are none the less
ours for their being implied in the narration. But the narration
guides the *form* our attitudes take. Mrs Norris for instance is hit
off in devices like understatement. Discussing the dangers and
difficulties of adopting Fanny Price, Sir Thomas explains that it
would be inappropriate if she came to see herself as an equal of his
daughters, Julia and Maria:

'Their rank, fortune, rights and expectations will always be different. It is
a point of great delicacy, and you must assist us in our endeavours to
choose exactly the right line of conduct.'

Mrs Norris was quite at his service; and though she perfectly agreed
with him as to its being a most difficult thing, encouraged him to hope
that between them it would be easily managed. (p. 11)

The understatement is telling. For not only is Mrs Norris always concerned merely to appear to be 'at his service' but, given the zeal with which she is to exercise this duty by constantly reminding Fanny of her inferiority, the tone of the narrator is ironic indeed and the criticism has far greater effect.

It is therefore surprising, though frequent, to find literary critics who feel that moral attitudes need not enter into our appreciation of literature and can actually be suspended. Patrick Murray, for instance, echoes what is often taken to be a necessary truth about the dramatic monologue in poetry that 'the reader takes up the speaker's view of things in order to understand him and he suspends moral judgement'.[13] Murray goes on to say that Browning's 'My Last Duchess' is a 'perfect specimen' of this:

Here the speaker is an amoral Renaissance Duke who has unjustly put his last Duchess to death and is arranging another marriage for himself through an ambassador, mainly for the sake of the dowry. But a necessary condition of reading the poem is the willingness of the reader to understand the Duke, even to sympathize with him. This is possible firstly because we are given the facts of the case from his point of view, and secondly because we admire him, however grudgingly, for his power of intellect and will, for his sheer affrontery, his aristocratic contempt for his listener's intelligence, and his highly developed artistic sense.[14]

It must be admitted that in reading Browning's poem we have an insight into the speaker and an interest in him that is not exclusively a moral interest. But no matter how true it might be to say that we (grudgingly) admire the Duke's audacity, we cannot both understand the poem and admire *him*. We are given, it is true, some insight into the way he sees things: his wife 'deserved' her fate since

> Sir, 'twas not
> Her husband's presence only, called that spot
> Of joy into the Duchess' cheek . . .

But what we actually discover is not an adulterous wife, but an unreasonably jealous and possessive husband who regards his wife's chief 'crime' as one of insufficient gratitude for the honour he has done by marrying her.

[13] *Literary Criticism: A Glossary of Major Terms* (London, 1978), 50.
[14] Ibid. 49.

> She thanked men,—good! but thanked
> Somehow—I know not how—as if she ranked
> My gift of a nine-hundred-years-old name
> With anybody's gift.

'I know not how' is one of several interjections which serve not as a genuine pause for thought, but as rhetorical flourishes which heighten the inappropriateness of the Duke's severe attitude. The speaker is sincere in his severity, yet insincere about himself:

> Who'd stoop to blame
> This sort of trifling? Even had you skill
> In speech—(which I have not)—to make your will
> Quite clear to such an one, and say, 'Just this
> Or that in you disgusts me; here you miss
> Or there exceed the mark'—and if she let
> Herself be lessoned so, nor plainly set
> Her wits to yours, forsooth, and made excuse,
> —E'en then would be some stooping; and I choose
> Never to stoop . . .

It is clear from the extravagance of the speech that the speaker's disclaimer about his lack of skill is disingenuous; and it is a further irony that such a lack of skill should be considered the only thing that might deter a husband from pointing out his wife's alleged deficiencies. The irony is greater still that, while clearly blaming her, he declines to accept the 'stooping' that attends it, and the even greater 'stooping' that is involved in arranging for her murder. It is not audacity but callousness that is revealed in the abrupt and deadpan

> This grew; I gave commands;
> Then all smiles stopped together. . . .

Instead of feeling remorse, he is proud that she is now captured on canvas, an image which is complemented by his reference to the commissioned statue of Neptune 'taming a sea-horse'.

In contrast to the curtain which is pulled back to reveal at one glance the portrait of a woman whose 'sin' consists merely in the 'earnest glance' and the 'spot of joy', the picture of the Duke is revealed bit by bit, each revelation showing something more to despise. It is true that the dry humour tempers our despite with a kind of astonishment that inhibits instant dismissal of the character; but that is hardly an argument for saying that we suspend moral judgement. The disapproval we feel exists because of, and not in spite of, the poet's slowly evolving 'portrait' of the Duke.[15]

Let us summarize the argument so far. In Chapter 3 I tried to show how moral attitudes are implicit in our understanding of human behaviour. Human actions are not mere bodily movements, nor mere imprints in the world: we see an intimate connection between the nature or character of a person and what he does. We cannot even begin to understand fiction unless we presuppose the same strength of relation between the fictional deed and the fictional doer. When we engage with a fictional work we do not understand or respond to fictional characters as peculiar creatures which are created by an omnipotent creator to go through the motions of doing; they must be seen as 'authors' of their own actions in the way that we suppose ourselves to be 'authors' of ours. In this sense they do not 'obey' a plot. From the internal convention there is no plot, but only the contingencies of various outcomes from the interactions of persons in their entanglements with good and evil, better and worse possibilities of human existence. To see fictional characters as moral agents involves accepting the conventions of fictional portrayal, which involves entering into a 'bargain' with the author. We see fictional characters as moral agents by contemplating a fictional world in which neither we nor the author can exist, and, in the case of the novel, by imaginatively adopting the role of implied reader to a fictional narrator. This does not involve a transformation of identity on our part. As a member of the implied audience/readership I remain the same person, but the role I imagine myself into is a passive one.[16] This means that I am distanced from some of the reactive attitudes and some of the feelings and emotions that are associated with them in actual cases.

That is so because in the actual world our understanding of the circumstances that surround us is often tied up in some way with what we are to do. To see that someone is in need of help, for instance, is not quite like simply noting a matter of fact. In many circumstances this judgement involves me in the question of

---

[15] 'My Last Duchess', in *Browning: A Selection by W. E. Williams* (Harmondsworth, 1954), 67–8.

[16] Not to be confused with the idea that our engagement with the *work* is passive, as will be seen later.

whether or not I am to be the one to provide the help. In other words my understanding of the other man as one who is capable of suffering and being harmed cannot be separated from my understanding of myself as a moral agent. Since we cannot enter a fictional world as an agent, we can enter it only as one who sees, hears, and understands. But since we can have *moral* understanding of fictional characters, this must be an understanding which does not rely on the above condition, for that condition cannot obtain: i.e. the plight of fictional characters cannot raise any questions about what I am to do about their plight. In the case of a novel we have no access to the characters except through the narrator, whose moral perception shapes the field of action we are to contemplate. No matter how 'impartial' the narration, there is necessarily a moral perspective, given that the narrator has subsumed the actions of the characters under particular descriptions and has selected some events rather than others for our attention, thus stipulating the focus of our concern with those characters.

In so far as we accept the narrator we come to share that perception, at least for the purposes of the work,[17] and see the characters through his eyes. In actual life it would be a shallow response indeed if we listened to gossip and formed opinions of people solely on that basis. But the pejorative force of the word 'gossip' depends on there being in principle other possibilities open to us—either to check the facts or to refuse to listen to the gossiper (who for that reason usually has an improper intention towards his victims). In fiction narration *per se* is not gossip, and we cannot depart from the fiction in order to check up on the characters. Of course it is possible for the narrator to be one of the characters who just happens to be a gossip; but in perceiving this we would rely on other features of the work to support the suspicion that the characters are not everything the narrator says they are. That is, we would have to entertain the idea that the author's presentation of the narrator is ironic. In the absence of any evidence from the text to suggest that it is an intention of the work that we distrust the narrator, we should then have to face the possibility that the work itself is shallow or misguided.

[17] What I mean by 'acceptance' here is discussed in Ch. 7.

THE MYTH OF THE DISAPPEARING AUTHOR

Although the concluding rider above brings the author back into focus, that in itself is not enough to counter the following objections to my argument so far. Two such objections might be (1) that it appears to drop out the author as the controlling voice and (2) that it says little about the possibility of moral disagreement with the implied attitudes of the narration and of the implications of this disagreement for our appraisal of the text as a work of art. I shall take up both of these objections in turn (dealing with (2) in Chapter 7).

The first thing to point out with respect to objection (1) is that I am not joining forces with the tendency in semiotic theory to 'drop out' the author. For on that view the 'text' becomes a rootless object which is fair game for the idiosyncrasies of any would-be critic to mould in the shape of his own choosing. That way of thinking has provided a background of opinion in which it is now considered permissible to treat the text as a political football and kick it around in a search for its alleged comment on any contemporary 'ideology', as though for example we should consider *Macbeth* as a feminist tract or condemn *Mansfield Park* for its inherent mercantile racism. To consider a literary work as a work of art means that it is to be distinguished from moral instruction, political propaganda, or a system of 'signs' to be 'decoded' or 'deconstructed': we have an interest in art that diminishes such preoccupations.

To return to the question of the author, my argument that our immediate negotiation is always with the voice of the narrator must be understood as a phenomenological observation. Since the author has in fact written every word of the narration, and since we read a book written by an author, the author never ceases to matter. In what I have described as a 'primary engagement' with the text we are interested in the characters as people and in the flow of the action. At this level of engagement the fictional personages are not fictional characters but real people, and their circumstances are not plotted but described. However, there is clearly more to a novel than a mere story. Complex philosophical questions are involved in giving an account of that 'something more' (to which I shall return), but given that a novel is not a yarn it seems that we shall look for a value or significance that cannot be found merely by viewing a novel as a concourse of fictional events. In the sense that the novel is serious and important, the narration is not all there is, even though it may be all we have to go on. In so far as we are concerned with the novel meaning something as a whole, we cease to be mere members of an implied audience/readership and become, however amateurishly, literary critics. In this capacity we are concerned with a text for whom an author is responsible. And the author is answerable to any criticism we make, i.e. criticism of the text is criticism of an author's creation.

That last point is emphasized by Colin Lyas in his retort to the tendency in the New Criticism to divorce the sincerity of the author from the sincerity of the work.[18] Yet it is possible to agree with Lyas that the author is implicated in the judgement that the work is 'insincere' (by which he seems to mean sentimental) without agreeing with his own inclination to play down the role of the fictional narrator. For, even in cases where they appear to coincide, there has to be a logical distinction between author and narrator given that we cannot literally be addressed by a voice from a fictional world. Lyas quite rightly opposes Beardsley's well-known dictum which effectively maintains that we cannot infer that the controlling intelligence behind the work is that of the author himself. Beardsley's attempts to separate the author from the work turns upon the mistaken assumption that all such references to the author would have to be inferential. Since we cannot, without engaging in airy speculation, infer anything about the mental states of the author from the text itself—or, more to the point, infer anything which would be criterial of what the work means—the thrust of the 'Intentional Fallacy' is that 'intention' is not relevant in appraising a literary text. But that argument misses the point by conflating 'intention' with 'prior intent'.[19] To acknowledge the importance of intention in a literary work of art is not to be committed to a speculative taxonomy of authorial motives but to be committed to considering the work itself as a vehicle of meaning.

To clarify this, one must refer here to the point made by Casey, Passmore, and others that there are two different models of

---

[18] 'The Relevance of the Author's Sincerity', in P. Lamarque (ed.), *Philosophy and Fiction: Essays in Literary Aesthetics* (Aberdeen, 1983), 17–37.
[19] See Peter Jones, *Philosophy and the Novel* (Oxford, 1975), 181–206.

'intention', the coherence model and the planning model. Clearly in forming an intention to do *X*, I may (in accordance with the 'planning model') consciously plan to do *X* and my intention in this sense would be explicit as a prior state to doing *X*. Yet to regard a man's behaviour as intentional we do not have to understand or explain it by reference to antecedent states called intentions, purposes, or deliberations. Rather, in regarding a man's behaviour as purposive we regard his behaviour as having some sort of coherent pattern, even if that pattern is not evident to the man in question. (John Casey has pointed out that this model is employed in psychoanalysis: the attribution of a given unconscious intention may help to make sense of a man's behaviour, and though his refusal to agree with that attribution may not entail that it is false, his agreement may be a criterion that it is correct.[20])

When a critic speaks of what a writer means or intends by his work he is using the 'coherence' model. Peter Jones for instance argues convincingly that any interpretation of a given work must proceed by selecting some *aspects* of the work and drawing them together (hence all criticism is, in this sense, 'aspectival'[21]). Again, the justification for employing this model of intention has to do with the kind of thing a work of art is. We regard a certain kind of complexity as one of the essentials of artistic quality: not in the sense that the work is necessarily difficult or opaque, but in that it is capable not only of provoking the reader to reread, but also of sustaining different readings and rewarding them with the presentation of aspects not previously noted (and, of course, not necessarily noticed by the writer). We must regard the work as purposive, given that it is the product of artistic creation, distinct from natural phenomena like sunsets and earthquakes, and from utilitarian artefacts such as beer mats and bus tickets. But, as Jones says, this is purposiveness without actual purpose. In interpreting a text we are concerned with what the writer might have meant (i.e. could have intended) without attempting to discover the mental states of the author. Hence any understanding we may reach is provisional without being subjective (interpretations need to be supported or justified, and not just anything will do).

We do not, then, need to *infer* anything about the author's

---

[20] John Casey, *The Language of Criticism* (London, 1966), 149.
[21] Jones, *Philosophy and the Novel*, 193–4.

sincerity or intention, for the author in that sense is revealed in the work. To that extent Lyas is right to say that the controlling intelligence of the *work* is not separable from the author. But it would be a mistake to suppose that we arrive at this judgement through choosing between two rival candidates for the job of controlling intelligence—the author and the narrator. Beardsley sets up the problem this way and plumps for the narrator. In rejecting Beardsley's choice, Lyas opts for the author. But to see the issue like that is to swallow too much of Beardsley's view of the problem: for there must be a distinction between author and narrator and, in the sense that there is a narration which is not the voice of the author, the narrator must for some purposes be considered the controlling voice. But the controlling intelligence of the *novel* is not a kind of super-narration concerned with the story behind a story: it is the novel itself, considered as a whole. As a work of art, a literary text is a unity which transcends the local and particular features of the story mediated through the narrator. The 'event language' of the narrator is an important element in the meaning of the novel, but when we step outside that discourse and concentrate on the significance of those events for the work as a whole, it is here that we are likely to find a crucial difference between art and life.

In order to illustrate and justify that last remark I shall in the following chapter take some examples from literature to show how events and experiences portrayed in a literary work can have a meaning and a significance that our experiences in life can never have. Further, this discussion will be intended to show that our concern with literature can never be a purely moral concern, even though it is a necessary condition of responding to literature that we do have moral understanding of the events and characters portrayed.

6
Life in Art

All life belongs to you, and do not listen either to those who would shut you up in corners of it and tell you that it is only here and there that art inhabits, or to those who would persuade you that this heavenly messenger wings her way outside of life altogether, breathing a superfine air, and turning her head away from the truth of things. (Henry James, 'The Art of Fiction'[1])

TRUTH IN ART

My discussion so far has rebutted the idea that there is an 'order of being' peculiar to art. But it is necessary to consider why so many have wanted to say that life in art is not like real life. I cannot discuss all the reasons, but the ubiquity of this idea cannot be brushed aside. It is not enough to detect fallacies; the insights underlying the tendency need to be brought to the surface and made more acceptable.

In the first place, if we had no feeling whatsoever for the difference between life and life as represented in art we should have no sense of embarrassment in making the most pedantic of objections to fiction which presents us with events which could not occur in 'real' life. If literal plausibility or abstract possibility were all, then we should expect *The Life of the Insects*, by Karel and Josef Čapek, to be laughed or booed off the stage. And since a woman cannot be changed into a laurel tree, we should regard Richard Strauss's opera, *Daphne*, as the work of a madman (in collusion with that lunatic poet, Ovid). What would be nonsense to say outside fiction is not necessarily nonsense within it, or at least not the same kind of nonsense. As Wittgenstein remarks in the *Philosophical Investigations*, 'Even a nonsense-poem is not nonsense in the same way as the babbling of a child.'[2]

---

[1] Henry James, *The Critical Muse: Selected Literary Criticism*, ed. Roger Gard (London, 1987), 205–6.
[2] *Philosophical Investigations*, trans. G. E. M. Anscombe (Oxford, 1967), I. 282.

It would be hasty to conclude from these examples, however, that a writer, simply because he writes fiction, can use that fact to claim a sort of diplomatic immunity against our possible outrage that what he writes is ridiculous, incoherent, unconvincing, or sham. Though fiction is not a speculative hypothesis (fictional worlds are not 'possible worlds' even where they do not contain logical absurdities), it is not some sealed-off realm in which anything goes. What we can go along with in a fairy-tale, such as a pot talking,[3] would not do in a kitchen-sink drama, and it would be difficult to stomach even in a science fiction movie. In *Cinderella* the fairy godmother can turn the pumpkin into a horse-drawn carriage. As R. F. Holland says, 'that little fragment of fiction is embedded in a larger story: nowhere else would it be at home'.[4] But it isn't just being embedded in a larger story that counts. It would only be 'at home' in something like a fairy-tale and not, say, in a Tolstoy novel (or even in a story by Kafka).

Though we have some sense of what is appropriate or convincing within a particular genre, that in itself does not mean that our understanding of life does not inform or bear upon what we understand in fiction. I have already argued that a fictional world is not a different 'kind' of world, and I am tempted to add here that though we have different kinds of fiction that is not to say that they portray or depict different kinds of 'life'. Yet the disjunctive 'this is art not life' is a perennial cry. At its most persistent and extreme, it settles into aestheticism, and the relation of morality to art is then finally obliterated. 'An artist, Sir, has no ethical sympathies at all. Virtue and wickedness are to him simply what the colours on his palette are to the painter.'[5]

In the case of Oscar Wilde, one gets the impression from his letters that he was driven to overstate the 'autonomy' of art in response to his philistine opponents. In a long and moving letter to Lord Alfred Douglas, written in HM Prison, Reading, 1897, he remarked:

[3] ' "But in a fairy tale the pot too can see and hear!" (Certainly; but it *can* also talk.)' (Ibid.)
[4] 'Lusus Naturae', in D. Z. Phillips and Peter Winch (eds.), *Wittgenstein: Attention to Particulars* (London, 1989), 50.
[5] Oscar Wilde's letter to the editor of the *Scots Observer*, 9 July 1890. (All refs. to Wilde's letters are taken from *Selected Letters of Oscar Wilde*, ed. Rupert Hart-Davis (Oxford, 1979).)

Truth in art is not any correspondence between the essential idea and the accidental existence; it is not the resemblance of shape to shadow, or of the form mirrored in the crystal to the form itself; it is no Echo coming from a hollow hill, any more than it is the well of silver water in the valley that shows the Moon to the Moon and Narcissus to Narcissus. Truth in art is the unity of a thing with itself.

Whatever 'truth in art' might mean, Wilde was correct to reject the idea that it must consist in a simple correspondence. It is not the artist's job to 'report' on the facts, in the way that a documentary might do. Moreover, the purpose of a documentary is to give information, to persuade, or possibly in some cases to goad men into action. Wilde was correct to insist that art cannot have a purpose in this sense. His famous dictum, 'all art is useless', is not likely to be better understood in our contemporary climate than it was by those to whom Wilde directed it in his own time. The point he was making is that things which are most precious to us are valued *precisely because* they are not merely a means to something else—i.e. they are valued in a different way from the way we value things we merely use. To see X as merely useful is not to see the same X that someone values as an end in itself; it is to have a different conception of X:

A work of art is useless as a flower is useless. A flower blossoms for its own joy. We gain a moment of joy by looking at it. That is all that there is to be said about our relations to flowers. Of course a man may sell the flower and so make it useful to him, but this has nothing to do with the *flower*. It is not part of its *essence*. It is accidental. It is a misuse.[6]

The man who sees the flower merely as a saleable item does not see it as a flower, but as a commodity. He does not appreciate its 'essence', for something else might have done just as well to procure ready cash.

Now one can agree with Wilde that art cannot be regarded merely as a means to something else without thinking of art as a self-contained game which has precious little to do with life. It is true of course that Wilde presented no systematic theory on this matter, that was not his job. But there is an instructive ambiguity at the root of his conception of art. Sometimes he speaks as if art is self-contained, either as an alternative to life or as something

---

[6] To R. Clegg, Apr. 1891 (emphasis mine).

which is superior to it: 'A thing in nature becomes much lovelier if it reminds us of a thing in art, but a thing in art gains no real beauty through reminding of us of a thing in nature.'[7] Here art and life are made to sound like two 'domains'. Yet on other occasions Wilde endorsed the idea defended in *The Decay of Lying* that instead of art imitating nature, nature imitates art: the point being that our perception of things in nature would not be the same if there were no works of art:

Where, if not from the Impressionists, do we get the wonderful brown fogs that come creeping down our streets, blurring the gas lamps and changing the house into monstrous shadows? To whom, if not to them and their master, do we owe the lovely silver mists that brood over our river, and turn to faint forms of fading grace, curved bridge and swaying barge? ... Nature is no great mother who has borne us. She is our creation. It is in our brain that she quickens to life. Things are because we see them, and what we see and how we see it, depends on the arts that have influenced us.[8]

There is an element of truth here, but one which should prevent us from drawing too firm a line between art and life. The relation is not between art and nature, but between art and our perception or experience of nature. The above passage is written for ostentatious effect. Nevertheless it is a view which Wilde defends in other places. The weakness in the argument is that it does not recognize the two-way transaction between art and our experience of the world. Certainly we see the world differently because of art, but there would be no art if men were not able to confront their actual experience in a certain sort of way. Neither the artist's perception, nor our response to his work, can dispense altogether with a concern for truth.

In John Donne's poem 'A Valediction: Forbidding Mourning' for example, the image of a pair of compasses is, to say the least, not an obvious or initially plausible representation of the union between lovers. We do not associate the closeness of love with a geometer's implement. Yet we find truth in the image, not merely because of some internal consistency within the poem (though this is important) but also because it is in tune with our capacity to recognize the difference between deep and shallow love.

    [7] To the editor of the *Speaker*, Dec. 1871.
    [8] 'The Decay of Lying', in *The Complete Works of Oscar Wilde*, introd. Vyvyan Holland (London, 1966), 986.

> Dull sublunary lovers love
> (Whose soule is sense) cannot admit
> Absence, because it doth remove
> Those things which elemented it.[9]

The absence between those who love is profound, however, does not diminish the relationship: it is not 'a breach' but 'an expansion'. The lovers, like the extended points of the compasses, are physically apart, yet their souls move in accord. Far from being just an artificial conceit, the image of the compasses conveys a truth about genuine or deep love: the paradox of being two, yet one.

> If they be two, they are two so
> As stiffe twin compasses are two,
> Thy soule the fixt foot, makes no show
> To move, but doth, if the'other doe.

The concern for truth in Donne's poem should be contrasted with the instant gratification of Craig Raine's 'Yellow Pages':

> all day he listens to the squeak of puppies,
> litters he is paid to drown and strangle.

> All day he sees himself in the glass darkly
> and waves goodbye, goodbye, goodbye.

> ('The Window Cleaner')[10]

Although there are those who have likened Raine to Donne, the resemblance between the two poets is superficial indeed. Raine's metaphors are clever and cheeky without earning their keep. They startle without justifying the surprise, entertain without enlightening. Whereas Donne's image of the compasses presents us with an idea through which we can understand something that is true of love, Raine's image of the puppy strangler has little to do with truth. There is a resemblance between the sound of leather on glass and the squeak of a puppy, just as there is between the visual impression of rinsing leather and drowning puppies, but not one that deserves the severity of metaphor. The effect is trivial, as it would not have been had the comparison been intended the other way round. Had Raine been attempting to convey the detachment needed to kill an animal, the image of leather would have been

---

[9] 'A Valediction: Forbidding Mourning', in Helen Gardner (ed.), *The Metaphysical Poets* (Harmondsworth, 1957), 71–2.

[10] 'Yellow Pages', in Craig Raine, *The Onion, Memory* (Oxford, 1978), 8.

close to the truth. As it is, the image is a departure from what the poem is about. It is about precariousness: 'The window cleaner cups a telescopic caber— | Blondin never trod so warily.' But even if we take the poem to be about the precariousness of man's existence, the strangling of puppies departs from this in being a deliberate act, not an accident.

> The college quad is cobbled like a blackberry
> and shining in the rain and dangerous . . .

The opening couplet introduces the idea of danger. But the image of the blackberry, though initially impressive (blackberries do look cobbled), is not only gratuitous but inappropriate (where is the danger in a blackberry?). Lest we have not caught the crude pun on 'glass darkly' and the allusion to death in 'waves goodbye', the message is hammered home:

> All day he wrings his hands, crying buckets,
> He'd rather shave shop windows clean
>
> than climb this bendy Jacob's ladder
> and risk the washboard fall of seraphim . . .

Any attempt to appraise either of these poems must therefore take into account considerations to do with the internal organization of the poem, but this does not mean that a poem has nothing to do with the actual world, and the same goes for novels and plays:

DUNCAN.   Dismay'd not this
  Our captains, Macbeth and Banquo?
SERGEANT.   Yes;
  As sparrows eagles, or the hare the lion.

> (I. ii)

If it were not actually the case that eagles are not afraid of sparrows or that lions are not afraid of hares, we would not be able to appreciate that the Sergeant's reply of 'yes' has the real force of 'no'. As R. K. Elliott has argued, if truth (in the sense of verification) were always aesthetically irrelevant then the 'no truth' theory could not account for the possibility of irony: 'When a poet makes a statement that is obviously false we normally assume that he did so intentionally and look for the point of the falsehood.'[11] This of

---

[11] 'Poetry and Truth', *Analysis*, 27/3 (1964), 77–85.

course means that it must be possible to speak of a poetic proposition being true or false. But, as Elliott shows, it is not necessary to put the point negatively, for in our experience of poetry it can be, and often is, that the poetic quality of a statement consists precisely in stating 'neatly, economically, and elegantly what is the case'.[12] And he reminds us that in Pope's couplet, 'So well-bred spaniels civilly delight | In mumbling of the game they dare not bite', we cannot divorce our pleasure here from the recognition that a spaniel is the appropriate breed of dog to convey the thought, since it illuminates the meaning of 'civil' in this context. Pope is not suggesting that Sporus (Lord Hervey) is polite, but that his 'civility' is a front. In fact if I may quote the line that precedes the couplet that Elliott cites—'Yet wit ne'er tastes, and beauty ne'er enjoys'—the further point of the spaniel image is to throw light on Sporus's insincerity: Sporus carries the game between his teeth, but is so preoccupied with his 'good breeding' that he lacks the sensibility actually to appreciate the finer things of life.

> Eternal smiles his emptiness betray
> As shallow streams run dimpling all the way.[13]

Again, if it were not actually true that the shallowness of a stream is linked with its bubbling or dimpled surface Pope would not succeed in conveying Sporus's duplicity.

This particular section of the poem coheres, in the sense that the separate images need to be considered in relation to each other, but this only works, at least in the given case, because the similes and metaphors are each good enough to stand alone. In a poem of my own, long since committed to the shredder, I had a line which ran: 'The audience of leaves heaves with surprise.' And the purpose of the image (or so I thought) was to fit in with the idea of a garden scene being seen as a circus. Though the idea of bushes encircling the garden like a circus audience fitted the schema, it was pointed out to me through honest criticism that an audience *qua* single mass, has a unity which a bush does not. The leaves of a bush do not react to the breeze in unison: the leaves and branches twist in different ways and in different directions. I had thus falsified the

---

[12] Ibid. 80.
[13] 'Epistle to Dr Arbuthnot', in *Alexander Pope: Selected Works*. ed. Louis Kronenberger (NewYork, 1951), 177–88.

bush by imposing upon it qualities it did not have simply in order
to fit the metaphorical theme. A poem may, as it were, transpose
reality, but it cannot forget it. The true poet is not concerned
merely with technical considerations of form, but with the world
as it is.

That is not to say, of course, that truth (in the sense of
verification) is a sufficient condition of artistic merit. Nor, since
there are poems to which this set of conditions may not apply, can
we have the confidence to call it a necessary condition. As both
R. K. Elliott and Malcolm Budd[14] have indicated, different types of
poem may require different kinds of evaluation. A lyric poem, or a
poem by Coleridge, may for instance actually violate truth in the
sense explained above; but that is not to say that poetry is
impervious to truth in some sense of the word 'truth'. It is not
merely representations of physical objects or processes which may
be false, but expressions of emotion too.

In Robert Frost's poem 'Acquainted with the Night' considerations of truth apply, not in the sense that we are concerned with
whether the speaker actually had the experience relayed in the
poem (a poem does not supply information in this way[15]) but in
the sense that the mood or expression of the poem seems genuine.
Had Frost ended the poem with some such line as 'And into my
cheeks the long, sad tears did bite', the line would have fitted in
with the rhythm and rhyme 'scheme', but it would have been cheap
and corny—soliciting our sympathies in a way that the poem
otherwise would not be doing—and thus would amount to
'posing', or 'striking an attitude', or revelling in the sadness such
that it becomes an excuse for an 'emotional debauch' (phrases I
borrow from Malcolm Budd[16]). John Casey has persuasively
argued that certain forms of expression may introduce an element
of insincerity into the actual feelings being expressed.[17] With the
present example, I think it is clear that my 'alternative ending'
would cheapen the whole poem: for it changes the significance of

[14] Malcolm Budd, 'Sincerity in Poetry', in Eva Schaper (ed.), *Pleasure, Preference
and Value: Studies in Philosophical Aesthetics* (Cambridge, 1987), 137–57.
[15] Because the speaker, like a novel's narrator, is a fictional voice, and because
even if the poet had the experience in question, the experience is fictionalized simply
by being expressed in a poem.
[16] Budd, 'Sincerity in Poetry', 143.
[17] 'The Autonomy of Art', in G. Vesey (ed.) *Philosophy and the Arts: Royal
Institute of Philosophy Lectures*, vi (London, 1973), 63–87.

what precedes it. As it stands, the speaker does not entreat us to sympathize with him: he just appears to list his observations.

> I have been one acquainted with the night.
> I have walked out in rain—and back in rain.
> I have outwalked the furthest city light.[18]

And when he says 'I have looked down the saddest city lane', it is clear that the sadness is attributed to the people who dwell there, not to himself. In his solitary state, the speaker rises above the self-pity and wallowing that could be introduced by my ending. This is confirmed when in passing 'the watchman on his beat' he 'dropped his eyes, unwilling to explain'. The mood of the poem has a sadness about it, but one that does not conflict with or undermine the speaker's detachment:

> And further still at an unearthly height
> One luminary clock against the sky
> Proclaimed the time was neither wrong nor right.

This image of the moon testifies to the speaker's having emancipated himself from the daily round, from the sense of time that pervades the little details of shared experience. He is thus not only outside time, but the slight catch on 'luminary' suggests that it is not a way of life that is regrettable, but one which provides insights (and ones which he is not prepared to share with the watchman, who presumably would not understand in any case). In being 'acquainted' with the night, he is in some sense at home in it. The truth or sincerity of the poem, then, does not have to do with verification, or with its communicating an actual state of affairs; rather, truth here amounts to integrity in the way that the poem communicates a state of consciousness. The mood of detachment is corroborated throughout, in such a way that we have a genuine sympathy for the speaker.

FICTIONAL LIFE NOT CONTINUOUS?

Though what I have said above hardly exhausts the topic, I cannot pursue the question of truth in art any further here, since I have other concerns. There is nothing yet to endorse the 'gulf' between

---

[18] 'Acquainted with the Night', in *Robert Frost: Selected Poems*, ed. C. Day Lewis (Harmondsworth, 1955), 161.

art and life. And certainly nothing in the following observation by Robert Liddell: 'For life and art are very different things and existence in one is very different from existence in the other. For one thing life enforces on us a continuous existence, whereas a character in fiction does not exist except at such times as he appears on the scene.'[19]

It is one thing to say that a fictional character only exists in the fictional world of a particular work, and quite another to say that he pops in and out of existence. Yet there are literary men who repeat this and similar fallacies over and over again. Liddell tells us:

Not only does man in fiction commonly omit such external acts as washing his teeth, but his interior or mental life is correspondingly simplified. He proceeds from thought to thought, or from feeling to feeling, either in accordance with reason or with an easily understood process of association of ideas. He will not suddenly burst out singing, nor will suddenly be overwhelmed with misery—he will be better controlled than real people are.[20]

That statement in turn relies on a misconception about human emotion. For no matter how passionate, 'moody', or changeable they might be, people are not (except when under the influence of drugs or affected by illness) suddenly overwhelmed by misery or joy in the same way that inanimate objects are pulled about by gales or earthquakes. Evidently Liddell has not appreciated what is involved in our 'continuous existence'. The continuity of our existence is not just a matter of duration: we have a *life*. The force of referring to our mode of existence as a 'life' is brought out in what Peter Winch says here: 'Unlike beasts, men do not merely live but also have a conception of life. This is not something that is simply added to their life; rather, it changes the very sense which the word "life" has when applied to men. It is no longer equivalent to "animate existence".'[21] The experience of misery or joy is only possible for a rational creature who has some conception of his life in relation to the world. Liddell tries to have it both ways. Fictional characters are, apparently, more rational than we are—yet, *ex hypothesi*, they lack the essential conditions of rationality: 'Fictional characters are not real people: they do not have to function

[19] *A Treatise on the Novel* (London, 1965), 91.
[20] Ibid. 92.
[21] 'Understanding a Primitive Society', in Peter Winch, *Ethics and Action* (London, 1972), 44.

in life, but in the novel which is an art form. They function in plots, which are abstractions, patterns, conventions.'[22]

I will not repeat my rebuttal of this point about characters being 'abstractions'. What I do want to emphasize is that we do not understand a fictional character's motive by simply noting that the plot requires it. (Indeed any novel or play giving that impression will be remarkably deficient as a creation.) Nor is it the case that to understand a character's motive is to point to a blind force that impels him: it is to understand how things seem to him. In order to understand Macbeth's motive for killing Duncan we have to enter Macbeth's mind. We need to understand the psychology that leads up to 'I go; and it is done.' For this we need to put ourselves in his place and imagine, as through the play we do imagine, what it feels like to have that kind of ambition and to be in love with a woman like Lady Macbeth, who eggs him on, partly through sexual persuasion. It is not possible to understand why Macbeth did what he knew to be wrong without understanding *him*. The relation between motive and deed is not like that of cause to effect. Macbeth is not pulled into action but allows himself to be tempted. To understand this is not like understanding a proof in mathematics: it involves, in a way, sharing his temptation.

Yet for all that, novels and plays are not 'real' (i.e. actual) life. First, because it is part of what we mean by the term 'fictional world' that no matter how great its resemblance to actual life or to actual events it is not an actual world. Secondly because a representation is not just a copy of life, but life seen under the perspective of the artist's work. There is a tendency among some philosophers to say that life in art is more ordered than actual life can ever be. This idea is worth exploring though I think it is wrong as it stands and needs considerable modification. For the moment, however, let us consider through one or two examples this idea that fictional situations can have a meaning they would not have if they were actual. In what follows I shall give detailed consideration to aspects of Jane Austen's *Mansfield Park*, and I have been awakened to the potential of this example through a stimulating essay by Tony Tanner.[23]

---

[22] *A Treatise on the Novel*, 97.
[23] 'Jane Austen and "The Quiet Thing"—a Study of Mansfield Park', in B. C. Southam (ed.), *Critical Essays on Jane Austen* (London, 1970), 136–61.

ORDER AND MEANING IN ART

There is an early episode in *Mansfield Park* which, when related to the novel as a whole, has a meaning it does not have when considered just as a development of the story-line. I have in mind chapters 6–10, the trip to Sotherton. Viewed merely as one sequence of events among others, these chapters just happen to be full of things which reveal more about the characters. The sequence of events is as follows. It is revealed during dinner that Mr Rushworth, who is engaged to Maria Bertram, wishes to improve the grounds of his estate, Sotherton Court. Henry Crawford, who has improved his estate at Everingham, offers his services. An outing to Sotherton Court is arranged, and a party consisting of Julia and Maria Bertram, Fanny Price, Mrs Norris, Mary Crawford, and Edmund Bertram travel there to tour the house and grounds. After a meal they are shown round the large house, and their tour concludes with the chapel, which is no longer used for family prayers. It is here that Mary Crawford learns of Edmund's intention to be ordained. It is noticed that there is a door 'temptingly open' to the pleasure grounds: a lawn bounded on each side by a high wall. Beyond the first planted area and bowling green is a terrace walk backed by iron pallisades, overlooking an adjoining wilderness.

The assembly move outside, eventually forming into three separate parties: Edmund, Miss Crawford, and Fanny; Rushworth, Henry Crawford, and Maria; Mrs Rushworth, Mrs Norris, and Julia (who is jealous that her sister, Maria, seems to be gaining most of Henry's attentions). The first party make for the terrace and go through a door, discovered by Mary Crawford, into a wood. It is here that Mary raises the subject of Edmund's intention to become a clergyman, and considers it to be an unfashionable, unprofitable career. Leaving the fatigued Fanny on a bench the couple move further into the wilderness. The second party find Fanny. Maria expresses a wish to go through the iron gate, which is locked, and Rushworth goes to fetch the key. In his absence, Maria finds the spectacle of the locked gate oppressive and feels impatient to go through it. Fanny exhorts the couple to wait for Mr Rushworth, but Henry and Maria pass through the side of the gate and walk off together in an extremely circuitous route. Julia Bertram arrives. She too ignores Fanny's plea for her to wait, and scrambles over the fence to follow Henry and Maria. When Rushworth eventually arrives he is surprised and vexed that the others had not waited. He opens the gate and goes in search of the others. Eventually the parties converge and return to the house. After dinner they return to Mansfield Park.

Viewed in isolation, there is nothing special about this episode. Like many others in the novel, it is a convenient background against which particular qualities of character are revealed. We learn of Mary Crawford that she has a restless energy, and is more at home with the fashionable bustle of London than with the quiet sense of the past found in rural England. Mr Rushworth is made to look increasingly stupid. Henry knowingly flirts with another man's fiancée. Fanny, as usual, is left alone to contemplate the foolish goings-on of the others, and she is made jealous by the way that Edmund's attention is lured away by the 'light and lively' Miss Crawford. Mrs Norris, having been the one to mastermind the visit, for no apparent motive except to be the mastermind, nevertheless returns with food she has 'sponged' from the housekeeper and the gardener.

At this level, the visit is just one incident among others. The foibles of the characters might just as well have been revealed by a day-trip to Brighton. And if one views the visit in that spirit, no doubt Fanny Price might appear to be a dull and boring girl who deserves to be neglected by those who have more about them. This is in fact a common criticism of Fanny Price as heroine. And such criticisms often proceed as though we could lift her out of the fiction and contemplate how boring she would be as a dinner-date at the White Elephant Nightclub, or how useless she would be as a companion on a skiing holiday. But there is a way of viewing this episode which not only renders Fanny's attitudes more intelligible, but ties in with key ideas in the novel as a whole. It has been said that *Mansfield Park* is a novel about ordination. But it is also about order. It is about the value of the past and respect for tradition as they affect the moral life. Neither the Crawfords nor Mrs Norris are consciously wicked. The former base their morality on the value of the present moment, while Mrs Norris bases hers on what might seem to others to be right. In this way the novel is as much concerned with the gap between the inner and outer man as is Shakespearian drama.

The Crawfords and Mrs Norris live on the surface of things.

Henry Crawford's penchant for play-acting (equally at home with all roles) is testimony to his lack of consistency and inner depth. Mary Crawford is outwardly sympathetic and attractive, but has a mind 'darkened, yet fancying itself light'. Mrs Norris has no real insight into what must lie behind a good act for it to be good. Goodness to her consists in the trappings of virtue, in the outward display—the 'deed'—rather than what comes from deep within. She never confronts her own motives but displaces, or projects, her own selfishness onto the figure of Fanny in order that her own conscience will remain clear: 'It was impossible for her to aim at more than the credit of projecting and arranging so expensive a charity: though perhaps she might so little know herself, as to walk home to the parsonage after this conversation, in the happy belief of being the most liberal-minded sister in the world.' (p. 9)

Fanny, by contrast, examines and criticizes her own motives far more than she criticizes others. She is not the self-righteous prig some critics believe, because her conception of failings in others is not distinct from what she would equally criticize in herself. Her principles are neither sterile maxims, nor weapons to elevate herself by putting others down. They arise from her genuine love of harmony in nature and from a genuine respect for the spirit handed down in noble or fine traditions. Given the unpleasantness of her origins, the noise, chaos, and discord, she more than anyone else at Mansfield is in a position to appreciate the value of order, decorum, and good sense.

The education of the Bertram children was a shallow affair, inculcating in them only a minimal grasp of what is important in life. Edmund survived the experience, perhaps by identifying with the sense of propriety exemplified by his father. But he, like his father, sees only so far. He wants to do the right thing, often without knowing what it is. Both he and Sir Thomas share a dullness that is not found in Fanny. She is dull only to the eyes of those who cannot see what lies beneath. She has a sensitivity they lack, one that feeds on her closeness to the order in nature that transcends even the values of Mansfield Park; Mansfield Park is just a place in which these values are given expression and can be preserved. It is significant that when she does condemn the behaviour of others, this is not because they are engaged in trivial enjoyment or self-satisfaction, but because they have exhibited a lack of respect for place or persons.

'But was there nothing in her conversation that struck you, Fanny, as not quite right?'

'Oh! yes, she ought not to have spoken to her uncle as she did. I was quite astonished. An uncle with whom she had been living so many years, and who, whatever his faults may be, is so very fond of her brother, treating him, they say, quite like a son, I could not have believed it.'

'I thought you would be struck. It was very wrong—very indecorous.'

'And very ungrateful I think.'

'Ungrateful is a strong word. I do not know that her uncle has any claim to her *gratitude* . . . she is awkwardly circumstanced . . . I do not censure her *opinions*; but there is certainly impropriety in making them public.' (p. 52)

The contrast between Edmund and Fanny is clear. While Edmund's criticism is to do with what is not seemly, Fanny's concern is rather more to do with justice.

In a sense, disputes about the character of Fanny Price are moral disputes (how could they not be?). But they, in turn, reflect different interpretations of the novel. It is not possible to side with, say, Lionel Trilling or with Marvin Mudrick in their lack of sympathy with the leading character without one's view of the novel as a whole being affected. Returning to the Sotherton episode with this in mind, it makes a difference to how we are to interpret these events. It is significant for example that the circumstances of the visit have to do with the idea of 'improvement'. Time and time again (as in the case of the amateur theatricals) the novel seems to ask: where's the harm in that? And the answer is that the harm can only be appreciated by looking beneath the veil of appearance. On the face of it, the idea of improving Sotherton estate seems innocuous enough—especially for readers today. But within the terms of the novel, the 'improvement' is really assault. The first thing that is entailed is the destruction of an avenue:

'Cut down an avenue! What a pity! Does it not make you think of Cowper? "Ye fallen avenues, once more I mourn your fate unmerited."'

Typically, it is again through Fanny that we are made alive to what is at stake. Sotherton represents an old order that is now going to give way to fashionable innovation. The established order is to be destroyed in the name of an improvement, on little more than a whim. Sotherton is to be 'improved' in the same way that the old morality is to be 'improved', and in the way that Mary seeks to 'improve' Edmund, by making him more go-getting in seeking worldly esteem and worldly rewards. The values that fashion would destroy are so quiet and unostentatious as to be scarcely noticed—indeed they are imperfectly represented by their very guardians. It is a subtlety of this novel that the values lying behind Mansfield Park are so inadequately upheld by those who have grown up there. This places those values in jeopardy and open to external, corrupting forces. It is against this setting that the 'improvement' is to be seen. It is slightly sinister, for it consists not in a drive to build upon values worth preserving but to eliminate them altogether. It is fitting that the first reference to Mary Crawford's harp ('fit accessory for the siren she is'[24]) occurs during the discussion of plans for the visit, and that Rushworth refers to the old order (Sotherton) as 'a prison'. What the improvers are after is a breaking down of constraints.

Like most fashions, the idea was conceived on the basis of a whim and sustained by the sheep-like element in human nature. Rushworth was impressed by a friend who had bragged that he had had *his* estate 'improved'. But in fashion's grip, the improvers embark on a course of action which threatens more than the destruction of an avenue. The decency and decorum of the moral life is to be undermined by removing the limits that social custom places upon conduct. In the chapel, significantly no longer used for family prayers, it is noticed that Rushworth and his fiancée are standing by the altar as though to be married then and there. But the 'ceremony' is turned into something rather satanic as Henry Crawford murmurs flirtatious remarks to Maria. The door to the garden is 'temptingly open' to the 'sweets of the pleasure grounds'; and the temptations of the 'wilderness' lurk therein. It is in the wilderness that Mary tries to dissuade Edmund from his religious vocation. There are further symbolic suggestions to be found in the image of the locked gate, and the behaviour of Henry and Maria, which are brought out excellently by Tony Tanner:

Maria, always impatient of all restraints and enclosures, wishes to go beyond the gates and into the wider freedom of the park. The gate—perfect image for the rigid restrictions imposed by the conventions of civilized life—is locked. Mr Rushworth goes to fetch the key. Being engaged to Maria, he is in many ways the lawful person to 'open the gates'

[24] Ibid. 142.

(there is perhaps a reference to virginity here, just as the locked garden represents virginity in medieval paintings). But, in his absence, Henry engages in some very persuasive and suggestive *double entendre* with Maria. The improver of the estate is also the disturber of conventional life. The whole conversation should be looked at carefully; particularly when Maria complains that the iron gate 'gives me a feeling of restraint and hardship' and Henry answers: 'I think you might with little difficulty pass round the edge of the gate, here, with my assistance; I think it might be done, if you really wished to be more at large, and could allow yourself to think it not prohibited.' Their final adultery also a bypassing of the iron codes of society—is here prefigured. Fanny warns against the danger, but Maria manages to slip round the gate without any harm from the spikes. Subsequently the spikes of convention will damage her more deeply.[25]

There are other episodes in this novel (such as the card game and the amateur theatricals) which have a deeper meaning than appears at first sight: indeed their meaning is given partly in their relation— and Tanner discusses them. The point I wish to extract is that it is difficult to see how incidents or experiences in actual life could have this kind of meaning. Consider first what it is for things in life to have meaning. It is often supposed that things only have a meaning that human beings give them, or bring to them. This, however, is simplistic and misleading because it blurs the difference between different sorts of cases. Of the man who plays darts, we may say that darts has a meaning for him, but this may be no more than to say that the question of whether or not it has a point does not arise. It does not have a meaning beyond itself: he simply enjoys a game of darts, thus it has a meaning for him. This is what one might call the 'horse-racing' sense of meaning. The allusion here is to a talk given by John Wisdom entitled 'What is there in Horse-Racing?'[26] If someone sees horse-racing simply as 'a matter of whether one horse has his head in front of another', it is clear that no attempt to get him to change his mind by trying to describe what 'more' there is in horse-racing can possibly succeed. To say that horse-racing has a meaning is not to say that it has a purpose, or that there is something valuable about it which goes beyond the enjoyment of horse-racing. The meaning is in the enjoyment, not in some additional 'meaning' that horse-racing has. However, the

---

[25] Ibid. 151–2.
[26] Quoted and discussed by Dilman in Ilham Dilman and D. Z. Phillips, *Sense and Delusion* (London, 1971), 11–13.

meaning people do find in it cannot be reduced to the matter of this horse now beating that horse, even though the present excitement cannot be dismissed as irrelevant. The excitement that people find in it cannot be understood apart from the tradition that lies behind it. 'That small incident . . . is the last move in a long game which began before the colt was born . . . It is a game with something of the flavour of life itself.'[27]

But there are other cases where seeing the meaning of *X* does involve seeing *X* as part of something else. And this is more germane to my discussion, especially since it might appear to challenge the basis on which we are considering that art is different from life. In his notebooks, Henry James remarked that life was capable of 'nothing but splendid waste'—'Life being all inclusion and confusion, and art being all discrimination and selection.'[28] If, however, this is taken to be an observation about the psychology of the artist while creating, it is not then a point about the *kind* of life found in fiction. Indeed James, at least in 'The Art of Fiction', actually argued against the view that art is not like life:

As people feel life, so they will feel the art that is most closely related to it. This closeness of relation is what we should never forget in talking of the effort of the novel. Many people speak of it as a factitious, artificial form, a product of ingenuity, the business of which is to alter and arrange the things that surround us, to translate them into conventional, traditional moulds. This, however, is a view of the matter which carries us but a very short way, condemns the art to an eternal repetition of a few familiar *clichés*, cuts short its development, and leads us straight up to a dead wall.[29]

The literary artist, for the purpose and execution of his work, must select and arrange his subject-matter. He may draw upon actual events, as James himself did, but that does not mean that life in fiction is a rearranged kind of life. 'In proportion as in what [fiction] offers us we see life *without* rearrangement do we feel that we are touching the truth; in proportion as we see it *with* rearrangement do we feel that we are being put off with a substitute, a compromise and convention . . . Art is essentially

[27] Ibid. 12.
[28] Quoted and discussed by G. H. Bantock, *The Parochialism of the Present* (London, 1981), 26–9.
[29] *The Critical Muse*, 199–200.

selection, but it is a selection whose main care is to be typical, to be inclusive.'[30] What James means by inclusive is not that the artist must include each and every detail or aspect of life, but that there are not features of life which are or are not the proper subject-matter of art.

To return to our original thesis, the claim that life in art is more ordered than actual life cannot be made against the supposition that life has no order. Not only do we see an order and meaning in things—otherwise we should be insane, or hopelessly confused and depressed—but it is possible to see a significance in quite ordinary or commonplace things that transforms or illuminates our understanding of other matters. In her autobiographical writings, Virginia Woolf has given many such examples from her own experience. One of these is quite striking. It concerns her understanding of the bereavement of John Walter Hills (referred to as Jack), who in 1897 lost his wife, Stella. Some years later, her understanding of his grief is deepened by the significance she comes to place on a quite ordinary object, a tree, giving it symbolic meaning:

I could sum it all up in one scene. I always see when I think of the month after her death the certain leafless bush; a skeleton tree in the dark of a summer night. Inside I am sitting with Jack Hills. He grips my hand in his. He groans. 'It tears one asunder' he groaned. He was in agony. He gripped my hand to make his agony endurable, as if he were in physical torture. 'But you can't understand' he broke off. 'Yes, I can', I murmured. Subconsciously I knew that he meant that his sexual desires tore him asunder, together with his anguish at her loss. Both were torturing him. And the tree, outside in the dark garden, was to me the emblem, the symbol, of the skeleton agony to which her death had reduced him; and us; everything . . . The leafless tree and Jack's agony—I always see them as if they were one and the same, when I think of that summer.[31]

It is clear from this that the significance Virginia Woolf comes to see in the tree articulates the grief in a way that makes sense of it— though in retrospect. It helps to put it in a different perspective by comparing Jack's loss with the idea of loss and decay in the natural

---

[30] Ibid. 200 (emphasis orig.).
[31] 'A Sketch of the Past', in Virginia Woolf, *Moments of Being: Unpublished Autobiographical Writings of Virginia Woolf* ed. Jeanne Schulkind (London, 1976), 121.

world. It is the image of natural loss which illuminates the need for a kind of rebirth, which is also part of the natural process.

The leafless tree was a very painful element in our life. Trees don't remain leafless. They begin to have little red chill buds. By that image I would convey the discomfort and misery and the quarrels, the suppressed irritations, the sharp words, the insinuations—which as soon as family life started again in Hyde Park Gate began to cover over the fact that Stella's death had left us all to take up new relationships.[32]

It is a moot point whether this recollection *gives* meaning to the event, or whether it brings out the meaning that was already dimly recognized. But where do we look to bring out the distinction between this and the symbolic meaning of the fictional episode in *Mansfield Park*? The crucial difference seems to be that none of the characters, including Fanny, see the meaning in the Sotherton episode that we can see. Indeed they cannot; for the meaning we see in that episode consists in its relation to certain themes and ideas in the novel as a whole. The 'prefiguring' of Henry and Maria's adultery, for instance, is not in any way like a premonition; they are not fated or casually determined to commit adultery. It is, if you like, a kind of dramatic irony, and in that sense the characters logically could not be aware of it, for they cannot know themselves to be characters in a novel. We see a meaning that is only accessible to one who stands outside the fictional world. It does not exist in our 'primary engagement' with the contingency of events and the unfolding of personality. It has to do with our contemplation of the novel as a unity, a work of art, our attention to the way that parts of the novel unite into a larger whole—in this case in a symbolic way. As far as the story is concerned, the wilderness is just one place among others. As far as the novel is concerned, it represents something beyond the fragments of mere events: disorder, freedom from the constraints of civilization, a place of satanic corruption. The events described by the narrator of course do not lack order or meaning. Quite the reverse. Yet they are the raw materials for the further significance we see when we explore the meanings of the work. At this level it is relevant that the characters are fictions. We gain access to them by first thinking of them as persons, then step back and contemplate their function in the

---

[32] Ibid.

purposes of the work. At that level it makes sense to say that characters are embodiments of ideas, providing we remember that we can only reach this level of response while also thinking of them as persons. In a sense Lady Bertram and Mrs Norris represent opposite vices: indolence and busybodydom. In fact one could go right through the list of characters and find similar contrasts (e.g. the profligacy of Tom *v.* the miserliness of Mrs Norris). This would lend support to Ryle's suggestion about the affinity between Jane Austen's moral thought and the Aristotelianism she shares with Shaftesbury.[33] Yet this level of representation can only be effective if the characters are fully realized as fictional persons: they are not vices on legs.

Malcolm Bradbury's novel, *The History Man*, might at first appear to contradict my argument. Without loss to his art, his characters seem to be nothing more than representations of qualities, principles, and ideologies. Miss Callender, for instance, does not seem to be a fully-fledged person who just happens to be in sympathy with nineteenth-century humanism, as against the dreary, demoniac ideology that animates Howard Kirk. In a sense she is the past personified. When Kirk invades her nineteenth-century fortress, the description of the seduction is tellingly dehumanized:

In the dark he moves and feels the busy, energetic flesh of himself wriggling into her, like a formless proliferating thing, hot and growing and spreading. Unmitigated, inhuman, it explodes; the sweat of flesh, of two fleshes, is in the air of the dark room; their bodies break away from each other.[34]

Here, Howard Kirk, 'the historical rapist', has his final conquest. The last shred of the past has been deformed and defiled—and finally obliterated. In the end, Miss Callender accepts her reduction to a mere 'role' in the 'Marxist plot' of history. And at the end of the final chapter she appears willingly in Kirk's basement to consummate the destruction, the pair oblivious to the suicide upstairs which is to become just another statistic. 'In fact no-one hears; as always at the Kirks' parties, which are famous for their happenings, for being like a happening, there is a lot that is, indeed, happening, and all the people are fully occupied.'

---

[33] 'Jane Austen and the Moralists', in Gilbert Ryle, *Collected Papers* (London, 1971), i. 266–92.
[34] Malcolm Bradbury, *The History Man*, 213.

These two examples are not really parallel cases. In the case of Jane Austen's 'naturalistic' novel we still want to say that the card game has a meaning over and above its being a card game. This symbolic meaning, however, is part of our 'secondary engagement', for it is evident at the level where we have an interest in the work that transcends our interest in the story-line, and our explicit attention to the way that parts of the novel fit together in a larger pattern is not part of that 'primary engagement'. Yet the symbolism in *The History Man* does seem to be part of the primary engagement. Throughout the story, the parties are arranged 'forms of interaction' manipulated by 'a theoretician of sociability'. Even within the primary engagement none of the characters seem to be real: they are, yet they are not, persons.

Now without further qualification that example would cut right across everything I have said. The qualification that makes all the difference is this, that we see the events as they are first filtered through Howard Kirk's eyes, even though he is not the official narrator. Since Howard Kirk has no real identity of his own, the narration is mediated though a kind of continuous-present consciousness which renders events as empty and meaningless as they are for Howard Kirk. Since for the radical consciousness the past does not exist, Miss Callender herself has to be seen as a mere device in Kirk's malevolent schemes. To him she is not a person in her own right any more than anyone else is: people are not seen as ends in themselves, but as items of convenience or as obstructions to his plans and projects. The symbolic meanings are not therefore 'added meanings'. On the contrary, they serve to drain meaning from ordinary things and everyday human transactions, which we are invited to see through the distorting lens of the radical consciousness to which things can never be simply what they are, but representations of one or another ism or ideology: to Howard Kirk everything can be reduced to politics.

But now it is necessary to ask of the Virginia Woolf example: couldn't we also say that the meaning or significance she finds in the 'skeleton tree' is a meaning that logically could not have been part of the experience it is supposed to throw light upon? Indeed the editor of Virginia Woolf's unpublished writings states in her introduction that in 'A Sketch of the Past', Virginia Woolf is 'searching and probing the past for meanings that could not have been evident to the self who had the experience'.[35] I think, however, that the service this example provides is to lessen the distinction between art and life without obliterating it. The distinction cannot be between 'life with order and meaning' (art) and 'life consisting of fragments' (life). We do not pass from one episodic experience to another as a train runs over a row of sleepers. Such a 'life' would be meaningless indeed. Not only does this crude model fail to take account of the meaning that must already be present for something to count as 'an experience', but it also overlooks the fact of change and development in human life. Although a human being remains the same person throughout his life, he is nevertheless changing and developing in various ways (for good or ill). Not only are we changed through and by the experiences we undergo, but these changes can lead us to put our past experience into a different perspective from the one apparent at the time. In such cases we are led to have a different view of everything we have been.

Without that capacity it is difficult to see how moral development would be possible. A moral agent is not merely continuous through time, but is capable of the kind of thought that enables him to move about between past, present, and future. Animals are confined to a life of immediacy and cannot be liberated from the present. But we can, and must be if we are to have purposes, express regret, acknowledge responsibility for our actions, or resolve to mend our ways.

Indeed, one may wish to go further than that and argue as some philosophers have done that a moral consciousness that reaches towards the spiritual dimension of human life will not only be concerned with the potential for acting on the world but also with a sense of one's own finitude in a world which existed before we were born and will remain after we die. This is less a moral theory than a mystical view that seems to transcend what we ordinarily mean by morality. And such a tendency is found in that 'tradition' of moral philosophy which runs from Plato through Spinoza, Kierkegaard, and Wittgenstein to Simone Weil, which portrays the good life as love of the beauty of the world: love in the sense of patient attention to the truth about things, and beauty in the sense of 'order'. Recognition of oneself as a finite creature lodged between birth and death cannot thus be separated from recognition

[35] 'Sketch', 13.

of a world that transcends the self in space and time. This is what I understand Wittgenstein (and Spinoza before him) to mean in saying that the good life is the world seen *sub specie aeternitatis*.

The life according to the flesh—to be contrasted with what Wittgenstein called the life of knowledge—is one which disposes us to view all things in the world as a means to our satisfaction, or as 'amenities'. Thus in Wittgenstein's 'early' view of ethics there is a distinction drawn between seeing things 'from within their midst' and seeing them 'from outside'. Viewed in the 'ordinary' way, the world may be seen as a vehicle to the pleasure or displeasure of the self. The man who is ruthless, greedy, dishonest, power-worshipping, or opportunist thereby rejects any kind of acceptance of a world which might transcend his own importance or be indifferent to his whims and fancies. He is not happy with the world 'whatever it might be', but only happy with himself, hence not happy in the ethical sense.

With fiction, and more particularly with great literature, we do seem to gain some intimation of a world seen *sub specie aeternitatis*. We can see a fictional world also from the outside. But this vision, in which ethics and aesthetics seem to merge, is not a vision confined to our experience of art. Virginia Woolf's autobiographical writings show how her understanding of things can involve seeing them in some sort of relation. On more than one occasion she speaks of seeing a 'pattern' behind things, as though everything in the world were part of a single work of art. 'It is a constant idea of mine; that behind the cotton wool is hidden a pattern; that we— I mean all human beings—are connected with this; that the world is a work of art; that we are parts of the work of art.'[36]

This is what lay behind her perception of the significance of the tree; through relating Jack Hills's grief to something apparently unconnected with it, she was able to see a meaning in it that went beyond the particularity of the circumstances. She sees the matter *sub specie aeternitatis*; and 'this wholeness means that it has lost its power to hurt me' (p. 72). However, she also says that she achieves such 'wholeness' by putting her experience into words. It might be important therefore to consider whether this 'order' itself is conferred in or through the act of narration, even though in this case it is an actual experience which is being narrated.

[36] Ibid. 72.

Whether or not the order she comes to see in her recollected experience is due to her literary methods is a question she herself raises, though is unsure of the answer:

These scenes, by the way, are not altogether a literary device—a means of summing up and making innumerable details visible in one concrete picture. Details there were; still, if I stopped to think, I could collect a number. But whatever the reason may be, I find that scene making is my natural way of marking the past. Always a scene has arranged itself: representative; enduring ... Is this liability to scenes the origin of my writing impulse? Are other people scene makers? These are questions to which I have no answer. Perhaps sometime I will consider it more carefully. Obviously I have developed the faculty, because in all the writing I have done, I have almost always had to make a scene, either when I am writing about a person; I must find a representative scene in their lives; or when I am writing about a book, I must find their poem, novel ... But this may not be the same faculty.[37]

It is a plausible enough thought that narrating an actual experience, particularly narrating it in such a way that a scene becomes 'representative' of something larger, adds meaning to that experience. But whether or not narrating fact and narrating fiction stems from the same 'faculty', there is surely a difference in the finished product. Even though in narrating a recollected experience she may have come to 'give' it a meaning it did not have before, the 'pattern' she claims to be 'hidden' behind things is not one that has been put there to be discovered. In this case the meanings are found where they did not before exist. In the fictional case, the meaning of the Sotherton episode is not 'imposed' in this sense. Our experiences do not have greater meanings in the way that there is a greater meaning involved in events within a novel. And with a novel there is the further question of what function these greater meanings serve. The significance of the Sotherton episode is one which throws light on our understanding of the characters and of the moral ideas that are presented in the novel. But in appreciating the work, one is obliged to consider features of the work that are not exclusively moral considerations. The question of how the Sotherton episode fits in with other episodes such as the card game and the amateur theatricals (which equally have a symbolic significance within the work) is not itself a moral question. It is a matter to do

[37] Ibid. 122.

with artistry. The way that these episodes link together is an artistic, not a moral, achievement—even though it expresses moral insights.

Let me sum up this discussion by suggesting that the difference between 'art-life' and actual life is not, strictly speaking, the difference between a world with order and a world without it, but is rather to do with the mode of attention to it. There is not some different kind of life portrayed in art that, for instance, entitles us to say that Van Gogh grass is a different type of grass from actual grass, or that the lives the Bertrams lead are different kinds of lives from actual lives because they have a meaning that ours cannot. In saying that life in art is more ordered, the point is that it is in the way our attention to it is organized and directed that confers the meaning. This can be illustrated further by considering the Japanese print, *The Great Wave*, by Katsushika Hokusai. Despite the highly stylized presentation of the sea, it would be wrong to say that what we have here is a different sort of ocean from a real one. Rather, the point seems to be that if we were to witness such a scene in reality (the huge wave threatening to engulf the tiny boat) our attention would be focused on the horror of this peril to human life. But as Herbert Read points out,

If we look at this Japanese print, our attention ought to be taken by the men in the boats, and we should then feel sympathy for them in their danger; but contemplating the print as a work of art, our feelings are absorbed by the sweep of the enormous wave. We enter into its upwelling movement, we feel the tension between its heave and the force of gravity, and as the crest breaks into foam, we feel that we ourselves are stretching angry claws against the alien objects beneath us.[38]

Our experience in this sense is unlike 'real life', yet this is not because the print depicts a different kind of world from the actual world, but because it enjoins a different mode of attention to it. As Read says, we are directed to identify with the wave in such a way that we see not a cruel sea but a mighty one. We are thus invited to see something about our smallness and insignificance as human beings. This does not mean that art is the only access we have to realizing such things, that it is the only way to step out of our natural inclinations and see ourselves in relation to an impersonal universe. As Wittgenstein remarked, 'there is a way of capturing

[38] *The Meaning of Art* (Harmondsworth, 1949), 30.

the world sub specie aeterni other than through the work of the artist. Thought has such a way—so I believe—it is as though it flies above the world and leaves it as it is—observing it from above, in flight.'[39] The difference between art and life, then, cannot consist simply in saying that the first is more ordered than the second, but rather it has to do with the manner in which it reveals order; it has to do with the way it guides our perception (a matter I take up in Chapter 8). If this is right, then there is a distinction between art and life, but not one that justifies the aestheticism of Wilde. Perhaps one should lean towards agreeing with him in wanting to distinguish art from morality without agreeing with him that 'an artist, Sir, has no ethical sympathies at all'.[40] A literary work cannot be divorced from morality, for reasons I have given; but our interest in it, and the achievement of its creator, is one that must take account of other considerations too. As Wilde put it, 'It was necessary, Sir, for the dramatic development of this story to surround Dorian Gray with an atmosphere of moral corruption. Otherwise the story would have had no meaning and the plot no issue.'[41] But this still leaves the question of whether moral disagreement with a literary work entails adverse judgement of the work itself. Hence the next question to be considered must be: is bad morality bad art?

---

[39] *Culture and Value*, ed. G. H. von Wright and H. Nyman, trans. P. Winch (Oxford, 1980), 5e.
[40] To the editor of the *Scots Observer*, 9 July 1890.   [41] Ibid.

7

Bad Morality, Bad Art?

Writers do not have to be professors of morals, but they do have to express the human condition. And nothing concerns human life so essentially, for every man at every moment, as good and evil. When literature becomes deliberately indifferent to the opposition of good and evil, it betrays its function and forfeits all claim to excellence. (Simone Weil, *On Science, Necessity and the Love of God*, 169–9)

ARTISTIC AND MORAL APPRAISAL

The question that concerns us poses a dilemma. We have an interest in literature that is not simply a moral interest. To apprehend a work of literature as a work of art is not to regard it solely as a vehicle for moral instruction or moral enlightenment, nor would it be appropriate to appraise a work on the basis of its alleged moral message. Yet, on the other hand, normally a literary work will express some attitude to human life, or to an aspect of it, and therefore has a moral dimension. In this sense no work can be ethically neutral, despite Wilde's protestation. Indeed, *The Picture of Dorian Gray* is very much concerned with morality. It is about a man who tries to escape the consequences of his own evil actions and who necessarily fails, since no man can ultimately escape from what he becomes *in* doing evil things.

Despite his general remarks on the gulf between art and morality, Wilde did not deny that this story has ethical import. 'Each man sees his own sin in Dorian Gray.'[1] '[The story] will fill the cowardly with terror, and the unclean will see in it their own shame. It will be to each man what he is to himself. It is the spectator, and not life, that art really mirrors.'[2] Yet, curiously, he gave the impression not only that one can appreciate the story as a work of art without understanding its moral content, but that there are two modes of

[1] To the editor of the *Scots Observer*, 9 July 1890, *Selected Letters of Oscar Wilde*, ed. R. Hart-Davis (Oxford, 1979).
[2] To the editor of the *Scots Observer* (31?) July 1890.

apprehension, the aesthetic and the moral. 'For if a work of art is rich and vital, and complete, those who have artistic instincts will see its beauty, and those to whom ethics appeals more strongly will see its moral lesson.'[3] And, a month later: 'If a man sees the artistic beauty of a thing, he will probably care very little for its ethical import.'[4]

Wilde obscured the issue by conflating two different things. He rightly opposed the idea that the chief merit of a literary work lies in its moral 'lesson', while refusing to acknowledge that the moral ideas in a novel may be an important consideration in appraising the work as a work of art. Thus to accept Wilde's view is not only to believe that the content of a work is of minor significance, but that what is of value consists in some sort of technique or skill of presentation which has little to do with the vision of life that the work presents. This apparent dichotomy between ideas and presentation is not unrelated to the further dichotomy between seeing art (*a*) as a kind of instruction about life and (*b*) as a matter of sensuous enjoyment divorced from intellectual understanding. To accept the premiss underlying that 'choice' would commit us either to seeing art as something which is to be described or justified by reference to some 'external' condition (thus in principle art might be replaced by some other means to that condition) or to see it as a matter of rolling about in blind ecstasy. Clearly, neither 'option' is adequate. We can opt neither for the message nor for sensuous titillation, but for an understanding that only art can give. It is notoriously difficult to say what this understanding consists in, just as it is to give an account of the relation between form and content. We do not evaluate a work of literature solely on the basis of what we may extract from it and call 'the content' any more than we can discuss 'the form' in abstraction from what the work has to say to us. Our discussion of *Mansfield Park* and *The History Man* made this clear. For in both works it is difficult to see how we could separate the 'ideas' from the way that these ideas are conveyed in the organization and 'treatment'.

Yet if we grant that all too familiar point, it still leaves the question of whether moral disagreement with what the work says (in the fullness of its 'treatment') inclines us to consider the work

[3] Ibid.   [4] To the editor of the *Scots Observer*, 13 Aug. 1890.

diminished as an artistic creation. Here it is helpful to take some examples.

Consider first Lionel Trilling's lack of moral sympathy with Fanny Price as heroine. I said in the previous chapter that disagreements about the character or personality of Fanny Price bear important implications for one's interpretation of that novel as a whole. This is borne out in Trilling's criticism. 'Nobody, I believe, has ever found it possible to like the heroine of *Mansfield Park*. Fanny Price is overtly virtuous and consciously virtuous.'[5] Trilling's hostility, or lack of sympathy, is not a personal whim: it is related to his rejection of what he takes to be one of the moral premisses of the novel. We are asked, he says, to reject and condemn Mary Crawford's vitality 'in favour of Fanny's debility' (ibid. 117). Of the former, 'we are asked to believe that she is not to be admired, that her lively mind compounds by very reason of its liveliness, with the world, the flesh and the devil'. Thus in being asked to approve of Fanny Price we are asked to approve of the Christian tradition which rejects worldliness and which affirms 'the peculiar sanctity of the sick, the weak and the dying' (p. 115). And, in approving of this, we are asked to share the novel's 'preference for rest over motion'. 'No other great novel', he says, 'has so anxiously asserted the need to find security, to establish in fixity and enclosure, a refuge from the dangers of openness and chance.'

Incidentally, I do not agree with this criticism, as will be evident from my discussion in the previous chapter. We are not, for instance, asked to disapprove of Mary Crawford simply because she is lively, but because of the form her liveliness takes, and because of the ends to which it is directed. Neither are we asked to approve of Fanny's physical weakness. Since Fanny is perhaps not the flawless creature Trilling supposes, she too has her failings; and though the novel does not explicitly condemn her for them, it does not seek to gain our admiration for them either. Nor, without ignoring the gentle ridicule of Lady Bertram, would it be reasonable to say that the novel approves of inactivity. Indeed it invites us to see beneath these categories to find in Fanny not 'inactivity', but a kind of quiet depth that does not so much reject the world as perceive what gives it its value.

---

[5] 'Jane Austen and "Mansfield Park"', in Boris Ford (ed.), *From Blake to Byron: The Pelican Guide to English Literature*, v (Harmondsworth, 1957), 116.

Clearly these rival interpretations not only permit, but entail, a certain amount of moral disagreement. But the important point is that Trilling does not argue that, because he does not like its morality, *Mansfield Park* is less a work of art. 'Yet *Mansfield Park* is a great novel.' The novel, he tells us, offends our 'modern pieties'. He does not, however, see that as a reason for belittling Jane Austen's achievement. In fact he makes it sound as though the greatness consists in the way that it does disturb the reader's moral sensibility—'it's greatness being commensurate with its power to offend' (p. 116).

What does that suggest about the relation between art and morality? Before attempting an answer, let us take another case which is in some respects similar: Orwell's discussion of Swift. In 'Politics vs Literature', Orwell goes to great lengths to show how opposed he is to *Gulliver's Travels* 'in a political and moral sense', yet in the same breath Orwell tells us that Swift 'is one of the writers I admire with least reserve . . . if I had to make a list of six books which were to be preserved when all others were destroyed, I would certainly put *Gulliver's Travels* among them'.[6]

The first moral he extracts from his own example is that 'if one is capable of intellectual detachment, one can *perceive* merit in a writer whom one deeply disagrees with' (emphasis original). But this still leaves him with the problem of how it is possible to enjoy such a work. Orwell explains the problem away by saying that although we are tempted to pass adverse judgement on a work which 'wounds', 'alarms', or seems 'pernicious', we do so only by 'constructing' an aesthetic theory to fit our prejudices at the time. But when our enjoyment surpasses our disapproval we likewise separate the subject-matter from the aesthetic worth of the work of art in question. As an observation on human nature, that may have some truth in it. But it simply bypasses the problem to be explained: what can we say in principle about the relation, or lack of it, between agreement with a writer's opinions and enjoyment of his work? That is, what *ought* we to say about a work with which we are morally at odds?

---

[6] George Orwell, *Inside the Whale: And Other Essays* (Harmondsworth, 1962), 138.

AGREEMENT AND ACCEPTANCE

It seems necessary here to draw a distinction between agreement and acceptance. In the examples discussed, Trilling and Orwell disagree with the world-view they take to be expressed in the works they criticize, yet find it possible to accept it for the purposes of the work. How precisely is this 'acceptance' to be explained? One crucial difference seems to be that acceptance is not so tightly related to belief. To agree with what you say, I must believe that what you say is right; I share your opinion. This agreement need not be present for me to accept what I am told. Faced with a pupil accused of a misdemeanour, the headmaster may decide to accept the boy's story without believing it to be true. He is not necessarily convinced by the story, but the plausibility—or indeed the presence of doubt—may be a ground for acceptance. Acceptance is the willingness to 'go along with'. To accept the vote of the majority in a meeting, for instance, is to agree to abide by it without necessarily agreeing with it. The advantage of invoking this concept to explain our engagement with a work of art is that it overcomes the difficulty posed by the fact that we 'go along with' something we do not believe to exist. If acceptance is not itself a belief then we are not faced with the conclusion that we believe in an X we know not to exist, for acceptance is not 'belief in'. But if the argument is right, the further advantage is that we can 'accept' the moral presuppositions of a work without agreeing with them. That does not mean of course that we are prepared to write a blank cheque, allowing any author in advance to draw upon our tolerance; that tolerance must be, in one way or another, earned. In a different essay Trilling remarks that 'we can take pleasure in literature where we do not agree, responding to the power or grace of a mind without admitting the rightness of its intension or conclusion—we can take our pleasure from an intellect's *cogency*, without making a final judgement on the correctness or adaptability of what it says.'[7]

To understand Trilling's remark, we need to remind ourselves that in responding to a work we are responding to something written by another human being. If we were to think of the text

---

[7] 'The Meaning of a Literary Idea', in Lionel Trilling, *The Liberal Imagination: Essays on Literature and Society* (Oxford, 1978), 234 (emphasis orig.).

merely as a physical object, as black marks on a white page to be 'decoded' or 'deconstructed', a whole dimension of our engagement would be altogether lost. In fact it would be impossible to make sense of literature at all. Part of the value we find in literature consists in our negotiation with a human mind other than our own. As for Trilling's reference to 'cogency', it is necessary to indicate here that the context of his remark is one in which he has been discussing the aesthetic impact of forms of expression—an impact which he claims does not depend upon agreement with what is said. Having quoted a couplet from Yeats, Trilling goes on to identify such pleasure in Freud's *An Outline of Psychoanalysis*: 'It is the pleasure of listening to a strong, decisive, self-limiting voice uttering statements to which I can give assent'[8]—an assent which Trilling distinguishes from agreement. There is nothing in this example to challenge the principle that how something is said is part of what is said, for Trilling's purpose is not to separate sound from sense. The 'assent' he speaks of has to do with the compelling quality that certain forms of utterance may have. This is not a quality which is independent of thought; rather it is a quality of thought that is valued independently of the attitude or belief it expresses. One presumes that Trilling finds this quality of thought in *Mansfield Park*. Indeed had it not some kind of compelling quality, it could not challenge or violate the 'modern pieties' to which Trilling apparently subscribes.

Orwell's point, however, seems to be different. Not only does he fail to explain what it is he finds attractive or important in *Gulliver's Travels*, but he expressly rejects the escape-route which consists in separating the unacceptable or 'false' vision from the quality of the writing: 'But not all the power and imagination of Swift's prose, nor the imaginative effect that has been able to make not one but a whole series of impossible worlds more credible than the majority of history books—none of this would enable us to enjoy Swift if his world-view were truly wounding or shocking.'[9]

Orwell's move here is not to look for some redeeming feature in the 'quality' of the writing (in the way that Trilling's account suggests) but to come back on himself and now deny that Swift's vision is completely false. The argument thus runs as follows:

[8] Ibid. 273.   [9] 'Politics vs. Literature', *Inside the Whale*, 139.

Swift's vision is completely false, yet I enjoy the work; how can this be? Since it cannot consist just in the 'quality' of the writing, it must be that the vision is not as false as I first thought. (It is at this point that though Swift 'refuses to see anything in human life except dirt, folly and wickedness' we are exhorted to recognize that since dirt, folly and wickedness do indeed exist, there is *some* truth in the vision to which 'part of us' responds.) 'In his endless harping on disease, dirt and deformity, Swift is not actually inventing anything, he is merely leaving something out.'

I am far from convinced by this argument, for a number of reasons. First, if what Swift 'leaves out' is something which would show that life is not the total misery the work suggests, it is a fallacy to suppose that Swift was half right: the idea that life is a total misery remains completely false. Second, and more important, Orwell begs the very question at issue. He simply assumes that it could not be the case that it is possible to admire the artistry, while deploring the vision it expresses. The conclusion he draws is that all we can demand of a work, before rejecting it completely, is that it be 'compatible with sanity', 'that it shall not be blazingly silly'. Here the wheel has come full circle.

So far, then, we have established only a tentative line of enquiry, extracted from Trilling's distinction between agreement and assent, and that is that we might consider the idea that we can fail to agree with the moral attitudes (i.e. opinions) evinced in a particular work while nevertheless accepting ('going along with') those attitudes as a result of some 'quality' or 'force' in the work. (Indeed Anthony Savile points to a fact of our common experience that 'in the case of some contrivances indifference or even repulsion may co-exist with . . . their beauty'.[10]) For that argument to be successful it would have to show that moral agreement with the work is not a necessary condition of perceiving its artistic merit. Indeed Orwell's inclination to say that the world-view of *Gulliver's Travels* is 'not altogether false' might profitably be interpreted along those lines. It might be a better way of explaining the fact that he feels drawn to a work with which he disagrees. 'Why is it that we don't mind being called Yahoos, although firmly convinced that we are *not* Yahoos?'[11] There are at least two possible answers. The first,

---

[10] 'Beauty and Attachment', in Eva Schaper (ed.) *Pleasure, Preference and Value: Studies in Philosophical Aesthetics* (Cambridge, 1987), 105.
[11] *Inside the Whale*, 139 (emphasis orig.).

following Orwell's own argument, is that we recognize that there is something disgusting in human nature even though human achievement often rises above it. But this answer is not adequate since it does not distinguish the text as a work of art from an argument that is partly true (the work of art belongs to a different language-game from that of argumentation: while a work of art may suggest some view of human life, it does not establish it as the conclusion from an argument). The second answer is that there is a force or quality in the execution of the writer's task that compels our acceptance of that which we know, or believe, to be false or unjustified as a picture of human nature. This would also explain why we are prepared to 'go along with' the depiction of an impossible world in fiction. If the writer has done his job well enough, we accept that 'world' while never even for a moment believing that it is other than impossible.

There is, however, a problem raised by this analysis. As it stands, it gives the impression that the artistic status of a work of literature can never be diminished by the unacceptability of its vision. If we go too far in that direction we shall end up with the view that literary achievement is only to do with tricks and techniques, rhetoric, embellishments, and so on, and nothing to do with the writer's perception or understanding of the world or of human nature. That would not do at all. As Leavis put it, 'I don't believe in any "literary values", and you won't find me talking about them; the judgements the literary critic is concerned with are judgements about life.'[12] And indeed what he goes on to criticize in Forster is 'a grave defect of perception, human insight and essential valuation'.[13] Without commenting on that particular case, in general it seems reasonable to believe that a shallow man will, for that reason, be a shallow writer. Or as Henry James put it, 'No good novel will ever proceed from a superficial mind; that seems to me an axiom which, for the artist in fiction, will cover all needful moral ground.'[14] Where does that leave us? I don't think that it contradicts the argument I was trying to develop. All that argument sought to do was show how it is possible to reconcile perception of

---

[12] 'Luddites? *or* There is Only One Culture', in F. R. Leavis, *Nor Shall My Sword: Discourses on Pluralism, Compassion and Social Hope* (London, 1972), 97.
[13] 'Elites, Oligarchies and an Educated Public', ibid. 224.
[14] *The Critical Muse: Selected Literary Criticism*, ed. R. Gard (London, 1987), 205.

artistic merit with disagreement over attitudes or moral opinions. Neither Trilling nor Orwell based their disagreement on the idea that the attitudes revealed in the work were shallow or superficial. And presumably there would be a close relationship between shallowness of treatment and shallowness of vision, or, for that matter, shallowness of feeling—as Ian Robinson points out: 'a poet who satisfies himself that he has expressed his religion, or his love, in a sentimental, shallow poem is judging his religion or his love to be sentimental or shallow'.[15] In a literary work one would not expect profound insight to be altogether separable from the way that the work communicates itself to us. In *Macbeth* for instance Shakespeare's insights into the nature of evil cannot be appreciated except in relation to the quality of the poetry. The playwright conveys the emptiness of soul that is entailed in a life that turns towards evil, and the quality of this insight cannot be separated from the way he shows that emptiness through the poetry. The 'tomorrow and tomorrow' speech for example creates a sense of emptiness and does not merely describe it. A lesser poet could not have shown us what Shakespeare shows us.

ART AND EVIL

My previous discussion about 'acceptance' does not drop out the importance of the perception of the writer. But, given that, the question therefore remains: what are we to say about a work which endorses some view of life that is so morally repugnant as to appear to forfeit its claim to excellence? It is one thing to tackle the question of reconciling our moral disagreement with our perception of artistic merit. It is quite another to speak of a work which appears to express attitudes which are corrupt or evil. For here, our reaction is not simply one of *disagreement*. To perceive something as evil or corrupt is to condemn it utterly, to be sickened by it.

Let us therefore consider a case in which a critic has condemned a literary work precisely on those grounds. Writing about *Crow*, a series of poems by Ted Hughes, David Holbrook mounts an attack on what he takes to be their nihilism. It would be irrelevant for my purposes to enter into dispute about whether Holbrook has inter-

[15] *The Survival of English* (Doncaster, 1981), 195.

preted the poems fairly or adequately. Let us assume for the sake
of argument that his interpretations of the poems are ones we
share: the real point is what follows from this. Something of the
tenor of Holbrook's criticism can be gleaned from the following
extract:

'Unspeakable guts', 'messy blood', 'dragged under by the weight of his
guts', 'smashed into the rubbish of the ground', 'brains incinerating', 'loop
of his blood like a garotte'—after so many words thrusting upon us guts,
blood, impossible pain, distortion, dismemberment, and vile images of the
inside of the body, nothing is left but a mental rage, that is encapsulated
within itself. Max Stirner, the German nihilist, declared that the world
was nothing and that he was nothing—so, the only posture towards the
world was that 'the other' and the world were—'my food'. There is
nothing in *Crow* for which to have respect or for which to feel care or
concern: it belongs to the 'racking moment' of smashing everything to
pieces: in one's head, at least. There is no one to whom to render account:
there is no respect for 'community'.[16]

Now it will be conceded that art is not just a form of therapy;
and some of the old therapy-seeking Holbrook remains in this
essay: 'we go to the arts, in trust, expecting that we will be given
something to take into our inner dynamics to our benefit—to help
us find meaning. Instead we are raped.' However, that is not the
main thrust of his attack. What Holbrook finds is a debilitating
vision in these poems that challenges their right to be called art:
revulsion for the world and for humanity. Man is 'a nothing', lying
among garbage:

> He saw this shoe, with no sole, rain-sodden,
> Lying on a moor.
> And there was this garbage can, bottom rusted away,
> A playing place for the wind, in a waste of puddles.

Man's consciousness is 'merely a burden':

> Grown so wise grown so terrible
> Sucking death's mouldy tits.

There is a complete horror at all creation. The universe is meaningless; the stars are 'mushrooms of the nothing forest', 'the virus of

---

[16] 'Ted Hughes's "Crow" and the Longing for Non-Being', in Peter Abbs (ed.),
The Black Rainbow: Essays on the Present Breakdown of Culture (London, 1975),
33.

God'. In Holbrook's words, amply supported by reference to the poems, 'Hughes tries to lock us into the reductionist view of man as seen by the ironical (and "realistic") Crow . . . The world only "is"—there are no levels of being: there is no transcendence of the weight of one's guts—there is no meaning and there are no values.' (Ibid. 39.)

LOVE AND THE CREATIVE ACT

If Hughes is guilty as charged, then it is difficult not to sympathize with Holbrook's claim that the poems are deficient as artistic creations. This means that we need to look very carefully at what we value in the process of artistic creation. Certainly we cannot insist on optimism; naïve optimism would in any case be a form of sentimentality inimical to that concern for truth we value in art. Equally we cannot outlaw certain forms of pessimism. Of *King Lear*, A. C. Bradley remarked, 'This is certainly the most terrible picture that Shakespeare painted of the world. In no other of his tragedies does humanity appear more pitiably infirm or more hopelessly bad.'[17] Yet it remains one of Shakespeare's finest achievements. Nihilism is a different matter altogether. *King Lear* is not nihilistic. Although humanity must perforce prey on itself like monsters of the deep, there is a glimmer of decency in man that perceives the spectacle and is appalled by it. There is something in *King Lear* 'for which to have respect and for which to feel care or concern'. Yet if Holbrook is right, *Crow* is anti-human. In *Crow* there is no tragedy because there is no hint of anything worth valuing: we are expected to feel a kind of perverse delight in the images of horror.

I find myself agreeing with Holbrook's expectation of the creative act: that there is a fastidiousness of genuine art which is a creativity rooted in love. Alvarez praises Hughes for the opposite: 'Ted Hughes, who starts out as a nature poet, and whose work contains more animals than the London Zoo lavishes all that loving, sharp detail on his menagerie only for whatever corresponding sense of unpredictable violence he finds in himself.'[18]

---

[17] *Shakespearean Tragedy: Lectures on Hamlet, Othello, King Lear, Macbeth* (London, 1985), 225.

[18] Quoted and discussed by Holbrook, op. cit. n. 16 above, p. 35.

There does seem to be at least a prima facie contradiction in Alvarez's remarks. No matter how much it may display our imperfections, artistic creation has an ancient association with a search for perfection, meaning, and order. The connection between love and creation is brought out in these rather striking remarks by Simone Weil: 'One can use a watch without loving the watch-maker, but one cannot listen with attention to a faultlessly beautiful song without love for the composer of the song and for the singer. In the same way the watchmaker does not need love to make a watch, whereas artistic creation (that sort which is not demonic but simply human) is nothing but love.'[19] Some say that Pope's attacks on his contemporaries were inspired by bitterness and malice. Whether or not that is true (and it is easy to forget the moral emotions that fuelled these attacks) what speaks through the poetry is something that rises above, or transcends, hatred. In his introduction to his selection of Pope's works, Lois Kronenberger puts this very well in commenting on the following portrait of Narcissa:

> Narcissa's nature, tolerably mild,
> To make a wash, would hardly stew a child;
> Has even been proved to grant a lover's prayer,
> And paid a tradesman once to make him stare;
> Gave alms at Easter, in a Christian trim,
> And made a widow happy, for a whim.

Kronenberger writes, '"Narcissa" may be a sobriquet for some-body Pope disliked: but we feel here a malice—if malice it be—that has been so completely aërated into sheer wit, we feel here so much greater an impulse to create a portrait than to destroy a person, that no animus seems involved.'[20]

It is difficult, even embarrassing, to speak of art and love in this way in an age which is as cynical and despairing as ours now is. It is as if art has to be destructive to be in fashion. But it isn't merely the spirit of the age which makes it difficult to speak of art being rooted in love. One also has to wrestle with the vocabulary of criticism bequeathed to us by various pseudo-scientific and political

---

[19] *Intimations of Christianity among the Early Greeks* (2nd edn., London, 1987), 90–1.
[20] *Alexander Pope: Selected Works*, ed. L. Kronenberger (2nd edn., New York, 1951), p. xxvii.

fashions that no longer recognize the element of the sacred that attaches to great works of art and which for various reasons drop out what used to be called the author. With the disappearance of the author, as Trilling observes, we are less and less surprised by 'art' which is increasingly dehumanized:

Twenty-five years ago Ortega spoke of the 'dehumanization' of modern art. Much of what he said about modern art has, by modern art, been proved wrong, or was even wrong before he said it. But Ortega was right in observing of modern art that it expresses a dislike of holding in the mind the human fact and human condition, that it shows 'a real loathing of living forms and living beings', . . . a disgust with history, society and the state. Human life as an aesthetic object can perhaps no longer command our best attention; the day seems to have gone when the artist who dealt in representation could catch our interest almost by the mere listing of the ordinary details of human existence; and the most extreme and complex of human dilemmas now surely seem to many to have lost their power to engage us.[21]

An artist may express disgust for human beings or even for the human form either by reducing human beings to animals or by portraying them as hideous physical objects. The difficulty for this argument of course is that even great art is capable of doing this. In Ben Jonson's *Volpone* men are portrayed as animals, and any run-of-the-mill sixth former can spot the ubiquitous 'animal imagery' in Lear. But the subtle difference is that these are highly moral plays: we are not invited to share some Frankensteinish delight in the creation of monsters, and we do feel, beneath, some sense of what we ought to be. In contrast, as Anthony O'Hear points out in his humane and perceptive examination of the relations between art and human value:

. . . it must be admitted that while the human imagination can be used to enlighten and free us from the grosser aspects of our nature—the naked-ness of our greed and need—it can also be used to oppress us with these aspects of our lives. Art can treat human beings and human life in terms of the animal in them, without allowing any scope for graciousness, magnanimity, friendship, love, dedication to something other than one's own animal desires, sobriety, or the other virtues. If anything is significant of our age and of the contemporary artistic scene it is surely that painters

---

[21] 'Art and Fortune', in Trilling, *The Liberal Imagination*, 249.

who shout loudest and paint biggest in glorifying the animal and the grotesque in human life are the current stars of the artistic establishment.[22]

The examples O'Hear gives are 'such artists as Francis Bacon, who represents human beings as skewered carcasses and writhing meat, Franco Clemente, George Baselitz, A. R. Penck and many of the other contemporary expressionists represented in the recent "New Spirit of Painting" and "German Art in the Twentieth Century" exhibitions, to say nothing of the appalling Gilbert and George with their cruel and narcissistic fantasies'. Human life is not without its grotesque elements, but two wrongs do not make a right. 'To respond to evil with yet more ugliness is, in a way, to connive in it . . .'[23]

Someone who wished to say that art is beyond good and evil would have little conception of the humanness of art. And perhaps this is the key to the whole discussion. Not only are works of art created by human beings, and not only are these works made possible by the living spirit of various traditions that have been passed from one generation to another, but they have served to heighten, rather than to diminish, our feeling for human kind. The influence of the arts on our thoughts and feelings about human beings is not fully explicit or fully conscious, and almost impossible to explain except in relation to other things that have shaped the history of civilization. But it is not at all fanciful to suggest that had there been no works of art our attitude to human beings would be unrecognizable. Our respect, fascination, and even reverence for human life has been shaped by centuries of artistic exploration and celebration of the human in its various aspects. Through the arts we have been made aware of the heights of conduct to which we may aspire and of the degradation into which it is possible to sink. Or perhaps it is better to say that art has helped to create the possibilities of these heights and depths.

We do not expect, nor do we always find in art a eulogy of human nature. That we can recognize ourselves in works which display our wickedness, our folly, our jealousies, blindness, greed, and superstition, shows that we do not turn to the arts for flattery. Nor should we always expect our follies to be displayed with the kindly and forgiving eye of a Geoffrey Chaucer. Since art is open

[22] *The Element of Fire: Science, Art and the Human World* (London, 1988), 156.
[23] Ibid. 156.

to various possibilities of human experience, we shall not even shy away from works inspired by wretchedness and misery. But it does seem to be antithetical to the idea of artistic *creation* to be presented with a vision of life that malevolently revels in the worthlessness of life itself.[24] What distinguishes tragedy from nihilism is that the former does not suggest that life is meaningless, and neither does it delight in the spectacle of human misfortune. Tragedy finds a meaning, and even a value, in human suffering. As Aristotle pointed out, tragedy does certain things to protect itself from being merely cruel: the tragic hero has some complicity with his own fate. In *King Lear* the punishment far exceeds the crime, yet there is sympathy for the 'little world of man'; the work does not lick its lips in enjoyment of the spectacle. Simone Weil goes so far as to say of this play that it is 'the direct fruit of the spirit of pure love'.[25]

THE ARTIST AND MORAL RESPONSIBILITY

It is impossible to speak of literature in those terms without implying that there is a relation between the writer and his material which has moral implications. The artist is drawn into a nexus of moral relations. For a start he is not an isolated practitioner, but one whose achievements can only be fully appreciated against a background of tradition. Over the centuries, the achievements in science, literature, and philosophy are not to be thought of as manifestations of individual skill popping up out of nowhere, like lamps shining in the dark. All achievement is achievement within a tradition, even when it strikes out in a new direction. As T. S. Eliot put it in his *Notes Towards the Definition of Culture*: 'Only a Christian culture could have produced a Voltaire or a Nietzsche.'[26] Tradition and culture, however, need to be distinguished. The former is a human spirit which is larger than any individual and requires self-sacrifice: the loss of the ego to something more valuable. The poet does not merely exercise skill, does not just

---

[24] Cp. Holland's argument that evil is 'de-creative', ('Good and Evil in Action', in R. F. Holland, *Against Empiricism: On Education, Epistemology and Value* (Oxford, 1980), 118–19.

[25] *The Need for Roots: Prelude to a Declaration of Duties towards Mankind*, Trans. A. F. Wills, with a preface by T. S. Eliot (London, 1978), 225.

[26] *Notes Towards the Definition of Culture* (London, 1962), 112.

pour out his personality, and does not regard poetry as a collection of isolated products. If he has what Eliot calls 'the historical sense' he regards poetry as 'the living whole of all the poetry that has ever been written'. This 'organic' sense of art confers a responsibility upon the artist as well as informing our perception of his achievement. 'No poet, no artist of any art, has his complete meaning alone. His significance, his appreciation, is the appreciation of his relation to the dead poets and artists.'[27]

It follows from this conception that the artist who lacks integrity in his work, or who is careless, slipshod in its execution, or indifferent towards its merit, is not only deficient as a practitioner but in his attitude towards the strivings of other men, past, present, and future. For the writer's craft does not exist in a vacuum; it has been handed down through centuries of creative effort, a fact any writer must respect; and present achievements will have a significant bearing on the arts of our successors. Here I feel some warmth towards Michael Oakeshott's conception of civilization as a 'timeless conversation between the generations'. Civilization is, and must be, larger than any contemporary community that sustains it: 'As civilised human beings, we are the inheritors, neither of an enquiry about ourselves and the world, nor one accumulating body of information, but of a conversation, begun in the primeval forests and extended and made more articulate in the course of the centuries.'[28]

Taken out of context, that statement appears more plausible than it is when rendered in terms of Oakeshott's leanings towards a rather obscure doctrine that each 'mode of experience' is entire within itself and that there can be no real relationships between them—a doctrine I find very difficult to understand. But granted that the term 'conversation' in the quoted passage is metaphorical (and given Oakeshott's philosophy it could be nothing else) the question arises whether it is an appropriate metaphor. Given that the world did not spring into existence overnight, the various bodies of knowledge and modes of understanding peculiar to the intellectual disciplines are passed on to us, and it should be a central task of true education to pass them on to the next

---

[27] 'Tradition and the Individual Talent', in *Selected Prose of T. S. Eliot*, ed. Frank Kermode (London, 1975). 38.
[28] *Rationalism in Politics: and Other Essays* (London, 1962), 38.

generation. In being the inheritors of civilization it is as though we were involved with a discourse with the dead, and any artistic or cultural achievement is in that sense predicated upon a respect for our ancestors and, perhaps, even upon a concern for the yet unborn. But, again, 'discourse' here is a metaphor, for literally speaking there is no reciprocity. The dead cannot literally speak to the living. Nevertheless if we have the requisite humility that attends respect for tradition, we shall see our intellectual and artistic engagements as having an importance that transcends the particular and local features of the here and now.

This conception of the moral responsibility of the artist must therefore be sharply distinguished from the idea that art has a social or moral purpose. The latter idea suffers from a myopic perception both of art and of those to whom the duty is owed, hence it fails to distinguish art from utility: for the 'community' it serves is a contemporary group, to be edified, enlightened, or reformed by an art that is indistinguishable from propaganda. It is necessary for this reason to insist that aesthetic engagement is to be distinguished from the purely practical, but not in a way that trivializes our conception of 'the aesthetic' by regarding it as a matter of titillation or delight divorced from understanding. (This is Oakeshott's error, since he regards the 'voice' of poetry—by which he means all art—as one of pure contemplation which has nothing to do with moral understanding; hence, as we have seen, he argues that we cannot engage in moral evaluation of fictional characters.) It is not necessarily so, of course, that for the artist to possess this moral seriousness he must consciously recognize or explicitly formulate his duty in terms of paying homage to his artistic forebears, or in 'creating something for posterity'. Rather, this seriousness is manifested in his attitude to his work, and a lack of serious commitment in that respect is a criterion for failure in the larger respect. (This is paralleled in Eliot's claim that 'culture' is not composed of a collection of individuals struggling to contribute to 'culture', but instead that 'high' culture is generated out of specialists dedicated to the furtherance of their specialisms.)

But that is only one level at which we can say that the artist stands in a moral relation to his art. With a particular novel or play there is also the matter of the writer's attitude towards the characters and their circumstances. We have already discussed at some length the way in which we can preserve at least one sense in

which characters are independent of their creator: i.e. in understanding them as persons we cannot regard them as being mere
puppets pulled hither and thither by an author's will. However, I
have also tried to show how in our response to the work as a
whole we step back from this 'primary engagement' and contemplate the significance of the fictional world, the 'meaning' of which
cannot be understood apart from our conception of the work as a
product of human intention. Thus to engage with the work is to
engage with the mind that has produced it. It is not to contemplate
a physical object shorn of moral significance, but to engage with
the moral perspective, not lying behind the work but revealed *in* it.
Of the work, and at the same time of the author, we can ask: why
are we being shown this act of cruelty, this man's hopeless fate,
this callousness, or this apparent triumph of evil over good?

Since the author has selected certain events for our attention and
has stipulated that this or that shall happen, our understanding of
these events is at the same time an understanding of the attitudes
of the author towards his material. In rejecting those theories that
drop out the author we are not committed to the belief that we
need an access to the author's state of mind that is independent of
the work (though in *some* cases this might increase our appreciation or understanding). It does not seem to matter for instance
that we know relatively little of the life of Shakespeare. That in no
way reduces our appreciation of his work, nor is it a limitation
upon our capacity to understand it. As Helen Gardner points out,
Auden is correct in saying in his introduction to the Signet edition
of Shakespeare's *Sonnets* that establishing the identity of the
Friend, the Dark Lady, or the Rival Poet would not in any way
illuminate our understanding of the poems. This is not because
there is no relation between a poet's life and his works, but because
this relation 'is at the same time too evident to require comment—
every work of art is, in one sense, a self-disclosure—and one too
complicated ever to unravel'.[29]

If, then, the mind of the author is revealed *in* the work, the
moral vision of the work cannot fail to have aesthetic implications,
indeed it is difficult to see how they could be kept apart. Moreover,
to claim that the author is irrelevant to his creation would be a
claim that itself bears moral implications. Trilling touches on this.

---

[29] Helen Gardner, *In Defence of the Imagination* (Oxford, 1982), 171.

Here he has just been discussing Sartre's theory of 'dogmatic realism', according to which the novel is to be written off as if without an author, and therefore without a personal voice:

> The banishment of the author from his books, the stilling of his voice, have but reinforced the faceless hostility of the world and have tended to teach us that we ourselves are not creative agents and that we have no voice, no tone, no style, no significant existence. Surely what we need is the opposite of this, the opportunity to identify ourselves with a mind that willingly admits it is a mind and does not pretend that it is History or Events or the World but only a mind thinking and planning—possibly planning our escape.[30]

My interest in this passage differs from what Trilling seems to intend. He seems to be responding to Sartre by sharing the premiss that art should be evaluated in terms of its good or bad 'social effects', whereas—for reasons I shall go into in the concluding chapter—the value of fiction lies in its fictionality, and therefore in its being conveyed to us through the mind of an author.

Trilling himself seems to be ambivalent about the relation between morality and art, whereas Leavis at least has the merit of being unequivocal. In *The Great Tradition*, Leavis argued that 'a vital capacity for experience, a kind of reverent openness before life, and a marked moral intensity' are criterial of the good novel. *Emma*, he maintains, has indeed a 'formal perfection', but this is not merely 'an "aesthetic matter", a beauty of "composition" that is combined, miraculously, with "truth to life"': rather, it 'can be appreciated only in terms of the moral preoccupations that characterize the novelist's peculiar interest in life' (pp. 17–18). Admittedly that 'only' is rather strong, for, as I argued in the previous chapter, the depth of Jane Austen's moral insights in *Mansfield Park* cannot be appreciated apart from the artistry through which they are expressed. But that is different from Trilling's retort to Leavis:

> it isn't a lack of catholicity that one objects to . . . but a basic error about the nature of art—and of life. For Dr Leavis is saying in effect that art has its true being only in tension and direction, only in completely organized consciousness and moral clarity. He takes no proper account, that is, of the art that delights—and enlightens—by the intentional relaxation of

---

[30] *The Liberal Imagination*, 253–4.

moral awareness, by its invitation to us to contemplate the mere excess of irrelevant life.[31]

What Trilling seems to be saying in this essay is that the Leavis criterion is fine for some works, but that he is blind to an art which takes its virtue from sheer 'performance' or 'virtuosity'—from 'the mind's delight in itself, in its power of excess and fantasy, in its ability to play the game of freedom, even freedom from law and the moral order . . .' (ibid.). I find this argument mysterious. It is one thing to argue that a writer needs more than moral vision, and that the strength of the moral vision will only be conveyed through an artistry, a talent, which is irreducible to moral perception. It is quite another to suppose that a literary work can be evaluated only in terms of a 'performance' divorced from moral perception and, indeed, from a moral perspective. For once we have re-established the author into the arena of criticism—as indeed Trilling in other places argues that we should—the 'meaning' of the work implies the existence of a 'meaner'.[32] And disputes about the meaning of the work will inevitably make some reference to some implied (moral) attitude on the part of the 'meaner'. Indeed if we consider Trilling's essay, 'The Morality of Inertia', this point is borne out in his discussion of Edith Wharton. Axiomatic to his adverse criticism of her work is the following: 'Whenever the characters of a story suffer, they do so at the behest of their author—the author is responsible for their suffering and must justify his cruelty by the seriousness of his moral intention.'[33] Can this be the same critic who argued against Leavis? And can one discern any real ground of disagreement between them, as a principle of criticism, in the following judgement? 'The author of *Ethan Frome* . . . could not lay claim to any such justification. Her intention in writing the story was not adequate to the dreadful fate she contrived for her characters. She indulges herself by what she contrives—she is, as the phrase goes, "merely literary".'

D. Z. Phillips has opposed the interpretations of Edith Warton's novels given by critics such as Trilling on the grounds that they have not appreciated that the values endorsed in the novels go far

[31] 'Dr Leavis and the Moral Tradition', in Trilling, *A Gathering of Fugitives* (Oxford, 1980), 112.
[32] A neologism I borrow from Alistair Fowler, 'A Critical Path for Literature', *Times Higher Education Supplement*, 8 Mar. 1985.
[33] 'The Morality of Inertia', in *A Gathering of Fugitives*, 36.

deeper than 'the dull, unthinking round of duties'.[34] It is not my job to adjudicate between these differing interpretations: I am concerned with the philosophical basis of this criticism. In evaluating Wharton's novel, Trilling—by his own admission—is assessing the morality of the voice that speaks through it. This evidence of Trilling's actual practice in criticism repudiates, or at least contradicts, what seems to be his point against Leavis: that there can be merely literary qualities. For he does not fault Edith Wharton at that level: 'We can never speak of Edith Wharton without some degree of respect. She brought to her novels a strong if limited intelligence, notable powers of observation, and a genuine desire to tell the truth, a desire which in some part she satisfied.' What, significantly for our purposes, he does find lacking is her 'limitation of heart', and finds instead that the book is 'the product of mere will, of the cold hard literary will': '. . . she was a woman in whom we cannot fail to see a limitation of heart, and this limitation makes itself manifest as a literary and moral deficiency of her work, and of *Ethan Frome* especially.'[35] He finds it a defect of that work that it 'sets off no moral reverberation'; that the author's presentation of human suffering lacks 'propriety' in the sense that it is 'gratuitous', an end in itself. Whether it does or does not lack that 'propriety' is not to the point here. The point is that, if true, seems reasonable to describe that as a kind of literary failure, an aesthetic shortcoming in the work itself.

ART AND NEGATIVITY

While, then, it seems to be neither a necessary nor a sufficient condition of perceiving merit in a work of literature that we agree with the moral opinions it embodies or expresses, it is nevertheless possible to say that a moral failing in a literary work is at the same time an aesthetic failing. Though it is difficult, if not impossible, to lay out an abstract set of conditions for classifying something as a moral failing in a work of art, there are two broad observations we can make. The first is that whatever is to be counted as a moral failing will normally militate in some way against the spirit of love

---

[34] 'Allegiance and Change in Morality', in D. Z. Phillips, *Through a Darkening Glass: Philosophy, Literature and Cultural Change* (Oxford, 1982), 9–29.
[35] *A Gathering of Fugitives*, 112.

that shines through the creative act. The second is that a moral failing in this sense will be an intrinsic feature of the work, and will not be located solely in consequences or effects. As Casey argues:

It would obviously be absurd to judge works of art in terms of consequences. That Hitler found ideological inspiration in the music of Wagner is indisputable—but it does not follow that Wagner's music is bad. Indeed if an institution which we considered wicked constantly succeeded in expressing itself in works of the highest value, then this could be a reason for revising our view of its wickedness (it is not an accident that the artistic manifestations of Fascism were banal in the extreme).[36]

This argument can be explained and developed through considering pornography. It is now popular to believe that if pornography is to be condemned at all, it is to be condemned largely on the grounds of its potential to deprave or corrupt the future conduct of those who are exposed to it. Further, these consequences or effects will be thought of as some kind of objectively determinable or purely factual state of affairs, such as the committing of indecent acts in public (as though in private nothing is wrong) or the committing of other crimes such as rape, incest, child-molestation, or sex-crazed killings. Whether or not pornography corrupts in that very specific sense is a matter for speculation; so far there is no conclusive evidence to suggest that it does.

But to discuss pornography in those terms is rather superficial: for, penetrating beneath the consequentialist framework within which the question is asked or answered, it seems more appropriate to say not that pornography causes depravity and corruption, but that—as Ian Robinson argues—pornography *is* depravity and corruption.[37]

There is something misguided about treating what is to count as depravity and corruption as though it were purely a matter of fact. We cannot say what is to be counted as an instance of depravity or corruption, any more than we can specify what is to count as human harm, without thinking in evaluative terms, such that what is to be regarded as degrading, debauched, sordid, and unnatural is seen thus against a conception of human life, and indeed of the human body, which it violates and offends.

[36] *The Language of Criticism* (London, 1966), 53–4.
[37] *The Survival of English*, 146–89.

Once we look at the matter in that way, there is a moral shallowness even in asking such questions as 'is pornography offensive?' or 'is it harmful?', as though our real concern is with some actual or possible event or empirically observable state of affairs lying beyond the pornography itself. Indeed we could say that not to feel offended or violated by pornography is already to be depraved and corrupted: for it is tantamount to a loss of ability to recognize depravity and corruption when it stares us in the face. A powerful illustration of this is provided by Robinson, who first quotes the following letter from the *New Statesman*:

He showed a group of children, aged between 11 and 18, films depicting violence and sex, including one called *491* which showed a girl being raped by a group of intoxicated louts and forced to have intercourse with a dog. None of the children were frightened either during or after the film ... Curiously enough two adults, who saw the experiment, one a grandmother and the other a mother, were so upset that they needed psychological treatment for a month afterwards! In 30 years' experience of treating patients I have never seen anyone who proved to have been corrupted by pornography.[38]

Robinson himself adds, 'The writer has "never seen" because he doesn't know corruption when he sees it; the shock to the women suggests they were far better judges than he was.'[39]

My purpose is not to engage in a crusade against pornography. There are two philosophical morals we can draw from Robinson's discussion in that chapter. The first arises from his rather shrewd observation that it is not so much individual conduct, but the 'common language of sex' which pornography depraves and corrupts. Robinson elicits this point with a wealth of detail, and indeed with an eloquence, that I cannot hope to emulate here. A crude estimate of the argument is that since our language reflects and helps to determine our powers of discrimination, once infiltrated by pornographic conceptions of the sexual response—divorced as such conceptions necessarily are from the serious and important part that the sexual response plays in our lives—our very perception of human life becomes impaired. I shall not pursue that argument here since in the next chapter I shall have more general remarks to make on the relation between morality and language.

[38] Ibid. 168.   [39] Ibid.

What is more relevant to this chapter concerns the distinction between pornography and art. Defenders of pornography frequently attempt to ridicule or silence their critics by pointing to accredited works of art (such as Shakespeare's plays) which can be violent or to some degree sexually explicit. (Does not *Romeo and Juliet* begin with a series of obscene jokes about sexual organs and having maids up against the wall?) The crucial difference, however, is that our reactions to such scenes and images are controlled by the writer's handling of the representation. The sexual undertones of Othello's strangling of Desdemona are not put there to pander to our sexual and sadistic, or indeed voyeuristic, fantasies. A representation in art is not concerned with the mere display of an object or a situation but with an understanding of it. In fact I find it impossible to improve upon Robinson's suggestion that '[a] work whose sexual content is left deliberately uncontrolled by the artist is pornographic' (ibid.). In the previous chapter I argued that the depiction of a fictional world in literature, or indeed in painting, is not *ipso facto* a different kind of world or a different kind of life, but that it guides our perception and understanding of what is presented to us. Though in understanding a fictional world we must draw upon our understanding of the actual world, it nevertheless makes a difference to us that the representation is fictional: for that allows a contemplative attitude that provides, in some respects, a distance between ourselves and what is represented.

With pornography, however, that distance is not preserved, and the sexual or sadistic content, instead of remaining a fictional object of contemplation directed to our understanding, transmutes itself into reality such that it provokes or engages our ('real') violent or sexual feelings—even if, debased and impersonal as pornography makes them, the feelings also merge with our sense of disgust and perhaps self-disgust. One aspect of that 'transmutation' may for instance be that our attention in a play is not now absorbed by the characters but by the actors: 'the response to nude love-making is not to the play but to the real (or not) actions. We want to know how far they're really going and what they feel like doing it. And are they really doing IT?'[40] The impulse away from the fictionality is brought out even more starkly in the following

[40] Ibid. 168–9.

example, where the fantasized participation of the audience becomes even more than mere voyeurism:

> The bare-bottomed bouncings, grapplings, wide-eyed oohings and aaah-ings, the long-drawn gasps and sudden grabs now almost *de rigueur* in plays on BBC television are no more art than a brothel's exibeesh is. It is appropriate that the groups who specialize in stage copulation—reintro-duced for the first time since the days of Heliogabalus—should also wish to do away with the proscenium arch, the final development of the 'circumstances' of drama, when they cross it in order to lay the audience. This is a straightforward attack on the language of the art, a determination to destroy the art in favour of 'real life'—the real life in question being, again, strictly that of a brothel.[41]

The only quarrel I have with Robinson is where he tries to separate pornography from obscenity (arguing that great works of art can be obscene, though not pornographic). I think that distinc-tion falls with Anthony Savile's definition of obscenity as that which 'invites us to self-abasement through the breaking of some taboo', and he cites as one species of obscenity 'the deliberate and seductive degradation of what are proper objects of reverence and love, a degradation that unfits them for our attachment'.[42] This definition is compatible with my earlier discussion of 'nihilism' in art. Art that is essentially negative, as Savile persuasively argues, is also for that reason aggressive in its attitude. For the desire to destroy or deform such objects of reverence (e.g. sexual love, the sanctity of the body, the respect for the dead) is 'not just an attack on the object itself but through the object on those whom we think enriched by it'.[43] One can go even further and argue as Robinson does that pornographic 'art' is an attack on art itself: 'It is because pornography speaks the imaginative language of real poetry, real novels, that one can see it as an indecent assault upon the kind of seriousness which real literature makes possible.'[44] The other side of this coin, as I have tried to show, is that, generally speaking, truly creative work has respect for human beings and human life.

I have some doubts about Savile's attempt to explain or justify

---

[41]   Ibid. 169.
[42]   Anthony Savile, *The Test of Time: An Essay in Philosophical Aesthetics* (Oxford, 1982), 261.
[43]   Ibid. 263.   [44]   *The Survival of English*, 170.

the positive qualities of art in terms of its 'reparative impulse'[45] for the same reason that I objected to Holbrook's (sometime) view of art as a kind of therapy. There may indeed be such effects, but that is not what art is for. Nevertheless it must be agreed that there is a connection between what we value in art and what we value in life. Thus I agree with Savile's endorsement of Ruby Meager's argument that 'in the obscene we adopt or are given a double sense of ourselves . . . able to think humiliatingly of persons through their bodies as inescapably corrupt, dirty and diseased, *by standards to which we are ourselves committed*' (emphasis original), or, in his own words, 'we cannot explain obscenity except as an attack on what we prize'.[46]

It would be nice to be able to draw a neat and tidy conclusion from this discussion that wholly negative art is bad art, yet this cannot be said without qualification. Pornography aside, are there not cases in which we feel compelled to admire the sheer brilliance of some works of art in spite of their obnoxious or evil vision? Is there no room for the idea of evil genius, or of demented creativity? To rule out the possibility of such phenomena would not only amount to dogmatic legislation, it would also fail to take account of the fact that the ability of some works to make such a powerful assault on what we regard as precious or sacred (an ability not shared by feeble drawings on lavatory walls) may indeed reside in their creativity, even if used in a demonic way. This seems to be the case with the macabre paintings of Hieronymous Bosch, for instance, or some of the work of Salvador Dali. These examples create problems, but they do not completely overturn my thesis about the relation between morality and art. For even if we are forced to acknowledge the artistic brilliance of some works which contain a vision that is repulsive and disgusting, the moral grounds for our disgust and repulsion can still at the same time be seen as grounds for faulting the work at the artistic level. We do not regard the repulsiveness of the vision as something to shrug off as being irrelevant to the work's worth or its nature (as we may shrug off the fact that typewriters may be used for good as for evil): it remains an intrinsic defect in the work. What we are left with in such cases therefore is something like a sense of regret. This

---

[45] *The Test of Time*, 265.   [46] Ibid.

paradox, if paradox it be, is no more and no less puzzling than our inclination in certain cases to admire the apparently virtuous qualities in an otherwise evil person (a phenomenon Shakespeare was able to depict with some profundity).

In summary, what I hope has emerged from this chapter is that it is possible to say that a moral failing in a work of literature counts against it as an artistic creation. This does not commit us to the view that art has a moral or social purpose, but serves rather to remind us of the relation between the author and his creation. Although there are a number of ways in which an author stands in a moral relation to his art and the human context in which it flourishes there is also a more immediate relation which must be invoked in order to deal with our present question—and one that is not to be narrowly construed as an author's 'duty to society', or other similar notions which effectively reduce the status of art to that of a tool, but is instead to be understood in terms of his attitude to human life implicit in his representation of the characters and their circumstances. This attitude to life is not one that could be discovered by additional biographical detail about the author, but is to be found in the work itself—or in juxtaposing and considering a number of works by the same author: with Shakespeare for instance we can enrich our understanding of one play by comparing it with his other plays. Once the importance or 'relevance' of the author is admitted then our responses to the work will not only permit moral considerations, it will demand them—but in a way that is not neatly separable from our aesthetic judgements on the work. That we may disagree with the moral perspective of a particular work does not in all cases mean that we shall judge the work to lack artistic merit, but this is to be explained in terms of an acceptance which is distinguishable from belief. A work in which it appears that the author expresses an attitude to life that is so objectionable that we cannot even 'accept' it, is one we are likely to condemn as an artistic failing. This argument raises further questions about the relation between ethics and aesthetics that must be taken up in the next, and final, chapter which deals with the question of what we learn from literature.

8
Learning from Literature

And how? How? How shall we even begin to educate ourselves in the feelings?

Not by laying down laws or commandments, or axioms and postulates. Not even by making assertions that such and such is blessed. Not by words at all.

If we can't hear the cries far down in our own forests of dark veins, we can look in the real novels, and there listen-in. Not listen to the didactic statements of the author, but to the low, calling cries of the characters, as they wander in the dark woods of their destiny. (D. H. Lawrence, 'The Novel and the Feelings'[1])

THE PROBLEM

The most direct answer to the question 'what do we learn from literature?' is 'many things, depending upon what is read, by whom, and in what spirit'. However, my question is narrower. First, I shall be concerned with what literature can contribute to our education. The point of this distinction, as R. S. Peters has repeatedly affirmed,[2] is that not all cases of learning are cases of education. Fagin's boys learned how to pick pockets: they were not thereby being educated. I shall take it as axiomatic that education is concerned with what is good (Peters's celebrated use of the term 'worthwhile' seems to me to be too weak). Second, I shall be concerned in particular with what literature contributes to our moral education (though for reasons I shall not elaborate on here, I think that all education has a moral dimension). In exploring this question, I shall be forced to examine what is meant by moral understanding and elucidate its non-propositional features. I shall first reject one formulation of the 'cognitivist' account of literature and try to show how it is possible to learn from literature without

---

[1] D. H. Lawrence, *A Selection from Phoenix*, ed. A. A. H. Inglis (Harmondsworth, 1971), 465.
[2] e.g. in *Ethics and Education* (London, 1966).

accepting propositions about human life 'implied' by literary works.

We are confronted right at the outset with a dilemma about the nature of literature *qua* art. It is a deeply held piety (though not for those who would axe literature from the curricula of schools and colleges) that literature can and does contribute to our education such that we would be intellectually, perhaps even morally, the poorer without it. However, is there a risk of conflating two different things: the importance or value of literature and its educative power? That is to say, do we value literature *because* it contributes to our education, or does it do so because of some value or importance it has independently of its educative function? (The alternative possibility, that we do not learn from literature, in so far as it depends upon views such as those expressed by Oscar Wilde, falls with my earlier rejection of 'aestheticism'.)

This is no easy matter. It seems there must be some relation between the value or importance of literature and its educative power, the question is what kind of relation? If we try to specify what kinds of things we learn from literature in terms which are, so to speak, 'extra-literary', the immediate objection is that we are regarding art merely as a means to other things which might therefore, at least in principle, be obtained in some other way. Suppose that we say a serious engagement with literature (and regarding it purely as a means would not count as 'serious') can provide moral insight, deepen our understanding of human conduct, show us things about the nature of evil, help us to see beneath appearances and thus distinguish the genuine from the phoney— all fairly common claims—then it cannot be that it is the 'purpose' of literature to inform our understanding in this way. If our interest in art is not to be merely instrumental, literature must therefore be distinguished from propaganda, politics, or preaching. This in turn will affect our conception of what is represented in a literary fiction. The 'message-seeker' or 'ideology-hunter' will not see fictional characters as individuals, but as embodiments of this or that idea, this or that principle, this or that political innuendo— and the work will be judged or evaluated according to such criteria. Advocates of the 'autonomy' of art, on the other hand, may be unacceptably vague, perhaps even to the extent of claiming that art is one thing and life another. To such an advocate there is a firm separation between morality and art. What we look for in literature, he will say, is its artistry, not its comment on life. Thus if we do learn about life from literature this is purely a contingent matter, not part of its essence or value.

Clearly those two positions are equally extreme, and perhaps equally misguided. Certainly literature *qua* art cannot simply be a device for moral instruction, fuel for 'the cause', or a tool for Marxist revolution. Yet, as the previous chapter argued, what substance is there to the 'artistry' valued by the autonomist if literature is to be divorced from life? Mere 'style'? (As Collingwood put it: 'Subject without style is barbarism; style without subject is dilettantism.'[3]) When Leavis said that there are no such things as purely 'literary values', this much must be conceded to him: that the relation between literature and life is presupposed in our critical vocabulary. Works can be criticized for their sentimentality, shallowness, and their falsity, just as they can be praised for their depth, wisdom, and truth. Nor, despite Walter Pater, is music totally unrelated to life. Consider for instance Wittgenstein's remark that Mendelssohn's music lacks courage.[4]

But where does all this get us? We can argue against the 'message-seekers', 'ideology-hunters', or the utilitarians that art is not to be valued for anything so vulgar as a 'message'. And in steering a reasonable course between them and the autonomists[5] we can insist that literature in some sense confronts the world, and that it can be criticized on the basis of its quality of thought. But that does not explain what we learn from it. Given that novels and plays depict events, circumstances, and persons which do not exist, and given that we are not required to believe that they exist, how can literature give us knowledge of the actual world? And if it is not knowledge we gain from literature, what else do we gain that can be called 'learning'?

THE COGNITIVIST THEORY

First a note of caution about my use of the expression '*the cognitivist theory*'. The question of the relation between literature

---

[3] R. G. Collingwood, *The Principles of Art* (Oxford, 1958), 299.

[4] 'What did Mendelssohn's music lack? A "courageous" melody?' Wittgenstein, *Culture and Value*, ed. G. H. von Wright and H. Nyman, trans. P. Winch (Oxford, 1980), 35e.

[5] I use this term in a rough-and-ready sense, and am aware it hides a number of distinct positions.

and knowledge is most often interpreted as a question about the relation between literature and propositional knowledge. I shall first address myself to cognitivism in that sense. But, as will emerge later, 'cognitivism' is a much wider concept, and includes other kinds of knowledge which I shall discuss. On the cognitivist/ propositionalist theory we learn from literature by being led to accept propositions about life as implied in, or by, the work. There are a number of telling, if not fatal, objections to this view, but it is first necessary to examine how it is even possible for a literary work to imply propositions.

Stepping back still further, we may consider why any philosopher should find that position attractive. The temptation, it seems to me, is generated from the correct observation that we cannot, without obscurity or absurdity, relegate the use of language in literary works to the status of something 'non-cognitive' or 'emotive'. Neither can statements within fiction be regarded as 'pseudo-statements'.[6] In the first chapter I agreed that there are indeed conventions governing our use of statements about fictions, but I was also at pains to show that the 'internal convention' can never be entirely separate from, or impervious to, the rules and conventions of 'ordinary' discourse. Since we must reject the idea that literature employs some different or 'special' use of language, the way seems clear for the propositionalist to maintain that statements found in a literary work can be true and can therefore give us knowledge about the actual world. Thus for instance when Priestley's Arthur Birling states the weight of the *Titanic* to be 'forty-six thousand eight hundred tons', if his statement is true we thereby learn something we might not have known before: the weight of the *Titanic*. The objection that we could not learn this since Birling (trapped within his 'world') cannot be referring to the actual *Titanic* is demonstrably false. Indeed Birling's insistence upon the *Titanic* being 'unsinkable, absolutely unsinkable' would fail to gain its necessary irony were we not to make use of our knowledge that, since the actual *Titanic* did sink, Birling is not only wrong, but will be proved to be wrong by the subsequent events the play will not depict.

So far then it seems that we ought to concede to the proposition-

---

[6] For the 'emotive meaning' view of literary utterance see C. K. Ogden and I. A. Richards, *The Meaning of Meaning* (London, 1985).

alist not only that literature may provide us with true statements about the world, but also that our knowledge of the actual world must be utilized in understanding the fictional world. However, this thesis would be too weak. If all we learned from literature consisted of a few factual snippets here and there the learning would seem trivial indeed (and strangely roundabout: far better for us to be given history books, maps, and encyclopaedias). The propositionalist must show not just how literary works contain propositions (some of which may be true of the actual world), he must also show how the work as a whole, or substantial parts of it, 'contain' or 'express' propositions about life—e.g. 'man is a fragile, gullible creature' or 'indecision is the mother of catastrophe'. And—the argument runs—even though such propositions are nowhere explicitly stated in the work, they are implied.

But what sort of implication is this? According to John Hospers, we are not concerned here with the 'logic book' sense of 'implication' (as in 'Jones is a father' implies 'Jones is male'). We are concerned, he argues, with 'implies' in the sense of 'suggests'.[7] Hospers elucidates this by considering the everyday sense of the word in which a speaker's intention (to be sarcastic, say) is discovered by seeing beneath the apparent assertion made. Thus the teacher who says to a pupil after the examination 'some people don't do their own work' may be said to imply, in the sense of 'suggest', that the pupil has been cheating. There are two major difficulties Hospers has to deal with in order to apply this sense of 'implication' to what is 'suggested' by literary works. Whether or not the work suggests proposition P cannot depend simply upon either (1) the author's intention or (2) the perspicacity of the 'audience'. If (1) is made the criterion then we are saddled with the (legitimate) difficulties raised in the 'Intentional Fallacy', and no author can be the ultimate authority on what his work means. But since no reader can be the ultimate authority either, it makes perfect sense to say that P is implied even though no reader has yet grasped the fact. To make the 'meaning' of the work entirely dependent upon what the reader takes it to be results in a rather wishy-washy subjectivism that effectively denies the possibility of being right or wrong. (While it may be true that rival interpreta-

---

[7] 'Implied Truths in Literature', *Journal of Aesthetics and Art Criticism*, 29/1 (Autumn 1960), 37–46.

tions of a literary work do not invalidate one another, it doesn't follow that no interpretation can ever be wrong.) The need to avoid the second 'criterion' then is at one with the need to distinguish meaning and association.[8]

So far, then, I am in agreement with Hospers's argument that if a literary work can be said to suggest *P*, it is the *work* that suggests *P* whether or not this is in accordance with the author's explicit or unconscious intention and whether or not the reader/hearer happens to have grasped *P*. But the real issue is what one is to make of this in the light of the general problem I have outlined. Here, Hospers is not particularly helpful. He sets himself the task of explaining how truths can be implied in literature and comes up with the answer that a work may imply propositions about life which 'may be true' (and, presumably, may be false). But one wants to know what these 'implied truths' have to do with the essence of literature and therefore what they have to do with the question of what we learn from literature *qua* art. Hospers does not enlighten us. In fact his finding is rather negative since he explicitly denies that such 'implied truths' need have any 'aesthetic significance'—though he adds that with some works the 'implied propositions' may be 'the most important single feature' (meaning what for their status as artistic creations?).

It seems to me that to ask questions about what we learn from literature is really to ask about the 'essence' of literature. What propositions about life are implied in *King Lear* or *Macbeth*? Are we to understand that what we learn from *King Lear* is that it is foolish to renounce all that sustains a position of authority and yet still expect to be obeyed?—or perhaps that human kind is capable of monstrous cruelty and treachery? Well, there would be no prizes for learning that. Most of us know that already, and indeed we need to know it before we can even begin to make sense of the play. Similarly with *Macbeth*, do we learn that murder is a terrible thing, or that the life that commits itself to an evil course of action sets itself upon the slippery slope? Again, we already need to know such things as a prerequisite for understanding Shakespeare's tragedy.

I believe that to be one of the most telling indictments against

---

[8] Otherwise a text is reduced to the status of what Peter Jones aptly calls 'a Rorschach test' (*Philosophy and the Novel* (Oxford, 1975), 90).

the propositionalist theory, though to rest one's case there would leave one open to the objection, 'but what of works which do imply things we didn't already know, and didn't need to know before studying the work?' I shall not answer that question since the whole approach seems to be fundamentally mistaken. If this were all that learning from literature amounted to then one could ask (1) why any particular author or any particular work should be thought to have sufficient authority to furnish us with truths about human existence, and (2) how we can learn anything coherent from a wide experience of reading, given that in some cases different literary works imply contrary propositions. (1) encapsulates different questions: (*a*) why should we trust the word of writers (what gives them special pre-eminence such that they can pronounce on human affairs and expect us to take them seriously)? (*b*) Why should writer *A* carry more authority than writer *B*, given that they are both telling us something different? Any attempt to answer either question would then have to appeal to a notion of 'authority' which undermines the propositionalist thesis: what distinguishes some writers from others is an artistic merit that is not defined in terms of the propositional content of the work. This objection spills over to (2). If the propositionalist thesis were correct then some literary works would be contradicting each other. Yet that is not how we experience them. If *Hamlet* appears to criticize thought without action and *Othello* criticizes action without thought, we still do not see these plays as in any way opposed. They no more oppose one another than the Brahms Clarinet Quintet with its autumnal sadness opposes the 'Dance of the Sugar-Plum Fairy'. It therefore does not seem appropriate to say, as Hospers does, that literature presents us with hypotheses about life.

In view of those considerations I do not see much prospect for the cognitivist/propositionalist theory. The trouble is that the anti-cognitivist theory offers no great sustenance either. For either we are asked to accept, as I. A. Richards argued, that it is an illusion that we learn from literature (an illusion born of the fact that literature makes such an impact upon us), or that, as for instance Rush Rhees claims, we do learn but cannot say what we learn. In reading *King Lear*, he says, 'It does not show me how I might see any *other* events, the lives of other characters. And that would not be relevant. The drama shows me the sense of these developments here. This is what I want to see again or listen to.'[9]

Unsatisfying though this would undoubtedly sound to the ears of many contemporary educationists, it is difficult to dismiss Rhees's observation. If the propositionalist theory were correct then it would be impossible to give an adequate or plausible explanation of why we return to the same works time and time again. Certainly we might return to a work hoping or expecting to find things in it that we hadn't seen before, but this is not a search for 'implied truths' about life: for then the novel or play would not be a source of ideas but, as Rhees says, something merely used to illustrate them. I think he is quite right about that. For, whatever else it might be, *Macbeth* is not an illustration of a moral idea or set of ideas. Consider the proposition, 'the life of the evil man is empty and meaningless'. To begin with, it is little more than presumption to suppose that the character Macbeth in some way represents evil men in general. Even if we take it that the play shows us the shape and quality of a particular man's life being fashioned out of his own evil decisions, it does not illustrate that idea—as though what we are shown would remain the same if 'illustrated' in some other way. To think of a literary work in those terms would be to suppose that two different plays or two different novels, providing they 'illustrate' similar ideas, are effectively saying the same things. But literary works do not 'say' things or 'tell' us things in that way. A literary work (if it is any good) is not a series of edifying propositions dressed up in artistic clothes which may be stripteased away as the content reveals itself.

TELLING AND SHOWING

Leaving aside for the time being the 'instrumentalist' problem, it is worth investigating whether we can provide an answer to any of the above difficulties via a distinction between telling and showing. This distinction was made famous by Wayne C. Booth in *The Rhetoric of Fiction*, but I shall have little or nothing to say about his treatment, since it seems to me that he is chiefly concerned with different styles of narration. Indeed in what follows I think it will

---

[9] *Without Answers*, ed. D. Z. Phillips (London, 1949), 145.

emerge that I am concerned with a different kind of distinction from Booth's.

To say that literary works show us something about life would not be the same as saying that they tell us about life. Hospers is at pains to acknowledge that his 'implied truths' are neither simply 'deduced' from the text, nor wholly separable from plot, characterization, and so on. But his whole treatment appears to ride on the back of the assumption that for literature to give us 'truths' about the world it must cross a kind of boundary between art and life. In this respect, both the cognitivist and the anti-cognitivist position seem to speak of life as being 'beyond' the text. As far as the matter of learning is concerned, the cognitivist/propositionalist insists that literature tells us things about the world beyond the text, while the anti-cognitivist insists that what the work shows us is only itself— not 'life' or 'the world'. The latter need not deny that our experience of literature may in some sense rub off on us so that we face some situations differently because of it. But he will deny that it gives us knowledge of the world, and by 'knowledge' he will mean propositional knowledge in the sense of 'knowing that'— though he may also deny that it gives us knowledge in the sense of 'skill' ('knowing how'). I shall come back to those epistemological matters later, but, having observed the assumption these opposed positions appear to share, it is necessary to consider whether it throws any light on the problem if we say that literature has something to show us *of*, rather than merely telling us *about* life. And one thing which will be of interest here is whether the concept of 'showing' removes the difficulty of speaking in a way which first posits a 'gap' between art and life, and then either contends that the gap can be bridged or that it cannot (and if it cannot, then art is relegated to the status of a self-contained game).

Taken in one way, the distinction between telling and showing would not get rid of the problem. If 'showing' were simply another way of 'telling about', then all the original difficulties remain. Clearly, in common parlance the idea of showing as opposed to telling can have such force. I might tell a pupil how to construct an equilateral triangle by giving him instructions, or I might show him by demonstrating or by constructing one with him. In telling, both the instructions and those being instructed remain at a stage of remove from the actual operation to be performed. In showing, something is revealed, displayed, that is closer to the present understanding and experience of the pupil—though only as a means to something which in principle might be attained in some other way.

Beyond that, it would be foolish to generalize. No doubt different examples of 'showing' would bring out different aspects of the concept. With literary art, the point of using the distinction between telling and showing seems to be that the writer who merely tells us things is deficient in creative power.[10] Our complaint is not that such a writer is failing to explain himself, since explanation is not his primary purpose. And in any case we may be dissatisfied with a piece of writing that merely tells, even though it does not provoke the need for further explanation or further detail (indeed it seems likely that we are only provoked to ask further questions by works which are already vividly realized and have thus whetted our appetites). If someone calling himself a poet were to write (without ironic intent),

> I am very unhappy
> I got in debt through gambling
> Then they took my house away
> My wife deserted me
> And took the children with her

then it would seem legitimate to object that the 'poem' lacks artistic merit because it speaks by 'telling' and consequently says nothing. Why it 'says' nothing requires further explanation.

In *Zettel* (155) Wittgenstein remarks, 'A poet's words can pierce us. And that is of course *causally* connected with the use they have in our life.' Poetry does not depend for its impact upon something we could classify as poetic language. The difference between poetry and other discourse lies not in a special 'poetic' language but in the way the genuine poem 'speaks'. Sometimes the way that a poem speaks to us may be through an image or a metaphor, which is not a mere 'illustration' or a pictorial 'explanation' of something we might equally grasp in some other 'literal' or 'direct' way. The successful image or metaphor (which need not be pictorial) already speaks to us 'direct'; it is not a decoration but rather the substance of the idea, such that what is communicated is not just a thought

[10] Unless the telling is good enough to be a way of showing, as Wayne Booth points out in his discussion of Boccaccio: *The Rhetoric of Fiction* (Harmondsworth, 1987).

'about' something. It does not tell us what to feel: it is apprehended through feeling, in the sense that it provides an experience. But a poem can provide an experience other than through the illumination of image or metaphor, which is why some are driven to describe poetry as 'memorable speech'. John Clare's 'I am: yet what I am none cares or knows' has a memorable and haunting quality even though it has the surface appearance of merely stating something. It speaks almost as music 'speaks'. ('Do not forget that a poem, even though it is composed in the language of information is not used in the language-game of giving information.')[11]

On the 'make-believe' view I criticized in Chapter 2, we would 'pretend to believe' what the fictional speaker says and have make-believe feelings on the basis of what we make-believe to be true. One of my many objections to that view was that it has little to do with our experience of art. I spoke in that chapter of genuine art compelling a kind of assent, not to the 'truth' of a 'fictional proposition' but to the thoughts and feelings embedded in the artist's representation of an object or situation. With my bogus poem (above) all we seem to be given is a bare instruction to feel something, but it lacks the power to make us feel.

If those lines were spoken in a play, or by an actual person communicating his distress, our reaction might well be different. But the surrounding context would then make all the difference. We would not be responding merely to 'information' but to a concrete human situation, real or imagined, which the information confirms, changes, or illuminates. A poem, however, must provide its own illumination, and speak to us through the medium, not merely through the form, of poetry. If there were nothing more to a poem than a series of statements to be 'make-believed', in this case we would not be told nearly enough. In the absence of further 'information' our response is as yet 'so what?' or 'tough luck'. Yet further detail or explanation would not necessarily make it any better. Indeed as a poem, it already 'tells' us too much. To be told the exact amount of the debt, the method of gambling (whether horses or cards), the postal address of the house, and the number of children, would even make matters worse.

In *Culture and Value* (54e) Wittgenstein's rather cryptic remark,

---

[11] Wittgenstein, *Zettel*, ed. G. E. M. Anscombe and G. H. von Wright, trans. G. E. M. Anscombe (Oxford, 1981), 160, p. 27.

'An observation in a poem is overstated if the intellectual points are nakedly exposed, not clothed from the heart,' needs careful interpretation. Read unsympathetically, it would seem sentimental, or just plain wrong—as though the suggestion is that the poet must disguise or adorn the naked essence of what he would be saying if he just got on and jolly well said it. The fallacy there would be that the expression is something apart from what is being expressed, such that we could speak of the way that the poet 'puts it across' as though the 'it' remains the same if 'put across' in some other way, say by an editorial in the *Daily Telegraph*.

The key to Wittgenstein's remark lies in the word 'overstated'. Our interest in and response to a poem is not an interest in and response to 'information'. Where we do get the impression that we are merely being given information there is a breakdown in communication, either because the art is unsuccessful, or because of some incapacity or deficiency on our part. In the case of a painting our interest and understanding consists in seeing and experiencing what is represented, rather than merely knowing what the artist meant. If I may for a moment borrow one or two examples from Wittgenstein's *Philosophical Investigations*, even though my use of them may be tangential to the range of problems Wittgenstein was exploring: 'When I see the picture of a galloping horse—do I merely *know* that this is the kind of movement meant? Is it superstition to think that I *see* the horse galloping in the picture?—And does my visual impression gallop too?' (II. iv. 202e) Wittgenstein asks of this, and similar examples, when one should call one's experience a 'mere case of knowing, not seeing'. And, unless I have misunderstood the discussion, the answer is not so much to be found by analysing some inner experience or sensation, as by considering our attitude to the picture. 'For when should I call it a mere case of knowing, not seeing?—Perhaps when someone treats the picture as a working drawing, *reads* it like a blueprint.'

It is important that we do not have the same attitude to a painting or a drawing as to, say, a 'working drawing'. In a blueprint, a diagram, or a plan, we may know what is represented but we do not, as with a painting, *see* the object depicted.

'To me it is an animal pierced by an arrow.' That is what I treat it as; this is my *attitude* to the figure. This is one meaning in calling it a case of 'seeing'.

But can I say in the same sense: 'To me these are two hexagons?' Not in the same sense, but in a similar one. (II. xi. 205e)

What I am suggesting, though not necessarily as an interpretation of Wittgenstein, is that while a painting must aim at getting us to see something and not merely to know what is supposed to be represented, something analogous can be said about poetry and other literary art, such that what we receive from it is capable of 'living' in the imagination (even though it might not 'live' with the same intensity on each and every occasion of our acquaintance with it)[12].

Contrast my 'Thribb-style' poem with Pope's portrait of Lord Hervey in his 'Epistle to Dr Arbuthnot'. As G. K. Chesterton points out: 'a man writing prose in a passion of righteous indignation might perhaps say, "one can at least get rid of such a human insect, a creature who is malodorous and poisonous at once." But it would not have the special sort of ringing energy of a couplet to the same effect: "Yet let me flap this bug with gilded wings, | This painted child of dirt that stinks and stings." '[13]

It is an unfortunate choice of words on Chesterton's part to say 'to the same *effect*', but the point remains that Pope's portrait of Lord Hervey (Sporus) says something that could not be said simply by being stated. Contemporaries of Pope were not necessarily given any information about Lord Hervey they did not previously possess (or if they were, that would not make it better poetry), yet they were shown something about him (brought to experience his nauseating qualities), partly in the way that a caricature can illuminate our perception of a well-known face. I say 'partly', because a verbal portrait has ways of communicating that are not available through pictorial depiction—one of the many reasons that books cannot be adequately filmed. ('Jonathan Miller remarks that no film-maker can provide a visual equivalent for Dickens's verbal visualization of John Wemmick Junior in *Great Expectations*: "a dry man, rather short in stature . . . his mouth was such a post office of a mouth that he had a mechanical appearance of

---

[12] 'I might say: a picture does not always *live* for me while I am seeing it.' (*Philosophical Investigations*, trans. G. E. M. Anscombe (Oxford, 1967), II. xi. 205e.)

[13] G. K. Chesterton, *Lunacy and Letters* (London, 1958), 169.

smiling." Any attempt to reproduce that mouth would be a ludicrous disaster.'[14])

A pictorial caricature cannot speak in rhyme, nor use assonance and onomatopoeia and other figures of speech that make language the peculiarly rich medium it is for focusing our attention on an object in a number of different ways, aurally as well as visually. Consider how Pope's portrait of Hervey at the ear of Queen Caroline recalls Milton's Satan of *Paradise Lost* book 4; even the style of Milton's lines is echoed:

> Or at the ear of Eve, familiar Toad,
> Half froth, half venom, spits himself abroad,
> In puns, or politics, or tales or lies,
> In spite, or smut, or rhymes or blasphemies.

Pope's portrait exploits the inexhaustible fund of associations and resonances of speech that is denied to the visual medium. A visual caricature would have to content itself with one point of comparison, yet Pope is able to associate Sporus with a number of different images: a 'mere white curd of ass's milk', an insect, a reptile, and so on—and in ways which go beyond the merely visual. For the nauseating qualities of Sporus are also enacted in sound: not only in assonance, alliteration, and onomatopoeia, but in the rhythm (note how the last couplet appears to travel in little jumps, like a toad), in the cadences which 'clinch' the thought, and the caesura in 'Now trips a lady, and now struts a Lord.' The sound does not merely echo the sense; it is part of the meaning which is created.

Outside the context of art, the contrast between telling and showing may simply mark a difference in approach to the same thing, knowledge being the end and showing and telling being two different means towards it. However, the 'showing' appropriate to art is itself an end and not merely a means. Certainly we can speak as though the techniques through which Pope achieves his effects are in a sense a means towards communicating something, but our interest in this portrait and what we value in it are inextricably bound up with the craft that has made it what it is.

This does not mean that we search beneath the portrait for the underlying techniques that have composed it, as we might examine a table for its method of construction: for the poetry is not 'made'

[14] D. J. Enright, *Fields of Vision: Essays on Literature, Language and Television* (Oxford, 1988), 8.

of these in the way that Hungerford bridge is made of girders. And that is why a discussion of 'techniques' in artistic creation cannot proceed as though we were talking about methods of manufacture. No artist can have a method in this sense. There is no formula or recipe to be followed either for the creation of an aesthetic object or for the appreciation of it.

Not only may a writer not be fully conscious of how he achieves what he achieves, but in responding to the aesthetic object he has created we may not be conscious of how the sophisticated elements of its composition have worked upon us to elicit the response they do. In this limited sense there is an element of mystery both in the process of artistic creation and in our response to works of art. But this does not mean that the concept of mystery can be invoked, as it so often is, to say that 'anything goes' in artistic endeavour or in our response to the finished product. While there may be an element of luck, intuition, or inspiration in the process of creation, it cannot be pure chance: it must be the kind of luck that attends *mastery* in the disciplines appropriate to whatever art form is in question. Similarly, while we may not be conscious of all the elements that have worked upon us so that we respond in the way we do, the work could not speak to us in the way it does unless we in turn have the sensibility to be affected by these elements—a sensibility which can be educated, such that we can point to and discuss some of these features and learn to articulate them in the business of criticism and appreciation.

We have noted the inadequacy of supposing that art supplies us with abstract generalizations about life. Could one say, then, that the difference between telling and showing is that the latter presents us with something more concrete? This, unless I have misunderstood them, seems to be the way that philosophers such as D. Z. Phillips and Peter Winch would attempt to justify their use of fictional examples in moral philosophy: their argument being that an exclusively abstract approach to ethics not only encourages philosophical prejudice to ossify into dogma, but blinds us to the heterogeneity of moral phenomena. I cannot enter here into the dispute about the nature of moral philosophy (though what I have to say later may have some bearing on it, given that I shall deny, *pace* modern educators, that moral understanding is abstract and propositional). I refer to this matter only to focus upon the illuminating quality that literary examples are thought to have.

Winch in particular has self-consciously employed fictional
examples in preference to the 'trivial' or schematic examples
frequently used in 'recent Anglo Saxon moral philosophy',[15] while
others, such as R. M. Hare, have remained rather sceptical about
the use of fiction in this respect. Indeed, Hare refers to 'situations
described in literature' as only an 'adjunct to moral thought'; and
his point seems to be that examples drawn from literature have
limited value because literature could never be a substitute for
'some experience of actual moral perplexities, and of the actual
consequences of moral choices' and because such examples are
only as good as their resemblance to actual life.[16]

Hare's first reason seems redundant since no one with any sense
would argue that experience of literature can replace first-hand
experience. And in any case, someone who '[took] all the examples
in [his] moral thinking out of fiction, as the young and those who
have led sheltered lives are apt to do' (ibid.) would for that reason
not be in a position to understand novels and plays. Hare's second
reason is not entirely clear. Of 'situations' in fiction, he remarks
'these situations are not reported as actually occurring; but they
are claimed to be like situations which do occur—otherwise their
relevance to moral thought would be small.' I find all this rather
opaque. ('Claimed' by whom?) 'These situations are not reported
as actually occurring' is ambiguous, and on one interpretation
false.[17] Within the 'internal convention', fictional objects are presented as being actual. The question is whether or not the representation succeeds. And the criterion for success or failure cannot
simply be a matter of correspondence with what is actual (for
reasons I have already given). But neither can it be a matter of
probabilities (concerned with 'what is likely to happen'.) No one
believes that people have beaks or that animals double-cross one
another, yet the characters in *Volpone* are not implausible creations. Janáček's opera, *The Makropulos Case* does not present us
with something which is 'likely to happen', nor—in the sense that
Hare seems to intend by his words—does it present us with a
'situation' which is 'like situations which do occur'. In cases of this
kind we are prepared to discount the superficial lack of resemblance

[15] Peter Winch, *Ethics and Action* (London, 1972), 154–5.

[16] R. M. Hare, *Freedom and Reason* (Oxford, 1963), 83.

[17] Depending on how one construes 'reported'. The narrator may *appear* to be
reporting, but that does not turn fiction into the language-game of reportage.

to 'situations which do occur' and see the common elements of our experience portrayed beneath the empirical 'events' of the story.

The telling/showing distinction becomes crucial here. Hare's estimate of the educative value of fiction seems confined to the rather superficial level at which novels are merely stories: his use of the expression 'story-books' confirms this. Thus when he begins his argument by referring to 'situations *described* in imaginative literature' (my emphasis) he is reducing fictional portrayal to 'telling'. To think of literature as merely presenting us with 'descriptions' of situations would be to ignore the complexity of the author's achievement. For once I find myself in agreement with the lover of outlandish aphorisms, William Gass, when he says that the artist 'must show or exhibit his world, and to do this he must actually make something, not merely describe something that might be made'.[18] The contrast here approximates perhaps to Leavis's distinction between 'analogical enacting' and 'mere saying'.[19] Against mere 'telling' or 'saying' we must, it seems, posit some such idea as 'making' or 'enacting', or perhaps simply 'creating'. The latter is borne out in the following example from Harley Granville-Barker. In discussing Lear's 'storm speech' ('Blow winds . . .'), he remarks that 'this is no mere description of a storm, but in music and imagination suggests a dramatic creating of the storm itself; and there is Lear—and here are we, if we yield ourselves— in the midst of it, almost a part of it.'[20]

One more example. Commenting on the inanity of 'pop poetry', Ian Robinson quotes a typical specimen from a sickly anthology called *Love, Love, Love* which runs as follows:

> I will bring you flowers
> every morning for your breakfast
> and you will kiss me
> with flowers in your mouth
> and you will bring me flowers
> every morning when you wake
> and look at me with flowers in your eyes

---

[18] *Fiction and the Figures of Life* (New York, 1972), 83.
[19] 'Reading out Poetry', in F. R. Leavis, *Valuation in Criticism: And Other Essays*, ed. G. Singh (Cambridge, 1986), 267.
[20] *Prefaces to Shakespeare*, ii: *King Lear, Cymbeline, Julius Caesar* (London, 1963), 7.

Robinson rightly objects to this crass sentimentality that what the writer does not do is *create* his love there on the page (as Shakespeare does for instance in his sonnets).[21] I am not suggesting, by the way, that what is 'created' in this sense has an existence of its own divorced from the experience of the discerning reader, any more than I am saying that it will 'live' for each and every reader. In speaking of the quality of Shakespeare's poetry I am referring, here and later, to what Shakespeare *offers* to the attentive reader.

I think I prefer to explicate the concept of 'showing' through the idea of creating, rather than through the idea of 'making', 'doing', or 'enacting', since the latter seem rather neutral, given my attempt in the previous chapter to point to a connection between love and the creative act. If this distinction between describing and creating is to prove useful, however, it cannot be that the advantage of using literary examples in moral philosophy (if it is an advantage) is that they are more concrete *in the sense of being more detailed or more fully described*. If detail were all, there would be little to distinguish literary depiction from what we can find in an actual case-study. In fact a case-study might be more useful as an example (or counter-example) to a philosophical argument if the former were written in a concise enough way.

I do not wish to argue that it is improper to use fictional examples in moral philosophy. My point is simply that such a practice cannot be justified in the above terms without overlooking, or even distorting, the way that literature speaks to us and the kind of importance it has. Literature does not speak to us by providing 'descriptions' of the human condition, and it has an importance far more subtle and complex than would be suggested by regarding it as a repository of moral insights or as a well-stocked fund of case-studies.[22] I can think of no better way of expressing this than by referring to Granville-Barker's commentary on *King Lear*. In discussing the development in Lear's character (as Lear passes from 'personal grievance' to the 'taking upon him . . . the imagined burden of the whole world's sorrow') Granville-Barker comments on Shakespeare's artistry as follows, 'Shakespeare brings about this transition from malediction to martyrdom with great art, by contrivance direct and indirect, by

---

[21] 'Paper Tygers or, the Circus Animals' Desertion in the New Pop Poetry', in P. Abbs (ed.), *The Black Rainbow: Essays on the Present Breakdown of Culture* (London, 1975).

[22] I do not of course attribute this view to Peter Winch.

strokes broad and subtle; nor ever—his art in this at its greatest—does he turn his Lear from a man into an ethical proposition.'[23] Our interest in the character of Lear and in the play as a whole must be, in part, a moral interest. But Shakespeare would not sustain this moral interest were it not for the way the play works as a play. As Granville-Barker adds to his previous comment, 'The thing is achieved—as the whole play is achieved—in terms of humanity, and according to the rubric of drama.'

For an explanation of the telling/showing distinction in terms of 'concreteness' of presentation, then, it is necessary to seek an alternative way of construing the term 'concrete' so that it does not simply mean 'more detailed' or 'more fully described'. Here I think it is necessary to insist—not by a priori fiat, but by remaining true to our experience of works of art—that the qualities necessary for 'showing' are ones which, in the totality of their execution, 'draw us into' the poem, the novel, the drama, such that—in Granville-Barker's phrase—we are invited to 'yield ourselves'. Thus if we respond to what we are shown we are in some sense 'acquainted' with the imagined objects of attention. In reading an actual case-study we may of course be much affected by the details and, as a result, come to feel that we know a great deal about the person in question. But as David Hamlyn[24] and Ilham Dilman have, in their different ways, pointed out, there is a difference between knowing a person and merely knowing about him. To know *him* requires acquaintance (though whether this acquaintance need always take the form of a reciprocal relationship, as Dilman insists, is another matter).

Dilman has commented that it is an 'illusion' that we know characters in fiction. The reason one might expect to be given for such a claim is that fictional characters do not exist (though I do not see why that would make our commerce with fiction illusory: it is after all not an 'illusion' that we see a face in a portrait)[25]. That, however, is not the reason Dilman gives. His argument is that we cannot know a fictional character for the same reason that we cannot know a person simply by reading a biography: 'for what one imagines entering into is scripted and what one brings to it makes no difference to the scenario'.[26] (An almost identical sen-

[23] *Prefaces*, 32.
[24] David Hamlyn (see above, Ch. 4, n 15).
[25] See Richard Wollheim, *Painting as an Art* (London, 1980), 76–7, 185.
[26] *Love and Human Separateness* (Oxford, 1987), 123.

tence appears in one of Dilman's previous pieces, this time referring
not to biography but to fictional portrayal.)[27] It is a confusion,
however, to run these two cases together. If we have not actually
met, or been acquainted with, the person on whom the biography
is based that is a contigent matter, but it is a necessary truth that
we could not meet a fictional character. That, incidentally, does
not prevent me from 'knowing about' the character: I *know* that
Hamlet is the son of Gertrude, even though I do not believe that
Hamlet exists. Nevertheless even though I cannot know a character
in the way that I can know my next-door neighbour, I can have an
understanding of that character that is more deeply personal than
merely 'knowing about'—and one that derives from an imagined
acquaintance, rather than a reciprocal relationship. To say that
'what one enters into is scripted' is misleading in this sense: that,
within the terms of my 'internal convention', Hamlet's life is no
more scripted than yours or mine. Furthermore, that I have no
access to Hamlet other than through the play is not a restriction
upon my capacity to understand him, any more than not being
able to see the reverse side of an object in a painting is a restriction
upon my capacity to perceive that object; whereas having no access
to X except through a biography of X is certainly a restriction.

In art, we have to work upon what we are given, and 'the given'
here is a limit, not a restriction. The limit provides a frame of
reference within which our attention to an object is directed and
focused in particular ways. Providing we respect the limit given by
the form and content of the literary work in question, there is no
reason why we should not claim to understand fictional characters,
or indeed be legitimately accused of misunderstanding them. The
fact that one cannot interact with them is irrelevant because the
criteria for determining what counts as understanding here must
take account of what is and what is not intelligible as a response to
a work of art. Since it is logically absurd to speak of interaction
between fictional characters and ourselves, such 'interaction'
cannot be a condition which our presumed understanding fails to
satisfy—for it is no failure not to satisfy an absurd condition.
Nevertheless there is a sense in which fictional characters can act

---

[27] 'Dostoyevsky: Psychology and the Novelist', in A. Phillips Griffiths (ed.),
Philosophy and Literature: Royal Institute of Philosophy Lecture Series, xvi
(Cambridge, 1984), 111–12.

upon us (though not exactly in the same way as we as non-fictional agents act upon one another) and to understand fictional characters I must regard them as persons who are therefore capable of interaction one with another (within the same fictional world).

To have an understanding of fictional characters that goes beyond merely 'knowing about', we must therefore be in some sense acquainted with them via the power of the work to 'show'. Since this cannot be actual acquaintance, it must be an imagined acquaintance.[28] But that is in no way a restriction upon our capacity to learn from it. On the contrary, the fact that the objects art acquaints us with are non-actual provides the opportunity for discovering things we might be inclined to miss if the objects were actual.

Consider for instance the painting, *Répétition d'un ballet sur la scène*, by Edgar Degas. Here the dancers are on stage in a dress rehearsal. Stage-left, five girls rehearse under the direction of the master. Stage-right, five girls stand waiting, displaying various gestures of boredom, fatigue, and restlessness. At the front of the stage a girl is seated, skirt spread around her.

If we were actually present at such a scene, our attention might well be dissipated. Our eyes might register the fact, without making anything of it, that some girls are waiting, some dancing. Perhaps we might notice how dingy the walls look. The painting, however, unites these otherwise disparate and aimless perceptions into a mode of attention that has direction and meaning. The eye is led in from the bottom left of the picture, receiving first the waiting girls. Our eyes rest for a moment on the seated dancer, whose skirt seems to merge with the curve of the stage, at the far end of which five girls are still, yet dancing. The outstretched arms of two of the dancers direct our attention back to the outstretched arms of two of the first group. Spatially, the gestures resemble each other, yet the outstretched arms of the waiting group mean something different. One is stretching while yawning, the other is supporting herself on the wings. The whole atmosphere is empty, lacking the spirit and warmth of a public performance.

---

[28] There seem to be two sets of distinctions here (*a*) between the concrete and the abstract and (*b*) between the imagination and the intellect. There is a tradition from Kant, Coleridge, and Schiller, through Hegel to Croce and modern aesthetics that brings (*a*) and (*b*) together, equating the imagination with the concrete and the intellect with the abstract.

If art were merely to 'tell' us things, then, in this case at least, it would not tell us anything we do not already know. It is obvious enough to anyone that a rehearsal lacks the atmosphere of an actual performance. Yet in acquainting us with this scene, the painting shows us something we would not know simply by knowing the truth of the proposition 'a rehearsal lacks the atmosphere of a public performance'. The proposition is trivial, yet what we are shown is not. It is both subtle and complex. It unites several paradoxes to do with movement and stillness. Even though the scene seems static, the curve of the stage and the perspective in the picture suggests movement, leading the eye first from left to right, then back and forth between two sets of gestures that correspond as geometry but not as actions. The first group is waiting, yet the waiting is expressed in terms of bodily movement. The second group is active, in the sense that they are practising, yet the feet are closed, suggesting they stand still. This not only conveys the paradox of the dance itself in which movement can be depicted by a still figure, but also suggests that the empty stillness in the theatre is not due to lack of movement but to the absence of an audience.

There are further paradoxes to do with the idea of audience. Any audience is there and not there. The dance itself must proceed as though there were no audience, yet the picture implies that it does make a difference even to the dancer. Secondly, a large audience can provide a hushed and restrained stillness against which the performance can come to life—a stillness that is not simply absence of sound or movement but a sort of positive force. The stillness in this auditorium is more like the stillness of death. The edge of the stage, cold and hard as a curved blade, leads the eye not to the detail of empty seats but to a steep plunge into a darkness that has unspecified depth.

It is not clear which is illusion and which is reality: the life-giving spirit produced by the audience or the humdrum striving and suffering that goes into a performance that the audience perceive to be effortless, or even ethereal. In the furthest distance, not seen at first glance, the picture reveals the hint of several figures in the wings: they appear transparent and ghost-like. This confirms the ambiguity between appearance and reality. Furthermore, we view the scene as though from a box above stage-right. Yet there is no visible sign, other than perspective, to confirm that we are seated in the box: no pillar, no balcony, no ledge, to mediate between ourselves and the girls on stage. The spectator is there and not there. Since this is not a performance we cannot be there even as an audience of one, for we are being shown something that derives its character from being unobserved. In this sense the picture shows us something that we logically could not observe in actuality. This is a case of art showing us something which in principle we would not be there to see.

The last remark, being tied to the particularity of the example, is not intended to establish some thesis that art enables us to be 'a fly on the wall'. However, the fact that we are in one way 'drawn into' and in another way distanced from the objects of aesthetic contemplation means that we can be acquainted with things which if the acquaintance were actual might give rise to emotions or predicaments that would be a bar to this kind of understanding. As David Pole has put it: 'Were one to witness such a scene in reality, the suffering of a friend or an acquaintance, one would feel more, I expect, but see less.'[29] The point here is not that we have no feelings when confronted with fictional suffering, but that they are not 'mere feelings'. We are encouraged to 'dwell in the experience'. Pole's phrase, 'dwell in the experience' is a useful one in that it conveys both the involvement and the detachment of our response to imagined situations. If we were in no sense 'drawn in' we could not 'dwell' in the experience; yet the fact that we can dwell in it means that we are in other ways detached.[30] But, as I have tried to show, the 'dwelling' does not simply mean 'lingering'. It means having our attention organized and directed through the many subtleties of composition. We therefore experience a kind of intellectual activity that may not be present in cases of actual acquaintance with, say, anxiety, war, boredom, earthquakes, or bereavement.

I say 'activity' since our engagement with a work of art is not a passive one. In the experience of the Degas painting for instance, there are not two separate processes at work: finding meaning in the picture and learning from it. To find meaning in the picture *is* to learn from it. The fact that the picture does not necessarily

---

[29] *Aesthetics, Form and Emotion*, ed. G. Roberts (London, 1983), 11.

[30] The phenomenon of involvement-yet-detachment is also brought out in R. K. Elliott, 'Imagination in the Experience of Art', in G. Vesey (ed.), *Philosophy and the Arts: Royal Institute of Philosophy Lectures*, vi (London, 1973), 88 ff.

provide us with 'take-away' propositions about 'life' or 'the world' is neither here nor there. What the picture shows us, acquaints us with, is something that deepens our understanding of what we already know. In this sense it is a confusion to insist that 'learning' must be something which proceeds outwards from the picture to life, or the world, 'beyond' (as though the picture were nothing to do with life or the world). We apply what we already know of *this* life, *this* world, to the picture in understanding the interrelation- ships of movements and gestures that are presented to us; and in understanding these relationships, in grasping their point, in finding order and significance, we are for that very reason discovering something more about what we knew all along—but perhaps knew in a distant, 'formal', or theoretical kind of way. In understanding the picture, we come to know more *of* life without necessarily knowing more *about* it.

MORAL UNDERSTANDING AND AN EPISTEMOLOGY OF VALUE

The foregoing has been an attempt to explain what is wrong with the 'propositionalist' theory and to challenge an assumption that 'cognitivism' (in this sense) and 'anti-cognitivism' appear to share. In sketching the way forward for an alternative theory, it has been necessary to establish at least one way that we can be said to learn from works of art, without capitulating to instrumentalist theories. The distinction between telling and showing is intended not merely to reconcile the value of art as an end in itself with its educative power, but to insist that they are importantly connected. In showing, as opposed to telling, a work of art does not present us with descriptions of the world (from which we are left to infer propositions about life), it acquaints us with scenes, objects, people, and circumstances in such a way that we learn through that acquaintance.

That, however, still leaves the question: what do we learn morally? And in trying to answer that question it will be necessary to relate the preceding discussion about 'showing' to an examina- tion of its implications for epistemology. Since my position on the moral question will be made clearer via a discussion of the latter, I shall begin with the epistemological question.

The direction of my argument so far commits me to a defence of the idea that there can be knowledge which is non-propositional. That would not be controversial were we to remain within the tram-lines of Ryle's famous distinction between 'knowing how' and 'knowing that'. To 'know how' is to be in possession of a skill rather than a statable fact or body of doctrine. Nevertheless it seems right to argue, as David Hamlyn does, that there is a further distinction between knowing how to do X and merely being able to do X.[31] 'Knowing how' implies some understanding of the practice one is engaging in, even though successful performance need not depend upon the ability to state precisely how the performance has been accomplished.

The distinction between knowing how and knowing that is of little help in elucidating what we learn from art. Far too many objections stand in the way of claiming either that we gain propositional knowledge about the world or that we acquire some sort of skill in living, supposing such 'skills' even exist. Unless we accept that strain in classical empiricism that locates the value of art in the pleasure it brings, we are forced to seek out some epistemological category other than knowing that or knowing how. The category we are after seems to be 'knowledge by acquaintance', though this phrase needs to be purged of its association with the Russellian programme.[32] Russell's distinction between knowledge by acquaintance and knowledge by description was locked into the empiricists' attempt to find the direct and incorrigible units of awareness upon which all other knowledge is based. Once emancipated from that unreasonable workload, the phrase can be accommodated in the task, not of seeking some kind of awareness which is epistemologically prior to all others, but of distinguishing different kinds of awareness. To know what depression is, for instance, is not the same as knowing what it is like. Knowledge of depression can take the form of 'knowledge that' in the sense that I can offer various descriptions of it, make true statements about the condition, tell you how depression differs from sadness or laziness, and so on. But knowing what depression is like involves having experienced it. Knowledge in the latter sense is not necessarily propositional, for it does not depend upon the

[31] *The Theory of Knowledge* (London, 1971), 103–4.
[32] 'Knowledge by Acquaintance and Knowledge by Description', in Bertrand Russell, *Mysticism and Logic: And Other Essays* (London, 1963), 152–67.

ability to provide descriptions: it involves the ability to recall the experience. Of course if I know what depression is like I shall also 'know that' it is unpleasant in certain sorts of ways. But someone who has never experienced depression can know that (indeed he may know more 'about' depression that I do). But in 'knowing what it is like' I have an insight denied to the man who merely knows about it—but not one that takes the form of 'knowing that'.

It seems to be no accident that 'I have known depression' is interchangeable with 'I have experienced depression'. But the past tense is significant, for it would be mistaken to equate the mere experience of depression with knowing what the experience is like. Try establishing an equivalence between 'I am depressed' and 'I am knowing depression' and the result is comical. The equivalence between the past tense statements suggests a context in which the subject has an awareness that is also partly attributable to some kind of distance from the experience—though not necessarily in the temporal sense. Person *A* may now experience depression (e.g. for the first time) and now know what it is like. *B* may experience it, yet not know what it is like: he is simply depressed. *A* has an awareness that *B* does not have.

There is, however, a weakness in this argument. It might be objected that actually having experience *E* is not a necessary condition of knowing what *E* is like. Must we assume that Shakespeare must have experienced depression to be able to write *Hamlet*? It seems not. Yet does not the 'Oh that this too too solid flesh' speech show that the playwright knows what depression is like? If imaginative identification with an experience is to be called knowledge, then we need a further distinction between 'knowing from acquaintance what *E* is like' and simply 'knowing what *E* is like' (neither of which is reducible to 'knowing that'). Nevertheless it seems that the latter still depends upon some form of acquaintance, even if the acquaintance is imagined. One thing seems clear: Shakespeare could not write *Hamlet*, nor could we understand it, without in some way getting inside the mind of a depressed man and seeing what the world looks like through his eyes (e.g. 'an unweeded garden that grows to seed'). The second observation we need to make is that even though 'knowing what *E* is like' is non-propositional, that does not mean that it is totally unsayable, even in principle. It means that the ability to say it would have to amount to 'showing'—something which requires talent and imagination. Indeed it requires something approaching the condition of poetry to show what love, sadness, or grief is like.

I claim to be no pioneer with the argument that in addition to 'knowing how' and 'knowing that', there is a category which can be called 'knowing what'. Dorothy Walsh got there before me. And, further, she argued that the cognitive value of literature consists in providing knowledge of this kind.[33] Bearing in mind that I am not merely interested in the 'cognitive' value of literature, it is nevertheless necessary to bring ourselves up to date with the debate. Catherine Wilson's objection to Walsh's account is roughly as follows: I might as a result of reading a novel know what it is like to undergo a particular experience or to be in a particular set of circumstances; however, this will not necessarily affect or change my 'conception' of that experience or those circumstances (e.g. 'The person who knows what it is like to be poor and lonely in the big city has not necessarily been forced to alter his conceptions of poverty, or loneliness, or anonymity'[34]). To fill this logical gap, she suggests that Walsh's account can be saved by a further distinction between a 'deep' and a 'shallow' way of 'knowing what X is like'. If as a result of reading a novel I *really* understand (deep sense) what X is like, then my conception of X will be affected. 'A person may learn from a novel, I want to argue, if he is forced to revise or modify, e.g. his concept of "reasonable action" through a recognition of an alternative presented in the novel.' (Ibid.)

Wilson does not mean that a novel sets out to provide 'alternative conceptions' since she expressly repudiates the view that novels provide us with philosophical doctrines or general propositions about life. What she does appear to mean is that if we really understand what it is like to live a particular kind of life depicted in a given novel we shall thereby (indeed she seems to make it a point of definition) be forced to change our conception of the values implicit in such a way of life. This does not imply, she hastens to add, that we have to weigh up our conceptions against those presented in the novel and decide in favour of one or the other. She expresses that point by means of the following example:

[33] Dorothy Walsh, *Literature and Knowledge* (Middletown, Conn., 1969).
[34] Catherine Wilson, 'Literature and Knowledge', *Philosophy*, 58/226 (Oct. 1983), 494.

Consider the case of the young man who learns about kindness from his aged aunt. There need be no moment when the young man realizes that there is something defective about his conception of kindness. Nor need there be a moment when he weighs the behaviour of his aunt against his own and decides in favour of his aunt. The difference between the young man who learns from the example of his aunt and a similarly situated young man who does not, does not amount to a kind of mechanical failure in the latter case, but to a difference *in the way they regard their aunts.* For the second man, she is 'too kind' or 'impossibly kind' or 'kindness isn't everything'—or he may have failed to be struck by her kindness in the first place. The essentials are no different in the case of the reader who is left unmoved by e.g. Japanese or Existentialist literature.[35]

There is a great deal of insight in the 'aunt' example, to which I shall return in discussing moral understanding. The difficulty is how one applies it to fiction—and here Wilson's argument is, to put it mildly, not entirely clear. For all she says is 'the essentials are no different'. But which essentials? For the 'aged aunt' substitute Kent in *King Lear*. Now at what level do we apply the analogy? Do we say that the difference between the reader/ spectator who learns from the sincerity and loyalty of Kent and the reader/spectator who does not consists in the way he regards *Kent*? Well if 'learning from Kent' were the matter in question then perhaps this answer might do. But the question is not how we learn from Kent, but how we learn from the play. The problem here should not be confused with the question, 'how can we learn from Kent, given that he is fictional?' Given all my previous arguments, his fictional status is not itself a problem. Someone might of course learn something of sincerity and loyalty from the example that Kent provides. If we learn from actual people, there is no reason why we should not learn from fictional characters—and no doubt this is an important part of moral education. But it is not the kind we are interested in here, since that is to do with the instrumental value of literature. That we can, as a matter of fact, learn from Kent is not itself a sufficient reason for valuing the play.

Given the way that Wilson develops (or rather fails to develop) her example, the implication for a literary work ought to be: the distinction between a reader who learns from a literary work and

---

[35] Ibid. 496 (emphasis orig.).

one who does not consists in a difference in the way they regard that work. If Wilson intends the latter implication, then there are a number of puzzling holes in the argument. She is heavy on epistemology, but shies away from marrying that epistemology to a theory of literature. Indeed she even hints that the latter enterprise would be irrelevant: 'It is tempting, although I think ultimately a mistake, to raise questions at this point about the mechanics of the influence of literary works' (p. 495). Our need to clarify what form 'knowledge by acquaintance' takes in our experience of a literary work is hardly a question of 'mechanics', no more than to ask how the compositional 'elements' of a painting combine in our appreciation of the work as a whole is to ask a question about mere technicalities.

The predicament created by Wilson's argument runs as follows: since merely knowing what X is like (weak sense) does not qualify for 'learning', there must be a stronger sense of 'knowing what X is like' which does qualify. This argument loops the loop in an air-tight epistemological chamber. Learning is defined in terms of 'concept modification'; thus, given that learning must change us in some way, the knowledge we gain from literature must change or modify our concepts, 'which in turn is capable of altering [our] thought or conduct' (ibid.). Since this tight little system sees no need to examine what we are acquainted with in a work of literature and how we are acquainted with it, the question is dismissed as irrelevant. Yet it seems to me that if we do take account of these matters, this will in turn have particular implications for the epistemological argument.

The trouble starts when Wilson posits a 'logical gap' between 'merely' knowing what X is like and learning something. Thus, in attempting to fill the gap, she emerges brandishing a concept of knowledge which has such overwhelming dynamic powers that, if the model is applied to literature, it claims too much. Why must every case of learning from literature be construed as a matter of being changed as a result, or in having one's concepts changed or modified? To climb aboard that galloping thesis is to ride dangerously close to George Steiner's stipulation that 'He who has read Kafka's *Metamorphosis* and can look into his mirror unflinching may technically be able to read print, but is illiterate in the only sense that matters.'[36] It may well be, as Steiner claims, that 'a great poem, a classic novel, press in upon us' and exert a 'strange bruising mastery'. But to maintain as he does that to read 'in the only sense that matters' is to see the world differently as a result, is to turn his 'strange bruising mastery' into something that inflicts a permanent wound, and the wish to return to the same work into a form of needless masochism.

How then are we to deal with Wilson's 'gap'? The answer I think is that, in the sense that learning from literature is learning from acquaintance, there is no gap between what she takes to be the 'weak' sense of 'knowing what' and 'learning', so we do not need a stronger sense which is likely to prove too explosive. However, it is necessary to argue this via my concept of 'showing'. Given that we cannot be acquainted with Kent in the same way we can be acquainted with an aunt, if we know what it is like to be in Kent's situation this must be because the play has succeeded in showing us something (or, equally, we have succeeded in understanding something of what the work means). To be struck by Kent's sincerity and loyalty therefore is different from being struck by an aunt's kindness: for we cannot be 'struck' by the former without being 'struck' by many other things too. To appreciate Kent's sincerity and loyalty is at the same time to contrast it with the oily obsequiousness of Oswald, the mock-devotion and ultimate treachery of Regan and Goneril, and to compare it with the still waters that run deep in Edgar and Cordelia. Further, to appreciate the value of Kent's unconditional love for Lear is not merely to see the deficiencies in Lear that put such love to the test, but also to appreciate how this love is not a matter of blind devotion, but something anchored in a sense of duty and feeling for justice:

> Think'st thou that duty shall have dread to speak
> When power to flattery bows? To plainness honour's bound
> When majesty falls to folly . . .

> (I. i)

Given that Kent's unconditional love is the love that issues from a good and virtuous man, this also shows us something about Lear that we would not otherwise know: that there must be, despite his

---

[36] 'Humane Literacy', in George Steiner, *Language and Silence* (London, 1967), 28–9.

deficiencies, something in Lear that is worthy of respect. To regard Lear as simply a despicable old fool would in that sense be a failure to understand the nature of Kent's sincerity and loyalty; for these virtues are not merely dispositions which would have the same moral quality whatever objects they were directed upon—otherwise we may say that a sincere and loyal Nazi is a more virtuous man than one who is simply afraid to disobey orders.

In order to argue that we learn from Kent's moral qualities, it is not necessary to construe 'learning' as 'concept modification', or to think of learning in terms of changes that are brought about in one's life. It is a matter of coming to understand the play. And if we are to distinguish a strong from a weaker sense of 'understanding' here, that distinction can only be applied in terms of coming to see more and more meaning in the play (or, to avoid the elusive ambiguity of a word like 'meaning', perhaps it is sufficient to say 'coming to see more *in* the play'). Such a distinction would then mark a difference in degree of understanding, rather than a difference in kind (which latter is suggested by Wilson's analysis).

If that argument is right, it links the educative power of fiction with its artistic quality in that the 'learning' in question is intimately connected with the power of the work to show us something that could not be obtained by telling. Given that this distinction between telling and showing is tied up with the distinction between describing and creating, the epistemological link with knowledge by acquaintance is already implicit, since the work is successful in showing, only if it has the power to engage the imagination in such a way that, providing we have the capacity to meet the work halfway, we are drawn into an imagined acquaintance with what it portrays or depicts.

This still leaves something to be said about the part played by knowledge by acquaintance in moral understanding. As a moral agent, I am not a mere producer of deeds or a creature of unthinking habit who has been trained like a circus monkey to perform the right tricks. If I have been brought up properly I shall have acquired some understanding of right and wrong. Early moral training, as the word 'training' implies, is something imposed. But as fully-fledged moral agents we are neither parrots nor imitative apes. Our actions, words, and emotions are not merely 'responses' but, as Ryle puts it, they 'need a personal pronoun in their description'.[37] My actions are 'mine', not only because I am responsible for them, but because they testify to the kind of person I am and reflect my understanding of the world. The man who habitually lies, cheats, rapes, and steals is not merely one who has failed to pick up the right habits: he is deficient in the way he regards other people and therefore his own status in the world. He does not see others as 'ends in themselves' but merely as a means to the satisfaction of his appetites—appetites whose very nature is tainted by the means through which he is prepared to satisfy them, and which, if he regarded the world aright, he would learn not to have. (Indeed Aristotle's point that it is wrong even to desire the wrong things is a salutary one against the tendency of some philosophers to overlook the importance of feeling in morality, as for instance Kant does.)

It may be as Aristotle says that children 'enter the palace of reason through the courtyard of habit', but at the highest levels of moral understanding, virtue cannot be taught: for it is neither a matter of theoretical knowledge nor of skill. Knowing the difference between right and wrong, or between good and evil, is neither to be equated with the grasping of propositions, nor with the execution of some sort of competence. Yet for all that, there is a 'knowledge' here which is not simply identical with the performance or non-performance of particular deeds—and it is essentially non-propositional. We do not understand what is wrong with murder simply be grasping the tautology that murder is wrongful killing, or even by grasping non-trivial propositions such as 'murder is wrong because human life is sacred' or 'murder is wrong because, except in the most extreme and unusual circumstances, we do not have the right to take another's life'. We do not and cannot (as Ryle would surely put it) learn such things from a blackboard. There are some things that each man must see for himself 'in the silence of the heart' (Kierkegaard). But that does not mean that we discover them in the dark. Our sense of right and wrong is acquired not by the acceptance of slogans and maxims, but by commerce with the moral realities of good and evil: by our own experience of wickedness, cruelty, kindness, affection, guilt, remorse, and forgiveness.

---

[37] 'Can Virtue be Taught?', in R. F. Dearden, P. H. Hirst, and R. S. Peters (eds.), *Education and the Development of Reason* (London, 1971), 446.

As children we learn about wickedness by doing things that are wrong and by being forced to confront the nature of what we have done through punishment, remonstration, regret, and remorse (though of course that is only to state the negative side of the matter). As Ryle points out, we encounter a special seriousness in human attitudes towards wrongdoing that is of a wholly different order from attitudes towards mere deficiencies in skill. And to acquire these attitudes with anything that can be called real understanding is not merely to chime in with the bleatings around us: it is to be genuinely appalled by the repulsiveness of greed, the slime of dishonesty, the filth of obscenity, and the stench of corruption. It is surely no accident that our ethical vocabulary is rich with aesthetic overtones. If we were, as some philosophers portray us as being, mere 'rational agents', our moral concepts would be different—perhaps unimaginable. While it is true that only rational beings are capable of aesthetic appreciation, the fact that we are creatures who are sensitive to beauty and ugliness makes a difference to our moral perceptions—or, rather, helps to make them what they are. For they seem to be informed by a series of aesthetic contrasts between pure and impure, clean and dirty, savoury and unsavoury, harmonious and discordant, sweet-smelling and foul-smelling, natural and unnatural, humane and inhumane.

To bring out the importance of this suggestion, consider for instance the conflict between Goneril and Albany. What on the surface appears to be merely a difference in attitude—Goneril considered by Albany to be too harsh in her treatment of her father, Albany considered by Goneril to be too gentle and indecisive—is, upon examination, a mutual repugnance offset against different standards of masculinity and femininity and different conceptions of nature:

> Milk liver'd man
> That bear'st a cheek for blows, a head for wrongs;
> Who hast not in thy brows an eye discerning
> Thine honour from thy suffering; that not know'st
> Fools do those villains pity who are punish'd
> Ere they have done their mischief. Where's thy drum?
> France spreads his banners into our noiseless land,
> With plumed helm thy state begins to threat;
> Whilst thou, a moral fool, sitt'st still and criest

'Alack! why does he so?'

(*King Lear*, IV. ii)

Goneril's description of Albany as a moral fool is not a statement issuing from one who has decided to stand outside morality. Rather, it is a moral judgement issuing from the perspective of a woman whose conception of the important and rational concerns of life is shot through with ruthlessness and go-getting. Her malevolence neither renders her ineligible for the making of moral judgements, nor discredits the grain of truth in what she says—for Albany is at times impractical and indecisive. However, it is difficult to separate her evaluation of his conduct from her conception of what is fitting, and therefore attractive, in a man. Hence there is an aesthetic, even a sexual, dimension to her response here, and that is shown by her attraction to Edmund, of whom she says, 'O the difference of man and man! | To thee a woman's services are due; | My fool usurps my body.'

Since Albany is a humane and good man, it is tempting to construe his aversion to what he discovers in Goneril as straightforward moral condemnation. Moral condemnation it certainly is (and perhaps more straightforwardly so than Goneril's) but this is combined with his repugnance at the way his conception of womanhood has been so grotesquely transgressed: 'See thyself devil! | Proper deformity seems not in the fiend | So horrid as in woman.' This is not just added to his moral condemnation: it is bound up with it ('tigers not daughters'). His condemnation of her offence against her father is pivotal upon his conception of nature. Goneril offends nature ('That nature which contemns it origin | Cannot be border'd certain in itself . . .') and she, in the shape of a woman, is an offence against the nature of woman—a deformity.

The link between aesthetic and moral sensibility tightens the argument about the role of 'knowledge by acquaintance', and helps to elucidate what would be missing if we attempted to give an account of moral understanding in terms of 'knowledge that'. He who only 'knows' that vindictiveness is wrong because people say so, no more understands what is wrong with vindictiveness than the man who only 'knows' that the Atlantic Ocean is beautiful because it says so in the guidebooks appreciates its beauty. We do not understand or appreciate beauty and ugliness except by being acquainted with beautiful and ugly things. Similarly, we do not understand what is wrong with vindictiveness and spite unless, when they manifest themselves, we are repulsed by vindictive and spiteful acts, finding in them a coarse and vulgar brutality of attitude and a range of ugly passions. I do not mean to imply that, for all cases, we cannot sincerely apply moral predicates without first being actually acquainted with the particular phenomena of which they are predicated. After all, the growth of moral understanding should equip us to understand situations we have not yet met, and indeed to want to prevent some situations from ever occurring. As we shall see, this is one among other reasons why imagination is important to morality.

If we now apply this analysis to the question of the morally educative power of literature, a number of our original difficulties, I believe, disappear. We can say that literature contributes to our moral understanding through acquainting us (or even re-acquainting us) with things we could not know by description alone, and in a way that does not violate the 'autonomy' of art by regarding it in purely instrumental terms.

Let us return to the case of *Macbeth*. I have argued that the moral significance of the play cannot be adequately expressed by saying that it communicates general propositions such as 'murder is wrong'. We already know that murder is wrong, but it is a further question whether we understand, or are prepared to let ourselves admit, what it is about murder that makes it so dreadfully appalling. We can read reports in the newspapers, or hear announcements on television, and we are rightly sickened, depressed, or shocked. But the full horror is not disclosed by these means; and, because it is too painful and too terrible, we tend to close our minds to the full moral import of what we are reading or hearing about. Life must, as they say, go on. And we may shield ourselves from the moral reality of evil by dismissing murderers as psychopaths or helpless victims of social or economic deprivation. Indeed we seem to live in an age which defines away the very possibility of evil. The more monstrous a man's deed, the more it is likely to be regarded as a form of sickness (no less a superstition than attributing evil to alien forces such as possession by demons).

In confronting ourselves with *Macbeth* we have no such opportunity to anaesthetize our moral sensibilities. We cannot separate the nature of 'the deed' from the evil intentions involved in its execution. The horror of Duncan's death is not simply that of a body rendered lifeless and bloody by the point of a dagger (despite the self-indulgence of Polanski's film, which insists upon showing the murder scene). For the hand that consents to clutch the instrument of murder is morally different from the hand that wielded the 'brandish'd steel | Which smok'd with bloody execution' and 'like valour's minion' unseam'd Macdonwald 'from the nave to th' chaps'. As physical events, these two killings differ only numerically, separated in space and time. Morally, they are as different from one another as is the noble courage 'disdaining Fortune' (I. ii) from the vain and devil desperation that cries 'Come, Fate, into the list | And champion me to th' utterance!' (III. i)

We are acquainted with the horror of Macbeth's passage into evil, not merely because we witness it as spectators, but because we also make the journey with him. He is not the distant and indistinct figure we might read about in a newspaper, but a man whose doubts, fears, desires, ambition, and sense of guilt we are invited to share. In I. vii for instance, he seems to speak our own thoughts in producing reasons for not committing the murder—reasons which are not merely abstractions but proceed from the felt reality of Duncan being '*here* in double trust'. We are with Macbeth when he says to his wife, 'We will proceed no further in this business', and can understand how his doubt is converted to resolution by the taunts about his manhood and his courage. We share (through the power of words, rather than through the excrescent 'special effects' of Polanski's team) the 'vision' of the dagger that invites. And upon Macbeth's return we share the tension created in the staccato

> Did you not speak?
> When?
> Now.
> As I descended?
> Ay.
> Hark.

terminating in 'This is a sorry sight'. Subsequently, after the killing of Banquo we share Macbeth's vision of the apparition seated at the table, knowing it to represent the true horror, one 'which might appall the devil'. In seeing what Lady Macbeth does not see, but regards as mere appearance ('the very painting of [Macbeth's] fear'), we are aware that such 'appearances' are only appearances to one who has a shallow conception of reality. They are given their status as appearances through that conception that says 'what is done is done', but not through that conception that says 'what is done cannot be *undone*'.

Macbeth does not tell us about the true horror of murder: it acquaints us with a particular set of circumstances through which we experience the horror for ourselves. We are exposed, with all the safety that fiction affords, to face the uncomfortable truths of which we are in part already aware. Indeed, that we can so easily get inside the mind of Macbeth makes it seem as though the knowledge of evil we gain is partly a kind of self-knowledge.

To say that we learn from the play is not to confer some 'external' value on it, such that the play is only a means towards some understanding of the world. Try extracting a moral or a message and dressing it up, as some publishers have done, in a 'classics for children' comic-strip format, and it does not, and cannot, show the same things. Indeed it cannot be the 'same experience'.[38] Or, as Bantock elsewhere puts it, 'The morality of great art is never simple and unequivocal.'[39] In part, what we learn from the play depends upon Shakespeare's mastery of language. But it also depends upon his achievement as a dramatist. In our experience of the play we cannot dismiss the reality of evil in the way that we so often do by regarding murderers as not responsible for their actions, or as a special breed, a race apart. If the essence of drama is conflict, that conflict is achieved here partly by the portrayal of Macbeth, not as a monster or fiend from hell, but as a man among men, whose capacity for evil is dependent upon his capacity for good. And herein lies the tragedy: that Macbeth is not a puppet manipulated by the witches, but a man who freely consents to do what his conscience and imagination tells him is the work of the devil. The temptation does not spring from some unearthly love of evil (whatever that might be). Rather, it only gets its bite because Macbeth has qualities of character and aspirations that are in other circumstances marks of virtue. The valour and pursuit of an honour that makes him a fearless and noble warrior

---

[38] G. H. Bantock, 'The Attack on the Culture of Quality', in Dennis O'Keeffe (ed.), *The Wayward Curriculum: A Cause for Parents' Concern?* (London, 1986), 21.

[39] *The Parochialism of the Present* (London, 1981), 29.

is perverted in the self-defeating pursuit of an 'honour' and a 'greatness' that cannot be achieved by legitimate means.

It would be as well to pause here to consider the link between knowledge by acquaintance and the imagination, with a view to drawing out the implications of this link for practical and moral reasoning.

Propositional knowledge takes the form of 'knowing that *P*', and the object of the knowledge is a true proposition. In 'knowing what *X* is like' the object of the knowledge is not a proposition but an experience. However, as Roger Scruton has suggested in *Art and Imagination* (p. 105), there is an important distinction between knowing what an experience is like and knowing what a '(material) *object*' of experience is like. In knowing what a pillarbox is like I can tell you about its describable features—e.g. its shape, colour, size, and function—and thus describe it using true propositions. Knowing what an experience is like, on the other hand, does not depend upon the ability to provide descriptions, but upon the ability to recall (or imaginatively engage with) the experience. The link with imagination therefore seems to be this, that imagining what *X* is like, where *X* is not a material object, involves the ability to summon up images which 'match' the experience of *X*. In looser language, it involves the ability in some way to live or relive the experience. (Scruton: 'there is nothing more to be said about imagining what it is like to break a bone than that it is an image irreducibly analogous to the experience of breaking a bone' (p. 106).)

On the importance of this capacity for practical and moral reasoning the following can be said. No practical reasoning about his own future action can be adequately rational unless the agent is able to envisage what it would be like to achieve a given objective. I may for instance wish to give up living in the city and move to a house in a quiet country village. Without knowing what it would be like to achieve this objective, however, any link between achieving the objective and being happy or satisfied would be nothing more than accidental. It is not enough that I know that I feel irritated and weary with the clamour of city life and thus assume that a move to the country would solve the problem. If my decision is to be more rational than this, I must have some conception of what it would be like to live in Brambleweed Dell, with no immediate access to the facilities and amenities I may hitherto have taken for granted, and with only the wildlife for company. Despite the way that 'decision-making skills' are now being taught in schools (as though decision-making were a matter of calculation, and as though people have a discrete faculty for 'deciding' which can be tuned-up and brought to bear on any situation) it would not be enough simply to draw up columns of 'pros' and 'cons' and weigh one column against the other in the abstract—for in the abstract such pros and cons mean little. How do I know that when I put 'quietness' in the pro column I am not really wishing for a quieter *city* life? In short, I am required to acquaint myself in imagination with the concrete particulars not merely of a specific place in the countryside but with *my* living there. To know what it would be like to live in the country therefore involves self-knowledge, to the extent that I must know what it would be like for *me* to live there. I must not assume that I would be happy there just because Farmer Giles is.

As for practical reasoning generally, the kind of imagination discussed above plays a central part. As distinct from fantasy, the imagination involved in rational contemplation of a desired future state is essentially concerned with the truth about that state. And in the kind of context we have been considering, being concerned about the truth involves testing one's apparent desire for future state X against an imagined acquaintance with the realization of that desire. By imaginatively projecting myself into such a future state I may well discover that my desire for X is illusory, a romantic daydream. Where properly rational, practical reasoning is not merely some kind of strategy for attaining an objective: it is also concerned with discovering what we really do desire.

As moral agents, however, we are not mere centres of practical reason, and are thus prepared to frustrate some of our desires. Here the kind of imagination under discussion becomes crucial. Even on those ethical theories which are opposed to the utilitarian ethic of consequentialism, a moral being is necessarily concerned with the consequences of his past conduct and the possible future consequences of his present conduct. As against that tendency in utilitarianism that portrays moral reasoning as a species of calculation, the impact upon us of these (actual or likely) consequences is mediated through the imagination in such a way that we are drawn into some form of 'lived' acquaintance with the actual or probable consequences of our own agency. To recognize and acknowledge responsibility for causing unjustified damage or hurt to others through something I have done in the past is not an abstract exercise, but involves confronting myself with images of that suffering and hurt in concrete form, such that I am 'haunted' by it, and thus feel guilt and remorse. And if this concern with what I have done is to amount to self-knowledge (if, that is, the remorse is sincere) it will have a direct bearing upon what I intend to do in future. ('A confession has to be part of your new life.'[40]) I shall confront in imagination what I think to be the likely consequences of my present or future conduct, not as the strategist considers possible moves in a board-game, but in a way that almost enables me to experience them. The fact that there are people who lack the imagination to consider their effects upon others does not tell against this argument, but rather supports it: the imagination they lack, in this context, amounts to a moral failing, a debilitated conscience. If that is so, the kind of imagination required for 'knowing what it would be like to . . .' is something which is active rather than passive. It is a capacity which the experience of imaginative literature, and indeed painting, may feed and strengthen.

My argument so far, then, is that good literary works provide the opportunity for knowledge by acquaintance, and that the educative power of literature is linked with its artistic merit. The pitfalls of instrumentalism are avoided because learning from the work is not a further consequence of understanding: it is that understanding. Imagine someone discussing *Macbeth* in a way that shows he has appreciated something of its depth. Would it not be distinctly odd, and perhaps confused, to say to him 'yes, that's all very well, but what have you *learned* from the play?'

One might seek a parallel in cases where we speak of learning from knowing people. As Rush Rhees has pointed out in his discussions of education: I might learn a set of facts or pick up particular skills as a result of someone's teaching; but that is different from the case in which I want to say that I have learned from knowing him ('It was not just the things he taught me and the training he gave. I learned from *him*. And I may want to say "My education has come more from knowing him than from any

---

[40] Wittgenstein, *Culture and Value*, 18e.

schooling." '41 If an uncomprehending sceptic were to ask, 'but *what* did you learn?', the answer, in so far as any answer could be given at all, would have to consist not of a statement about the knowledge that he was a means towards, but of some sort of description of the man himself—one that expresses, say, admiration and respect, and therefore implies that I would have been the poorer for not knowing him. It is almost as though he has become a part of what I now am.

This analogy, while pointing up the non-propositional flavour of such knowing by acquaintance, also reveals a difference (and one not brought out by Catherine Wilson's otherwise perceptive example of the 'kind aunt'). What we learn, when we do learn, from knowing particular people has nothing to do with literary form. And it would be a mistake to treat 'literary form' just as a means towards the presentation of characters from which we can go on to learn through acquaintance. If Macbeth were an actual man, I should no more be the worse for not knowing him than I am the worse for never having known Hitler or Stalin.

Granted his being fictional provides opportunities for confronting moral realities that for one reason or another we might evade in everyday life (I do not wish to retract any of that argument) it seems that is not enough to explain how we have the sense that we would have been the poorer without the experience. The additional value (though of course it is not simply 'added on') cannot rest in the moral significance of the play, and this for two reasons. We need no special qualifications for exposure to people from whom we can learn simply by knowing them (though of course it is undeniable that the other person could not have this sort of impact upon me unless there were something in me to be reached). But it does require additional capacities, and of a particularly specialized kind, to gain access to the moral insights in anything so demanding as a Shakespeare play. The fact that great works of art, like Shakespearian drama, have qualities that we must be educated into appreciating confers further value upon those moral insights.

If the 'knowledge by acquaintance' argument were sufficient by itself, that would hardly explain why we are drawn to the same works time and time again. Literary works are not mere 'opportunities' for learning, and if they were their value would be expended,

---

[41] *Without Answers*, 149 (emphasis orig.).

as the value of any opportunity is, once seized and made use of. Again one may seek a parallel: people are not merely 'opportunities' either. And we would not learn from people in the way we do if our interest in them were purely instrumental. Indeed it may be that in many respects our interest in persons and our interest in works of art are one. But not in all respects. What this analogy misses out is that art in some way celebrates our interest in persons. My argument so far therefore has not sufficiently considered the fact that we do not merely understand works of art but also treasure them. We value them as lasting utterances. In my closing remarks I shall have something to say about this.

It is first necessary to confront some deficiencies in the present analysis. (1) I have so far taken 'knowing what' in the rather narrow sense of 'knowing what X is like' and have not said enough about other kinds of 'knowing what'. (2) Not enough attention has been focused on the role that genre plays in our ability to learn from literature, or rather, in the 'ability' of literature to provide such understanding. Given the hugeness of these topics, what I say will be very sketchy. To write with any authority on (2) would require something beyond my present competence and what I do have to say has the force not of a comprehensive survey but of a pointer to further enquiry. It should be noted that the term 'genre' is itself ambiguous. The idea of a genre is that of a kind, class, type, or sort, and as Martin Dodsworth has indicated, precisely what we are referring to here is a matter for complex dispute.[42] I shall use the term in a rather rough and ready way, since I shall only comment here on one important distinction between tragedy and comedy.

In this connection, let us return to my comments on *Macbeth*. Here I gave some indication that we cannot properly discuss what we learn from the play without remembering that this work is a drama, and one of a special sort: tragedy. The reason we cannot learn from it as though it were one of the many 'issue-raising' plays on television is that such a reading would be a *mis*reading of the work. But neither can we regard Shakespeare's tragedy as though it were a Greek tragedy. Shakespeare's tragic heroes are not victims of destiny or fate. What we learn from *Macbeth* or *King Lear* for

---

[42] 'Genre and the Experience of Art and Literature', in Vesey, *Philosophy and the Arts*, vi. 211–27.

instance would not be possible were we in the former case to regard Macbeth as a puppet of fate's decree and in the latter case to blind ourselves to the self-pity of Lear's attempt to blame the gods for his suffering. Shakespeare enjoins our sympathies with his tragic heroes while sustaining our awareness of their responsibility for what happens. We do not pity them as we would pity victims of misfortune. What we learn through being led to sympathize with them is inseparable from finding meaning in the drama, the *kind* of drama it is.

Contrast this with our experience of comedy. Though we may in some instances sympathize with a comic figure, we need not in all cases have such sympathy. There is a tendency for comedy to thrive on a type of cruelty, which is what makes it funny. We might have a soft spot for Dogberry, but, as an object of our laughter, in no sense do we sympathize with him. Indeed our amusement depends upon some perception of our superiority to this bumbling idiot. Nevertheless there are limits—limits given by the genres of tragedy and comedy—to what we can find acceptable in the suffering of a comic figure. Had the playwright attempted to establish a link between Dogberry's bumbling and some sort of tragic downfall we would find a lack of intelligibility in the play. Here I am in agreement with Roger Scruton's point that 'The tragic suffering of a comic character is disgusting; our feelings are outraged by the demand that we sympathise with this character in a predicament that he lacks the virtue to bear. Our attention is taken away from the dramatic meaning, and directed towards the suffering itself: this alone now interests us, but with a horrifying force.'[43] (Perhaps it is no accident that Shakespeare leaves us wondering what happened to the Fool in *Lear*?) If *Much Ado* is to remain intelligible as a comedy, Dogberry's 'flaw' must remain inconsequential. Something similar could be said about the love–hate relationship of Beatrice and Benedick. Had Shakespeare 'rewarded' the pride of the lovers with, say, a depiction of suicide, we would fail to find sense in the drama—given that pride is not hubris. Learning from *Much Ado* has to do with finding meaning or sense in the play as a play; this 'meaning' or 'sense' must have to do with the genre of comedy. To be moved to tears of sadness rather than tears of laughter would be a failure to understand the drama. (Though I

[43] *Sexual Desire: A Philosophical Investigation* (London, 1986), 227.

am not suggesting that understanding involves *assigning* the play to a genre.)

Now this argument could be extended to other genres (in an elaboration of what in Chapter 5 I called the 'bargain' between author and reader/spectator). But I wish to establish a link between the present issue and different forms of 'knowing what'. It now emerges from what has been said above that understanding a work, and thus learning from it, involves 'knowing what' in the sense of 'knowing what to feel'. Given that understanding persons and understanding works of art are to be distinguished from understanding things like physics textbooks, the understanding here must involve knowing how to respond. Peter Jones has drawn attention to the equivalence between understanding a novel and knowing how to 'take it' in one way rather than another.[44] But he also compares this with a feature of our understanding of another person: that we know how to respond to him. In both cases this is not merely a matter of cognitive apprehension but something which involves establishing a certain clarity in our emotions: e.g. learning to feel the appropriate thing towards the appropriate object in the right degree (something central to Aristotle's conception of practical reason).

One can then connect this idea with the role of knowing what to feel in the realm of practical knowledge. Here, as Scruton has argued, there is a link between knowing what to feel and knowing what to do.[45] The latter cannot be simply a matter of skill, since it requires evaluation: right knowledge of the end to be attained. But neither is it theoretical knowledge. Practical knowledge is not merely a matter of knowing what I *should* do, rather the emphasis is on knowing what *I* should do. This, however, is not equivalent to 'choice' or 'decision', since if we are concerned with knowledge here, the knowledge is partly that of self-knowledge. This requires knowing what to feel, not in the sense of having an opinion about the feelings I ought to have, but in actually having the requisite feelings. It is at this point, if not earlier, that 'individualistic' theories give out, by positing 'autonomy' in a ('culture-less') vacuum. Divorced from the social framework of a common culture,

[44] *Philosophy and the Novel*, Ch. 5.
[45] 'Emotion and Culture', in R. Scruton, *The Aesthetic Understanding: Essays in the Philosophy of Art and Culture* (London, 1983), 139–52.

our picture of the autonomous individual is one who in some way stands outside social institutions and practices, and 'works out' appropriate modes of conduct. He is thus either a human calculating machine or a hedonistic centre of drives and desires seeking how best to attain his goals or how to minimize his frustrations.

It is revealing that utilitarian theories usually anchor themselves to a picture of 'human nature' as a constant that is supposed either to pre-date or transcend its local and particular manifestations in particular societies at particular times. Thus Warnock speaks of '*the* human predicament' and Mrs Foot of 'human good and harm' as a kind of datum, or as facts from which values can be derived.[46] Mary Midgley has tried to buttress the neo-naturalist position by reminding us that human nature is not 'infinitely plastic' and that 'everything must have *some* internal structure'.[47] Quite what might count as the 'internal structure' of people remains a puzzling question. Neo-naturalistic arguments of this type try to isolate and contemplate the framework of human nature in itself (divorced from the social context) and while this may not be an error of the same kind as trying to contemplate roses and fountains shorn of their perceptual qualities, it is an error of the same magnitude.

One does not have to hold that man is 'infinitely plastic' in order to hold that he is not fixed and determinable in the neo-naturalists' sense. We do not have to jettison the idea that there is such a thing as human nature in order to suggest that, within a particular epoch of civilization, or within a particular culture, conceptions of what it is to be fully human may be importantly affected by different presuppositions of value. Indeed, the moral conflict we see develop in Macbeth, and the moral disagreement between Macbeth and his wife, involves differing conceptions of what it is to be a man. This is one of the themes of the play: what it is to be a man cannot be separated from what conduct is worthy of a man.

MACBETH. I dare do all that may become a man;
    Who dares do more is none.
LADY MACBETH.   What beast was it then
    That made you break this enterprise to me?
    When you durst do it, then you were a man;

---

[46] G. J. Warnock, *The Object of Morality* (London, 1971); Philippa Foot, 'Moral Beliefs', in Foot (ed.), *Theories of Ethics* (Oxford, 1967), 83–100.
[47] 'Is "Moral" a Dirty Word?', *Philosophy*, 67/181 (July 1972), 222.

And to be more than what you were, you would
Be so much more the man.

(I. vii)

As I have tried to show with the Goneril/Albany example, ideals
of conduct have an aesthetic element. Given all this, knowing what
to feel can be separated neither from one's sense of the social
context that determines certain possibilities of feeling, nor therefore
from the conventions or modes of utterance which impose order
and intelligibility upon the feelings themselves. Roger Scruton has
illustrated this by referring to a passage from *Odessey*.[48] One can I
think support this illustration by considering IV. III of *Macbeth*,
when Ross tells Macduff that his wife and children have been
slaughtered:

MALCOLM. Merciful heaven!
　What, man! Ne'er pull your hat upon your brows;
　Give sorrow words. The grief that does not speak
　Whispers the o'erfrought heart and bids it break.

Without some conception of what would be appropriate as an
expression of the grief, Macduff cannot properly be said to know
what to feel. In the light of modern psychological theory, the
passage would probably be interpreted on the model of the blocked
chamber that needs to be relieved in order to prevent some sort of
implosion, but that is not the point here. The point is that until
Macduff aligns himself to one of the conventions open to him for
expressing his reaction to the grief he cannot make sense of his
feelings. Malcolm advises him,

　　　　　　　　Be comforted.
　Let's make us med'cines of our great revenge
　To cure this deadly grief.

but Macduff first expresses his grief in such a way that his loss
becomes palpable enough to grapple with:

MALCOLM. Dispute it like a man.
MACDUFF.　　　　　　　　　I shall do so;
　But I must also feel it as a man.
　I cannot but remember such things were
　That were most precious to me. . . .

---

[48] *The Aesthetic Understanding*, 145–52.

Malcolm's advice is not that of therapist to patient, but that of one whose conception of manhood is essentially connected with what is regarded as noble. And when Macduff expresses his grief in terms of anger, it changes what he feels and channels it into a definite course of action. Malcolm replies, 'This tune goes manly', not meaning simply that he is putting a brave face on it, but that he is now turning a senseless event and the chaos of feeling into a genuine and intelligible cause for overcoming Macbeth's tyranny ('Macbeth is ripe for shaking').

What this example brings out is that knowing what to feel is not an individualistic exercise of rumination, but a matter of latching on to modes of expression that are publicly given and shaped by the ideals and aspirations within a common culture. There is no doubt that Macduff thinks and feels as an individual, but his individuality is only possible within shared forms of thought and expression.

There is another way of bringing out the import of the above discussion, and that is by considering a rather puzzling paradox of moral experience, that (1) as rational agents we are individuals who are 'autonomous', in Kant's sense, albeit in accordance with the moral law, yet (2) as members of a cultural community we have duties and obligations that are 'given' to our understanding through participation in the community of which we are a part. On the second model, moral concerns are not 'chosen' or reached through 'decision' but often forced upon us in various ways. Much confusion in ethics is created by following model (1) to the exclusion of (2), and vice versa. In some way one feels that (1) and (2) must both be true, yet how can this be?

In trying to answer this I take some inspiration from Stuart Hampshire's suggestion in *Morality and Conflict* that there is both a rational and a non-rational element in moral thought. There seem to be two, ostensibly conflicting, requirements for moral understanding. The first is that we do not merely imitate the actions, thoughts, and opinions of others, but make our own moral evaluations. According to this model the *sine qua non* of being a moral agent is that of being a rational agent: on this even the Kantians and the utilitarians are in agreement. To do what is morally right and to do what is rational are one and the same. The difference will consist in the *kind* of reasons thought to justify moral choices. For utilitarians the justification consists in the instrumentality of particular moral choices towards a non-moral goal, or empirically identifiable state, whereas for a good Kantian a morally good act is good in virtue of its being in accord with the moral law, though of course performed from, and not merely in accordance with, that duty. Incidentally, it is quite wrong to parody that duty as 'a Sense of Duty' akin to military duty, as Geach does.[49] The psychological 'must' implanted by military training or by a totalitarian regime is not the Kantian unconditional 'ought' which must be grasped by an individual doing his own moral thinking—a position which is antithetical to unquestioning obedience to arbitrary authorities, or to a failure to question the spurious 'duties' enjoined by a ruling power. Against Geach's own example of the ardent young Nazi who machine-guns a column of refugees 'till he bleeds to death', the chief objection is surely that it is not a Kantian finger that presses the trigger but one that is not Kantian enough.

Ignoring the difficulties internal to both variants of the first model, we must point to an inevitable difficulty in regarding morality as a matter of calculation (a feature both variants share). Too exclusive a regard for this model of moral reasoning commits us in the end to regarding the moral/rational agent as one who, so to speak, stands *outside* the contingencies and conventions of his particular society. Thus every institution, every tradition, every social practice will be subjected to a searching scepticism and be required to prove its legitimacy before loyalty, or conformity to it, is exacted. This view is in part a legacy of the Enlightenment. And the view it takes itself to be rejecting is that morality consists in blind conformity to a particular moral code, practice, or convention—a way of life informed by little more than 'prejudice' or superstition (consider Rousseau's strictures against the corrupting influence of poetry on the child's 'autonomy').

What this caricature misses out is that it is a necessary condition of moral understanding that we are first inducted into the culture into which we are born. We learn our morality through social relations which are to some extent informed by the settled pattern of expectations rooted in a common culture. And any subsequent

---

[49] Peter Geach, *God and the Soul* (London, 1969), 121–2. (To be fair, the identified target is post-Kantian moral philosophy; though Geach does not seem to want to rescue Kant from some of the unfortunate manifestations of that tradition.)

questioning must succeed, not precede, our grasp of the moral certainties of our surrounding order. These certainties are acquired, not through manipulation of abstractions, but through learning to feel—love, loyalty, obedience, duty, respect, reverence, and so on. This learning does not stand outside our capacity for rational thought, but it is not, and cannot be, simply a product of reasoning. Indeed, without these elemental feelings our capacity to reason is itself impaired. Further, the peculiar importance of the respect for other persons that we gain from our social environment derives its authority from its being taken for granted, and not open—as so many other things are—to debate. We do not receive it as *hypothesis* that murder is wrong. The authority or legitimacy here is amenable to explanation in terms of history rather than in terms of any form of reasoning that can loosely be termed 'scientific'. As Burke maintained, there are some duties and obligations which are inherited, rather than created through deliberation or choice.

Morality as convention does not necessitate relativism, in the troublesome sense of the term; what it does involve is a distinction between those loyalties, duties, and allegiances which are binding upon us simply because we are human beings, and those which arise from 'a valued way of life which might, however regrettably, change radically and which might not continue for ever'.[50] The 'valued ways of life' given by convention are, like aesthetic preferences, susceptible to conflict. In fact this second model gets its bite upon the inadequacy of the first model, which posits 'a good life' valid for all men whatever their circumstances. It is clear therefore that 'learning what to feel' within a common culture involves not so much some abstracted conception of rightness and wrongness, but rather appropriateness (and it is here that the link with aesthetics is forged). It is the second model which can accommodate the notion of a social role and the duties that are appropriate to it. Thus the model not only permits the existence of moral conflict, but insists upon it as a permanent possibility. My duties and obligations enjoined by one particular role or institution may conflict with the duties and obligations enjoined by other roles or institutions that either I cannot avoid or which seem to have some claim upon me. The self that feels, or tries to resolve, such conflict is, however, not one that stands outside all conventions and

---

[50] Stuart Hampshire, *Morality and Conflict* (Oxford, 1983), 143.

institutions, but rather one that acts or feels by reference to one set of allegiances as opposed to another. (It is here that the utilitarian's question, 'why should I be moral?', can be seen for the self-defeating abstraction that is is—since it posits one who stands outside the moral community *tout court*, which is impossible.)

MORALITY, LANGUAGE, AND CULTURE

Once this emphasis is placed upon the role of feeling in morality, we can see the need for further comments about the value of literature. Any writer of any art proceeds from and encourages a respect for the quality of language. And the relevance to morality is this, that a culture in which language becomes in certain respects enfeebled or debased may in some circumstances prevent certain possibilities of feeling. This has been argued vehemently by cultural commentators such as Leavis, Robinson, and Bantock, as well as by philosophers such as John Casey.[51] But nowhere with more passion than by Simone Weil in her comments on the responsibility of writers. In identifying the 'essential characteristic' of the first half of the twentieth century as being marked by 'the growing weakness, and almost the disappearance, of the idea of value', she points to something important in lamenting that

Words like virtue, nobility, honour, generosity, have become almost impossible to use or else they have acquired bastard meanings; language is no longer legitimately equipped for praising a man's character. It is slightly, but only slightly, better equipped for praising a mind; the very word mind, and the words intelligence, intelligent, and others like them, have also become degraded. The fate of words is a touchstone of the progressive weakening of the idea of value, and although the fate of words does not depend upon writers alone one cannot help attributing a special responsibility to them, since words are their business.[52]

It may be that the responsibility Simone Weil confers upon writers is too great, but that does not undermine the strength of her observation on the connection between language and the quality of thought and feeling. Can one even imagine what Simone

---

[51] John Casey, 'The Autonomy of Art', in Vesey, *Philosophy and the Arts*, vi. 65–87.

[52] *On Science, Necessity and the Love of God*, trans. and ed. R. Rees (Oxford, 1968), 168.

Weil would make of things today when pressures towards egalitar-
ianism seek to remove words like 'able' and 'gifted' from the
English language?[53] The kind of praise involved in calling someone
gifted has nothing to do with keeping scores or winning in the
horse-race of life: it is an attitude of wonder to achievements that
seem to flow from the very soul and confer added beauty on the
world. An attack on the word 'gifted' is not only an attack on the
kind of value we place on achievements which rise above mere
competence (which is always just 'good enough' for a purpose or a
preconceived end), it is also an attack on the disinterestedness of
our admiration. To see a particular musician, artist, or writer as
gifted is to marvel at his work; it draws upon our sense of wonder,
our sense of the miraculous that is also expressed in the phrase 'the
gift of life'. A gift is not something 'due' to a man: it is something
he is blessed with, it is given to him through what the religiously
inclined would call grace. An attack on the very means by which
one could express such praise is an attack on the meaning of 'gift'
in its purest sense. And it is perhaps no accident that the very word
'gift' (like the word 'charity') has itself been corrupted and
degraded. The idea of a 'gift' now is virtually equivalent to the idea
of a reward, or a gratuity (by no means merely gratuitous) for
service received, or it connotes the habitual and compulsory
'exchange' of presents, as though in fulfilment of contractual
obligation.

If John Casey is right in his sympathy with the philosophical
idealism that regards 'modes of expression of a particular period
as creating, in a real sense, the possibilities of feeling'[54] (the
epistemological analogue being that possibilities of thought create
possibilities of what can be perceived), then we have much to fear
from the contemporary linguistic habits in which moral concepts
are gradually being evacuated from the increasingly influential
language in which some psychologists and sociologists describe
and explain human behaviour. And in no sphere does this influence
have greater effect than in education. The language of 'behavioural
objectives' for instance, redolent of Skinnerian behaviourism, treats
education as a form of sausage-making, in which predicted and

---

[53] See Anne Sofer's personal column, *Times Educational Supplement*, 6 Dec.
1985.
[54] 'The Autonomy of Art', 84.

measurable units of 'behaviour' (or even, as the Americanism has it, 'behaviours') and sets of 'attitudes' are to be pulled into existence by 'programmes' and step-by-step 'objectives' in which the teacher is demoted from his status as a human being to that of one more 'teaching aid' among others. (Indeed, teachers are now redescribed as 'facilitators', 'enablers', and 'managers of learning experiences'.) The term 'moral education', already suggesting something that has a life of its own apart from 'ordinary' education, has now acquired Brave New World connotations, consisting in the implanting of specific 'attitudes' to specific 'issues'.

When language is debased and corrupted in this way it carries in its train a potential for debasing and corrupting the human conduct it already misperceives. The adolescent, or rather hooligan, who uses violence as a first resort will not be treated to the disapprobation he deserves, nor as one who has failed to benefit from a humanizing education, but more likely as one whose 'teachers' have failed to implant the requisite social 'skills'. As I now put the final touches to this manuscript I find that even that example is out of date, and, incredible though it seems, far too optimistic. If the thinking behind the latest innovation 'Personal and Social Education' known for short as PSE (taught as a 'cross-curricular area' in many British schools) flourishes as other curriculum innovations and 'initiatives' have done during the past twenty-odd years, the conduct of pupils emerging from such courses will be beyond moral assessment. Their behaviour will consist in their having made and having been encouraged to make 'informed life-choices'. The Australian name for PSE is 'Values Education', and the purpose of values education it seems is to teach pupils that there are no values: 'The core theme of values clarification is that there are no right and wrong values. Values education does not seek to identify and transmit "right" values but to help children to discover the values that best suit them personally. . . .'[55]

Leavis's protest against the American influence on the English language in this country was not a protest against 'distinct American usages' as such, but against 'the characteristics that betray (or inculcate) the crude human attitudes of the civilization implicit in

---

[55] From a report on a conference opening address by Melbourne barrister, Jim Bowen ('Why Classrooms Have Become a Battleground', *News Weekly*, 3 Mar. 1990.)

them'.[56] Casey makes a similar point: 'it is worth considering what effect certain celebrated American funerary rituals must have upon the *experience* of grief.'[57] One can also ask what the language of 'skills' does to the quality of our relationships. In an age in which it is becoming second nature to speak of communication and personal relationships in terms of 'strategies' (an insidious metaphor connoting war-games) one has to look hard to perceive the sheer ugliness embedded in that conception of sexual love revealed by the term 'sexual dysfunction'—hot from the Masters and Johnson clinics of the USA. The emphasis on what are called 'skills' in personal relationships is one which puts a premium on the idea of 'success' at any price: success in personal relations, success in decision-making, success with a lover, success in avoiding moral dilemmas. Indeed given that the idea of a skill implies the successful and non-accidental attainment of a given end, the idea that there are human dilemmas, formerly known as predicaments, is likely to be ousted in favour of the view that in life there are merely 'problems' which therefore admit of neat solutions. The more this view becomes ossified in the language, the more we are likely to regard such difficulties as malfunctions in a machine. The language of 'skills' (once confined to management training courses) has begun to affect even the way that informal relationships are described. The implication is that the other person is a pawn to be manipulated in the hedonistic life-games of wants and satisfactions.

This bland pragmatism is brought out tellingly by D. Z. Phillips in his essay, 'Some Limits to Moral Endeavour':

in a society where 'success' is the key word, the notion of living with insuperable difficulties is likely to decline. This is seen most clearly in changing conceptions of marriage . . . When marriage vows are thought of as eternal and unbreakable, difficulties, when they arise, must be met in terms of them and, if needs be, lived with despite the cost. When such difficulties are regarded as things to be helped, coped with, ironed out, their persistence might well be regarded as a proof that an experiment in co-habitation has failed. The vows which once were eternal may become, as they have become for some, the tentative terms of reference for a trial period. Similarly if success and achievement are emphasized to the exclusion of all else, a sense of tragic inevitability such as that depicted by

[56] *Nor Shall My Sword: Discourses on Pluralism, Compassion and Social Hope* (London, 1972), 185.
[57] 'The Autonomy of Art', 84.

Hardy is likely to diminish. Life can be only too difficult, it will be said for those who fail to take advantage of the services and help at hand. It is not hard to see how such ideas would have a direct effect upon what people think of pity and compassion.[58]

It is clear here that Phillips does not take pity and compassion to be the gratuitous overflow of sentimental feelings but, instead, forms of acknowledgement of our common imperfection: forms of understanding which are rooted not in the self-indulgent delights of one-upmanship, but in the knowledge that we are finite and fallible creatures, subject to the vicissitudes of circumstance and the limits of character.

Not through a theory of literature but through his own approach to moral philosophy, Phillips has often drawn attention to the power of literary works to challenge particular philosophical presuppositions and assumptions.[59] A. C. Capey similarly makes out a case for saying that the study of literature 'inoculates us against the tyranny of catchword and cliché'. His discussion of an example taken from *Anna Karenina* is interesting:

The Steeplechase chapter, without intending to do so, disposes of the doctrine of 'audience-participation', exposes the phrase as a glib simplification of the delicate and shifting relations between 'done', 'shown', 'observed' and 'shared'. The scene on the course, where Vronsky rides his horse confidently at first, then carelessly and disastrously, is observed by Anna, agitated in the stand; and Anna's exposed feelings (so much more than observations) are observed by her husband, who is implicated in the drama and yet insulated from it. No one who has read the Steeplechase chapter can again utter the catchphrase with quite the ease it requires; his sensibility has been modified too far to permit it.[60]

There are two distinguishable, though related, morals which may be drawn from arguments of this type. The first is that literature, and especially the novel, penetrates beneath appearances, giving us, in Trilling's words, 'the look and feel of things, how things are done and what things are worth and what they cost and what the odds are'.[61] But the second is that literature in its

---

[58] *Through a Darkening Glass: Philosophy, Literature and Cultural Change* (Oxford, 1982), 48–9.

[59] See e.g. ibid. 64–81.

[60] 'The Language of Enlightenment', in Abbs (ed.), *The Black Rainbow*, 95.

[61] *The Liberal Imagination: Essays on Literature and Society* (Oxford, 1978), 199.

fastidiousness with language ('My language is the universal whore whom I have to make into a virgin'[62]) provides a safeguard against other forces which corrupt and debase the language. That is where thinkers like Leavis take over from where thinkers like Phillips leave off. On the latter conception, literature is not a form of philosophy but a sort of injection into our semantic habits, and the needle penetrates into the heart of the culture in which the language has its life. But it seems that only the greatest works of literature are likely to do this—which is perhaps why Wittgenstein remarks, 'I do not believe that Shakespeare can be set alongside any other poet. Was he perhaps a creator of *language* rather than a poet?'[63] (Though my difficulty in interpreting this passage is not made easy by Wittgenstein's other reservations about Shakespeare.)

If there is anything in the above argument, then what the second moral throws light on is that 'learning from literature' is too narrowly conceived if we restrict ourselves to considering what an individual can learn from an individual text. What we learn from literature is not the sum total of a series of 'learning experiences' and this for two reasons. (1) Growth of literary understanding does not run in serial progression; our understanding of particular works of art is affected, sometimes in retrospect, by an increasingly wider and deeper experience not only of works in the same genre, but of different art forms which, if sufficiently appreciated, throw light upon one another. (2) If the greatest works leave something of their character on the culture in which they are studied, they can contribute even in an indirect way to the lives of the individuals who have never even studied them. To pursue (2) fully would be to enter into a detailed examination of the complex relations between 'high' and 'common' culture. My observations will have to be brief.

High culture grows out of common culture, but transcends it in the sense that its survival depends upon more than the local and transitory shared values of the community that sustains a common culture. In this sense the products of high culture speak to men in different cultures and different times, and are thus 'universal'. It therefore shows a serious misconception when pundits dealing with the products of high culture of the past translate them into vehicles

---

[62] Karl Kraus (quoted in W. H. Auden, *The Dyer's Hand: And Other Essays* (London, 1975), 23).
[63] Wittgenstein, *Culture and Value*, 84e.

of immediate and locally applied 'relevance' (the American film *Joe Macbeth* is an example of this, since it extracts a 'message' from an established masterpiece and applies it only to the transient circumstances of gangsterdom in a particular era). *Macbeth* gains its status as a masterpiece precisely because it is not immediately 'relevant' to such a particular set of circumstances and so outlives them. To study great works of art is to be emancipated from such narrowness of vision and to link hands with a wider humanity. Even to people who do not themselves study great works of art, the presence of high culture breathes a greater sense of meaning into civilization by intimating the presence of enduring or even permanent values against which our immediate desires, needs, and petty concerns can be seen for what they are. In so far as formal education cynically abandons these values, or even fights against them, our lives cannot but be impoverished.

As things have turned out I think Leavis was understating the matter when he pointed to the link between what he called 'spiritual philistinism' and empty lives:

I spoke earlier of the collaborative interplay that sustains cultural continuity as creating the human world; for 'the human world' I might have said 'reality'. By 'spiritual philistinism' I mean the implicit belief that the only reality we need take account of in ordering human affairs is what can be measured, aggregated and averaged. With this philistinism goes the elimination of the day-by-day creativity of human response that manifests itself in the significances and values without which there is no reality—nothing but emptiness that has to be filled with drink, sex, eating, background music and what the papers and telly supply.[64]

A little over two decades have elapsed since Leavis wrote that, and we can now see to our cost that people have other ways of compensating for the emptiness: in increasing violence, cruelty, viciousness, and aggressiveness; or even in the self-congratulatory fanaticism that feeds on the overwhelming desire to seek out, denounce, or even kill those who are rendered enemies in the glowing light of some moral, political, or religious obsession.

Human beings have a need for significance and meaning, and when this is not intimated through the bonds of the civilization in which they live, and where they do not have the personal resources to find it for themselves, they will find some substitute for it in the

---

[64] 'T. S. Eliot and English Literature', in *Valuation in Criticism*, 142.

most destructive ways. We should look to the decline in civilization itself for the decline in morality, and not to some particular local cause such as the easy availability of hard drugs and alcohol, knives and daggers, firearms and ammunition.

It is symptomatic of the spiritual philistinism Leavis described that the most vocal of our moral guardians are less concerned with the way people treat one another than with the physical condition of 'the environment', 'the ozone layer', with cleanliness and hygiene and physical fitness. Anyone who speaks of moral or spiritual pollution on the other hand is likely to be dismissed as an eccentric fool, even by some leading members of the Church.

Even to attempt to describe the decline in civilization would require a vocabulary in discord with the very language in which that decline is reflected. To refer to the 'sanctity' of the body is to invite the accusation of being sanctimonious. To use words like 'sacred' or 'spiritual', especially in connection with works of art, is thought pretentious. The word 'precious' is now a term of abuse. Indeed, if some of the anti-intellectual forces at work in education eventually succeed we should not be surprised if in the future it is no longer a compliment to describe someone as cultured or academic, and if words such as 'excellence' and 'taste' suffer a similar fate.

The corruption and debasement of language I noted earlier is not the result of some impersonal force in nature: it springs from fashionable mores and trends—often sustained by vested interests. This means that the 'non-rational' (not equivalent to 'irrational') element in morality cannot be defended by appealing to some spurious value of blind obedience to a contemporary *Zeitgeist* as it applies to particular ways of life and to particular institutions. For evaluations of such ways of life and such institutions are bound to conflict (how else would it be possible for me to criticize the trends and fashions I have mentioned?). But where contemporary fashions are challenged, if only by passive or spiritual resistance, they are not challenged from a viewpoint outside society, but from an allegiance to other customs and traditions which still survive, though muted, and have been passed on in various ways, not least through great works of art which are kept alive through high culture.

What comes down to us by this means is something difficult to put into words for the very reason that it has an 'unspoken' quality.

It has to do not only with a kind of reverence for human life, with a sympathy for human kind, but with something sustained upon that 'unspoken' respect: an exploration of the ends of human conduct and of the meaning of our existence. If that remark is obscure I can at least try to clarify it by means of an example. As a young schoolboy, hostile as many schoolboys are, even to the very name 'Shakespeare', and the expression 'classical music', I was awakened to their importance not initially by being in a position to *understand* high culture, but by having its significance conveyed through sensitive teachers who communicated a feeling, more common than now, that there is something of great human importance about works of art—something that strikes to the heart of the soul.

My awakening to the beauty of classical music came at the age of 9, a discovery that developed with the realization that classical music was not something that grows like a vegetable out of the dust of some remote archive, but is composed by human beings. The teacher in question gave a talk on Handel's boyhood and followed this by playing on the piano the famous march from *Scipione*. The melody had a simple beauty that haunted me and the way it spoke to me seemed inseparable from the feeling of being spoken to by another human being from the past, in a way that made the distance of time seem irrelevant.

My change in attitude to Shakespeare came at the age of 15. Dragged on a school trip to the cinema to see *Henry V*, I was virtually asleep with boredom until Act IV scene i. Halfway through Olivier's soliloquy I was stirred by the following,

> 'Tis not the balm, the sceptre, and the ball,
> The sword, the mace, the crown imperial,
> The intertissued robe of gold and pearl,
> The farced title running 'fore the King,
> The throne he sits on, nor the tide of pomp
> That beats upon the high shore of this world,—
> No, not all these, thrice gorgeous ceremony,
> Not all these, laid in bed majestical,
> Can sleep so soundly as the wretched slave
> Who, with a body fill'd and vacant mind,
> Gets him to rest, cramm'd with distressful bread . . .

I had no firm intellectual grasp of what those words meant, and certainly nothing which would be good enough to pass an examination, but the poetry seemed to speak, or rather sing, as it was meant to sing, of some hidden gold beneath the fool's gold of appearance. I was dimly aware, though not sufficiently so to articulate the thought in this way, that the King was standing outside the immediate action, and the role imposed upon him, questioning the hollowness of 'ceremony' and the accident of birth that confers the crown, thus setting the King apart from the strange comfort of the routine labours of those who merely serve. Had that thought been expressed in prose I should not have listened, for I was not interested in the thought but in the King's act of contemplation. The magic of the poetry through Olivier's delivery of it, the impossibility of escape from the onward flow of the lines, seemed to lift me out of the everyday world while looking back upon it. It had the intensity of a religious experience, and no 'analysis' of the lines could have induced that. Auden has said, 'One cannot be taught to recognize a sacred being, one has to be converted.'[65] A conversion does not merely pull one towards something, it pushes something else away: a content, perhaps, with wilful ignorance or prejudice; a smaller world.

Even in such an unintellectual and inchoate form, the experience of great art can have an impact that puts one in touch with something that can only be called spiritual, with something that not only transcends the little world of the self, but the humdrum experience of everyday life. So I am drawn to sympathize with R. F. Holland, who claims that poetry and music, if of the right quality, have the capacity to 'breathe spiritual dispositions into people',[66] and with R. K. Elliott, who speaks of imagination in art taking us out of the body:

If we find ourselves wandering in a picture of Corot's, for example, then it is as if the self has suddenly been set free from its imprisonment in the body, and in our naive depth we do not fail to take the hint that the given world of ordinary perception may not be the only one in which we can live and move and have our being. Thus the second import of imaginal experience is of the existence of the separate soul, and not far beyond that is an intimation of immortality.[67]

---

[65] *The Dyer's Hand*, 56.
[66] *Against Empiricism: On Education, Epistemology and Value* (Oxford, 1986), 73.
[67] Above, n. 30, p. 103.

There is of course no necessary connection between such rapture or exaltation and our subsequent conduct as moral beings. It is utterly baffling that a man of fine artistic sensibilities may, in other respects, remain a swine: so in words to that effect remarked Fenby of Delius. Perhaps a better example is Tolstoy, whose sensitive and sophisticated moral insights are at odds with the man he actually was. But for all that it still seems reasonable to say that to be moved in the way that great art can move us is to be put in touch with something that in a way dwarfs our own little concerns, which is a step nearer to being sensitive to the 'reality' of other people. I am reminded at this point of something Bernard Levin wrote in *The Times*. He was referring to an increasingly familar incident. 'In New York, a gang of youths set upon a 28-year-old woman who was jogging in an unfrequented part of Central Park. They attacked her with bricks, a metal pipe and a knife, then gang-raped her. She was found lying unconscious in a pool of her blood. Her injuries have apparently left her brain-damaged.'[68] Levin reports that among one of the comments made by the perpetrators after being arrested was 'she was nothing'. Levin's own analysis of this otherwise unintelligible affair is that the perpetrators lacked the imagination to grasp the nature of what they were doing. They of course knew what they were doing in the sense that they were not mad, or drugged, or hypnotized. But they lacked the imagination to confront themselves with the nature of what they had done. 'Has our junk world of instant gratification uncoupled from any idea of consequences destroyed the capacity to change places, imaginatively, with another?' I have some sympathy with Levin's question and the implied answer. But to appreciate the 'reality' of another person involves not just an act of identification with him, but a sense of his 'otherness'. The reality of the other is that he is not me. To regard him as a mere instrument to my evil satisfactions, is to lack the imagination to appreciate that the world is not my plaything, that others have a reality which is independent of mine and which I should not trespass upon. In saying that the woman was 'nothing', her attacker was denying her independent reality, making her dwell like a puppet in his own vicious fantasy where she could be ripped to pieces. He and his confederates, could not accept the 'mystery' of otherness.

[68] 'Blind in the Mind', *The Times*, 15 May 1989.

It is often said that great works of literature have universal significance. It seems to me that point is misconstrued if it is taken to mean that, for instance, Shakespeare's heroes 'stand for' or 'represent' men in general. Given all my previous arguments about characters being individuals, that cannot be so. Rather, the universality consists in the fact that these plays speak to people living in different societies and at different times. Hence there is a double aspect to this universality. The first aspect is this, that throughout different ages and different cultures, Shakespeare's characters and their human problems show certain constancies in human nature that different peoples can recognize. But secondly, the universality of the plays has something to do with the fact that they can survive different interpretations. This does not mean that just anything will do as an interpretation (e.g. feminist readings of *Lear*—readings which are *imposed* upon the text). This brings me to the point that genuine interpretation requires a certain humility. We must not only concern ourselves with what the playwright might have wished to convey, but also respect the characters he has created, in a way that is not totally removed from our respect for actual persons. Among other things, we need to consider how things would look through their eyes. In considering and *re*considering the play from different points of view we are often put in touch with the kind of sensitivity and integrity required for our understanding of actual people: for rarely, if ever, can we 'sum up' a character completely so that we have him 'taped' for good and all. In art, as in life, our estimates of character are defeasible. Indeed it seems reasonable to claim that in various ways art in general, and tragedy in particular, puts us in touch with the mystery of the human personality, and even with the mystery of life itself. Literature can add to our knowledge of human nature by showing us how little we do know. Literary works do not consist of codes to be cracked or crossword puzzles to be solved. In the case of Regan in *King Lear* David Pole aptly remarks, 'Instead of a psychological puzzle we have something more like a cosmic mystery.'[69] This perception is rooted in an understanding of the play, rather than in a failure to understand it. A. C. Bradley observes that in our experience of Shakespearian tragedy we are left not

---

[69] 'Art and Generality', in Pole, *Aesthetics, Form and Emotion*, 154.

merely with pity and fear, but with an overwhelming sense of mystery and waste:

> We seem to have before us a type of the mystery of the whole world, the tragic fact which extends far beyond the limits of tragedy. Everywhere from the crushed rocks beneath our feet to the soul of man, we see power, intelligence, life and glory, which astound us and seem to call for our worship. And everywhere we see them perishing, devouring one another and destroying themselves, often with dreadful pain, as though they came into being for no other end. Tragedy is the typical form of this mystery, because that greatness of soul which it exhibits oppressed, conflicting and destroyed, is the highest existence in our view. It forces the mystery on us, and it makes us realize so vividly the worth of that which is wasted that we cannot possibly seek comfort in the reflection that all is vanity.[70]

Given the degree of humility needed to interpret fictional characters (where the art is sufficiently good to sustain their complexity), it would be surprising if there were no potential connection between that and our understanding of human beings, no feeding back from it to the circumspection needed in our dealings with people, so that our awareness of the mystery of the human personality awakens 'a salutary humility . . . in the august presence of another soul'.[71]

That last remark, and the remarks that preceded it, seem on the surface to have transgressed our principle that art is not a mere instrument. But it is not necessary to go all the way with utilitarianism. That art can feed back into our quality of life can be part of its value without being part of its purpose (or indeed part of *what* we value when we value it). Friendship for instance contributes to our happiness, but that consideration need not enter as a reason for valuing a particular friend: indeed it cannot, if the friendship is true or sincere. Similarly, the heteronomous benefits cannot be 'my' reason for attending to a work of art. Our interest in a work as a work of art cannot be a practical interest, for that would rob it of its value. What I have tried to stress in this book is that the significance of fiction must have something to do with its fictionality. The object of aesthetic contemplation is thus divorced from the

---

[70] *Shakespearean Tragedy: Lectures on Hamlet, Othello, King Lear, Macbeth* (London, 1985), 16.

[71] A. O. Cockshut (quoted by Helen Gardner, *In Defence of the Imagination* (Oxford, 1982), 154). The remarks pertain to literary biography, but are apposite here.

self-interest and practical considerations that would otherwise prohibit understanding. Our engagement with literature, as with any art, depends upon a particular kind of loss to the self, and one that we may therefore call love. (A point that also pertains to the activity of the artist in creating. As Auden put it, 'unless the poet sacrifices his feelings completely to the poem so that they are no longer his but the poem's, he fails'.[72])

Here there is a parallel with love for a person. One way of putting the point is to say via Kant that we treat the other person as an end and never merely as a means. But the spirit of Kant's imperative also shines through Simone Weil's observation that love for another recognizes the 'distance' between self and other. Thus to recognize and respect the 'reality' of another is to be concerned with truth. In her discussion of the 'attention' a human being can give to a sufferer the link between otherness and truth is brought out in her comment that 'warmth of heart, impulsiveness, pity are not enough', since

The love of our neighbour in all its fullness simply means being able to say to him: 'What are you going through?' It is a recognition that the sufferer exists, not only as a unit in a collection, or a specimen from the social category labelled 'unfortunate', but as a man, exactly like us, who was one day stamped with a special mark by affliction. For this reason it is enough, but it is indispensable, to know how to look at him in a certain way.

This way of looking is first of all attentive. The soul empties itself of all its own contents in order to receive the being it is looking at, just as he is, in all his truth.[73]

If engagement with a work of art is seen under the aspect of love, we can neither project our fantasies onto it, nor keep looking over our shoulder for the heteronomous rewards; for what we have here is a mode of 'attention' that is antithetical to a concern for self-interest and consonant with a search for truth. That such engagement confers some 'external' enrichment in 'my' life is not totally irrelevant to an estimation of the value of literature. All that we must insist upon, to preserve a workable notion of autonomy, is that we do not regard it purely as a means to an end: for so to regard it drops out the condition that makes it lead to anything.

---

[72] *The Dyer's Hand*, 70.
[73] *Waiting on God*, trans. Emma Crawford (London, 1959), 75.

RITUAL AND CELEBRATION

I said earlier that cognitivist theories—even of the kind that I have ultimately defended—cannot account for the fact that we wish to return to the same works time and time again, and that we value them as lasting utterances. Here, in closing, it is necessary to point out that works of literature are important to us in a number of different ways. At one level we may regard them as a form of philosophy. Even at that level, however, it is philosophy made concrete. While imaginative literature may draw upon or express philosophical ideas it does so in such a way as to 'enact' or 'embody' such ideas so that we experience them through circumstances made concrete through imaginative realization. And while philosophical activity must pay attention to concrete particulars it does so in order to inform its impulse towards abstraction. Our interest in a philosophical argument lies in what it points to, what it illuminates, or calls into question. The ambience of a philosophical discussion (even where it is an interior dialogue) consists in a shared search for clarification. Though philosophical texts are written objects, their role in the surrounding human context is that of a shared search for that which its very means make impossible: intellectual peace.

Literature is also a 'common pursuit', but not in the same sense. The surrounding human context behind the written literary work consists in the artist's desire to make or create and in the desire of readers to experience and to praise. Art can be food to philosophical insight, but our interest in works of art also derives from something more primitive: a deep human need for ritual and celebration. As young children our acquaintance with literary creation takes place in a ritualistic setting: the oft-repeated bedtime story, the chanted nursery-rhyme, the disturbing yet consoling magic of fairy-tales, and—in the infant school—the spellbound passivity of sitting cross-legged while teacher recounts the morning story.

To consider literary fiction as a language-game, or art as a 'form of life', one needs to look more widely at the part that literature plays in human life other than its role as a source of philosophical insight. Indeed the way in which it can be a source of such insight or illumination derives from its being art and not a substitute for some other discipline, such as philosophy or psychology, sociology or history.

'You need to think of the role which pictures such as paintings (as opposed to working drawings) have in our lives. This role is by no means a uniform one.' (Wittgenstein, *Philosophical Investigations*, II xi. 205e.) One 'role' is that paintings are hung on walls and displayed in galleries, not simply to serve the function of what we may get out of them by way of delight and edification: this practice also expresses our attitude to paintings. They are not put there as the staff timetable is pinned in the common-room or as the mechanic hangs his spanners on the garage wall, simply so they are easier to get at. The tradition of displaying paintings is a ritualistic form of praise—praise, not just of a particular painting, which may or may not deserve its pride of place there, but of painting as art: something to be treasured.

A similar argument can be adduced about the creedal and ritualistic aspects of religion. While organized religion would be nothing without some form of creedal commitment, it would lack its spiritual significance if robbed of the awe and sense of eternity that is created through ceremony. It would also be difficult to estimate the effects upon our feeling for law and order if courts of law were to lose the authority that derives from long-standing traditions embodied in the repetitive formality of court proceedings.

We cannot assess the value and significance of art in a vacuum, any more than we can adequately assess what we learn from art by speaking in terms of what we learn from a single work. The significance of art is deeply entwined with the significance of other major institutions that play a part in the life of mankind, and single works of art only speak in the way they do because the influence of art is cumulative rather than episodic. Great works of poetry, great novels, and great plays are not extinguished upon the one utterance, but grow in stature, leaving their mark upon the language we speak—contributing to its music and extending its field of reference. They derive their memorable quality, not from a set of abstract or formal requirements which they satisfy, but from a particular kind of authority that is created through repetition, the kind of repetition that keeps religious utterances alive and respected. A great poem that we return to time and time again is not metrified prose, but more like—in Herrick's words—a 'holy incantation'. As Auden put it: 'A poem is a rite; hence its formal and ritualistic character. Its use of language is deliberately and ostentatiously different from talk. Even when it employs the diction and rhythms of conversation, it employs them as a deliberate informality, presupposing the norm with which they are intended to contrast.'[74]

In visiting the theatre to see a great play, we do not enter a debating chamber or a lecture hall, but, as Chesterton put it, a festival.[75] In fact Helen Gardner makes it sound more like an act of religious worship: 'the hush of the audience that is truly absorbed in the play gives an experience that is comparable to the experience of public worship, in which the individuals are united while remaining themselves'.[76] This loss to the self is described by Nietzsche in *The Birth of Tragedy* as the Dionysian impulse. Under this conception, our experience of art is akin to a ritual of 'intoxication': 'the union between man and man [is] reaffirmed . . . each one feels himself not only united with his neighbour, but as one with him'.[77]

Caution is needed in interpreting this argument. If repetition alone were sufficient to confer legitimate authority, then we might as well attribute greatness to clichés and advertising jingles. The latter, however, have only the semblance of authority. They neither survive nor repay serious scrutiny, and their mesmeric force derives from a corrupted form of the need for ritual—derives, that is, not from a genuine desire to unite with others in celebrating what is important, but from a pusilanimous fear of appearing to be different. My argument is not that being handed on through tradition and celebrated in ritual is the only thing that gives works of art their value—no more than the formal traditions of court proceedings are the only things that make law and order important. It is that the repetition here consummates that importance, whereas on the instrumentalist theories I have rejected, art is merely consumed.

---

[74] *The Dyer's Hand*, 58.
[75] *Lunacy and Letters*, 43.
[76] *In Defence of the Imagination*, 57.
[77] *The Birth of Tragedy, and the Case of Wagner*, trans. and ed. W. Kaufman (New York, 1967), 37.

BIBLIOGRAPHY

ABBS, PETER (ed.), *The Black Rainbow: Essays on the Present Breakdown of Culture* (London: Heinemann, 1975)

ALTHAM, J. E. J., 'Reproach', *Proceedings of the Aristotelian Society*, 74 (1973/4), 263–72.

ARISTOTLE: *Aristotle/Longinus/Horace: Classical Literary Criticism*, trans. T. S. Dorsch (Harmondsworth: Penguin Books, 1965).

AUDEN, W. H., *A Selection by the Author* (Harmondsworth: Penguin Books, 1958).

—— *The Dyer's Hand: And Other Essays*, 2nd edn. (London: Faber & Faber, 1975).

AUSTEN, JANE, *Mansfield Park* (New York: Signet, New American Library, 1964).

BANTOCK, G. H., *The Parochialism of the Present* (London: Routledge & Kegan Paul, 1981).

BAYLEY, JOHN, *The Characters of Love: A Study in the Literature of Personality* (London: Chatto & Windus, 1968).

BECKERMAN, WILFRED, 'The Problem of Judging Evil', *The Times*, 17 Dec. 1986.

BEST, DAVID, *Feeling and Reason in the Arts* (London: George Allen & Unwin, 1985).

BOOTH, WAYNE, C., *The Rhetoric of Fiction*, 2nd edn. (Harmondsworth: Penguin Books, 1987).

BRADBURY, MALCOLM, *The History Man* (London: Secker & Warburg, 1975).

BRADLEY, A. C., *Shakespearean Tragedy: Lectures on Hamlet, Othello, King Lear, Macbeth*, introd. John Russell Brown (London: Macmillan Education, 1985).

BROWNING, ROBERT, *A Selection by W. E. Williams* (Harmondsworth: Penguin Books, 1954).

CASEY, JOHN, *The Language of Criticism* (London: Methuen, 1966).

—— (ed.), *Morality and Moral Reasoning* (London: Methuen, 1966).

CAVELL, STANLEY, *Must We Mean What We Say? A Book of Essays* (New York: Scribners, 1969).

CHESTERTON, G. K., *Lunacy and Letters* (London: Sheed & Ward, 1958).

COLLINGWOOD, R. G., *The Principles of Art*, 2nd edn. (Oxford: Oxford University Press, 1958).

DANTO, ARTHUR C., *The Transfiguration of the Commonplace: A Philosophy of Art* (Cambridge, Mass.: Harvard University Press, 1981).

DEARDEN, R. F., HIRST, P. H., and PETERS, R. S. (eds.), *Education and the Development of Reason* (London: Routledge & Kegan Paul, 1971).

DILMAN, ILHAM, *Love and Human Separateness* (Oxford: Blackwell, 1987).

—— and PHILLIPS, D. Z., *Sense and Delusion* (London: Routledge & Kegan Paul, 1971).

EAGLETON, TERRY, *Marxism and Literary Criticism* (London: Macmillan, 1976).

—— *William Shakespeare* (Oxford: Blackwell, 1987).

ECO, UMBERTO, *The Role of the Reader* (Bloomington, Ind.: Indiana University Press, 1987).

ELIOT, T. S., *Notes Towards the Definition of Culture*, 2nd edn. (London: Faber & Faber, 1962).

—— *Selected Prose of T. S. Eliot*, ed. Frank Kermode (London: Faber & Faber, 1975).

ELLIOTT, R. K., 'Poetry and Truth', *Analysis*, 27/3 (1964), 77–85.

ENRIGHT, D. J., *Fields of Vision: Essays on Literature, Language and Television* (Oxford: Oxford University Press, 1988).

EVANS, GARETH, *The Varieties of Reference*, ed. John McDowell (Oxford: Clarendon Press, 1982).

FALK, COLIN, 'Fictions and Reality', *Philosophy*, 63/245 (July 1988), 363–71.

FINN, F. E. S. (ed.), *Poets of Our Time: An Anthology* (London: John Murray, 1965).

FOOT, PHILIPPA (ed.), *Theories of Ethics* (Oxford: Oxford University Press, 1967).

FORD, BORIS (ed.), *From Blake to Byron: The Pelican Guide to English Literature*, v (Harmondsworth: Penguin Books, 1957).

—— (ed.), *The Present: The New Pelican Guide to English Literature*, viii (Harmondsworth: Penguin Books, 1983).

FOWLER, ALISTAIR, 'A Critical Path for Literature', *Times Higher Education Supplement*, 8 Mar. 1985.

FROST, ROBERT, *Selected Poems*, ed. C. Day Lewis (Harmondsworth: Penguin Books, 1955).

GARDNER, HELEN, *In Defence of the Imagination* (Oxford: Clarendon Press, 1982).

—— (ed.), *The Metaphysical Poets* (Harmondsworth: Penguin Books, 1957).

GASS, WILLIAM, H., *Fiction and the Figures of Life* (New York: Vintage Books, 1972).

GEACH, PETER, *God and the Soul* (London: Routledge & Kegan Paul, 1969).

—— *Logic Matters* (Oxford: Blackwell, 1972).

GRANVILLE-BARKER, HARLEY, *Prefaces to Shakespeare*, ii: *King Lear*, *Cymbeline*, *Julius Caesar*, illustr. edn. (London: Batsford, 1963).

GUSTAFSON, DONALD F. (ed.), *Essays in Philosophical Psychology* (London: Macmillan, 1967).

HALLETT, JOAN *The Bucking Chestnut* (London: Collins, 1950).

HAMLYN, DAVID, *The Theory of Knowledge* (London: Macmillan, 1971).

—— 'The Phenomena of Love and Hate', *Philosophy*, 53/203 (Jan. 1978), 5–20.

HAMPSHIRE, STUART, *Morality and Conflict* (Oxford: Blackwell, 1983).

HARE, R. M., *Freedom and Reason* (Oxford: Clarendon Press, 1963).

HINTIKKA, JAAKKO, '*Cogito Ergo Sum*: Inference or Performance?', *Philosophical Review* 71/1 (Jan. 1962), 3–32.

HOLLAND, R. F., *Against Empiricism: On Education, Epistemology and Value* (Oxford: Blackwell, 1980).

HOSPERS, JOHN, 'Implied Truths in Literature', *Journal of Aesthetics and Art Criticism*, 29/1 (Autumn 1960), 37–46.

HUME, DAVID, *Enquiries Concerning the Human Understanding and Concerning the Principles of Morals*, ed. L. A. Selby-Bigge, 2nd edn. (Oxford: Oxford University Press, 1962).

JAMES, HENRY, *The Critical Muse: Selected Literary Criticism*, ed. Roger Gard (Harmondsworth: Penguin Books, 1987).

JONES, PETER, *Philosophy and the Novel* (Oxford: Clarendon Press, 1975).

KENNY, ANTHONY, *Descartes: A Study of His Philosophy* (New York: Random House, 1968).

KNIGHTS, L. C., *Explorations: Mainly in the Literature of the Seventeenth Century* (London: Chatto & Windus, 1946).

KRIPKE, SAUL A., *Naming and Necessity*, 2nd edn. (Oxford: Blackwell, 1981).

LAMARQUE, PETER (ed.), *Philosophy and Fiction: Essays in Literary Aesthetics* (Aberdeen: Aberdeen University Press, 1983).

LAWRENCE, D. H., *A Selection from Phoenix*, ed. A. A. H. Inglis (Harmondsworth: Penguin Books, 1971).

LEAVIS, F. R., *The Great Tradition: George Eliot, Henry James, Joseph Conrad*, 2nd edn. (Harmondsworth: Penguin Books, 1967).

—— *Nor Shall My Sword: Discourses on Pluralism, Compassion and Social Hope* (London: Chatto & Windus, 1972).

—— *Valuation in Criticism: And Other Essays*, ed. G. Singh (Cambridge: Cambridge University Press, 1986).

—— (ed. and introd.), *Towards Standards of Criticism: Selections from the Calendar of Modern Letters 1925/27*, 2nd edn. (London: Lawrence & Wishart, 1976).

—— and LEAVIS, Q. D., *Dickens the Novelist* (London: Chatto & Windus, 1970).

LEVIN, BERNARD, 'Blind in the Mind', *The Times*, 15 May 1989.

LEWIS, C. S., *Selected Literary Essays*, ed. Walter Hooper (Cambridge: Cambridge University Press, 1979).

LEWIS, DAVID, *On the Plurality of Worlds* (Oxford: Blackwell, 1986).

LIDDELL, ROBERT, *A Treatise on the Novel*, 2nd edn. (London: Jonathan Cape, 1965).

LINSKY, L. (ed.), *Reference and Modality* (Oxford: Oxford University Press, 1971).

MAITRE, DOREEN, *Literature and Possible Worlds* (London: Middlesex Polytechnic Press/Pembridge, 1983).

MANNISON, DON, 'On Being Moved by Fiction', *Philosophy*, 60/231 (Jan. 1985), 71–87.

MIDGLEY, MARY, 'Is "Moral" a Dirty Word?', *Philosophy*, 67/181 (July 1972), 206–28.

—— *Wickedness: A Philosophical Essay* (London: Ark Paperbacks, 1984).

—— 'The Flight from Blame', *Philosophy*, 62/241 (July 1987), 271–91.

MISCHEL, T. (ed.), *Understanding Other Persons* (Oxford: Blackwell, 1974).

MURRAY, PATRICK, *Literary Criticism: A Glossary of Major Terms* (London: Longman, 1978).

NIETZSCHE, FRIEDRICH, *The Birth of Tragedy* and *The Case of Wagner*, trans. and ed. Walter Kaufmann (New York: Random House, 1967).

OAKESHOTT, MICHAEL, *Rationalism in Politics: And Other Essays* (London: Methuen, 1962).

OGDEN, C. K., and RICHARDS, I. A., *The Meaning of Meaning*, 2nd edn. (London: Ark Paperback, 1985).

O'HEAR, ANTHONY, *The Element of Fire: Science, Art and the Human World* (London: Routledge & Kegan Paul, 1988).

O'KEEFE, DENNIS (ed.), *The Wayward Curriculum: A Cause for Parents' Concern?* (London: Social Affairs Unit, 1986).

ORWELL, GEORGE, *Inside the Whale: And Other Essays* (Harmondsworth: Penguin Books, 1962).

PAVEL, THOMAS, G., *Fictional Worlds* (Cambridge, Mass.: Harvard University Press, 1986).

PHILLIPS, D. Z., *Faith and Philosophical Enquiry* (London: Routledge & Kegan Paul, 1970).

—— *Through a Darkening Glass: Philosophy, Literature and Cultural Change* (Oxford; Blackwell, 1982).

—— and WINCH, PETER (eds.), *Wittgenstein: Attention to Particulars* (London: Macmillan, 1989).

PHILLIPS GRIFFITHS, A. (ed.), *Philosophy and Literature: Royal Institute of Philosophy Lectures*, xvi: *1981/82*, Supplement to *Philosophy* (1983) (Cambridge: Cambridge University Press, 1984).

POLANYI, MICHAEL, *Personal Knowledge: Towards a Post-Critical Philosophy*, 2nd edn. (London: Routledge & Kegan Paul, 1973).

POLE, DAVID, *Aesthetics, Form and Emotion*, ed. George Roberts (London: Duckworth, 1983).

POPE, ALEXANDER, *Selected Works*, ed. Louis Kronenberger, 2nd edn. (New York: Random House, 1951).

PRICE, H. H., *Belief* (London: George Allen & Unwin, 1969).

PRIESTLEY, J. B., *An Inspector Calls*, introd. E. R. Wood, 2nd edn. (London: Heinemann Educational, 1965).

RADFORD, COLIN and WESTON, MICHAEL, 'How can we be Moved by the Fate of Anna Karenina?' *Proceedings of the Aristotelian Society*, suppl. vol., 69 (July 1975), 67–93.

RAINE, CRAIG, *The Onion, Memory* (Oxford: Oxford University Press, 1978).

READ, HERBERT, *The Meaning of Art*, 2nd edn. (Harmondsworth: Penguin Books, 1949).

RHEES, RUSH, *Without Answers*, ed. D. Z. Phillips (London: Routledge & Kegan Paul, 1949).

ROBINSON, IAN, *The Survival of English*, 2nd edn. (Doncaster: Brynmill Press, 1981).

RUSSELL, BERTRAND, *Mysticism and Logic: And Other Essays*, 2nd edn. (London, George Allen & Unwin, 1963).

RYLE, GILBERT, *Collected Papers*, 2 vols. (London: Hutchinson, 1971).

SAVILE, ANTHONY, *The Test of Time: An Essay in Philosophical Aesthetics* (Oxford: Clarendon Press, 1982).

SCHAFFER, PETER, *Amadeus*, ed. Richard Adams (Harlow: Longman, 1984).

SCHAPER, EVA (ed.), *Pleasure, Preference and Value: Studies in Philosophical Aesthetics*, 2nd edn. (Cambridge: Cambridge University Press, 1987).

SCRUTON, ROGER, *The Politics of Culture: And Other Essays* (Manchester: Carcanet Press, 1981).

—— *Art and Imagination: A Study in the Philosophy of Mind*, 2nd edn. (London: Routledge & Kegan Paul, 1982).

—— *The Aesthetic Understanding: Essays in the Philosophy of Art and Culture* (London: Methuen, 1982).

—— *Sexual Desire: A Philosophical Investigation* (London: Weidenfeld & Nicolson, 1986).

SEARLE, JOHN, 'The Logical Status of Fictional Discourse', *New Literary History*, 6 (1975), 319–32.

SMITH, FRANK, *Reading* (Cambridge: Cambridge University Press, 1978).

—— *Understanding Reading*, 3rd edn. (New York: Holt, Rinehart & Winston, 1982).

—— *Writing and the Writer* (London: Heinemann Educational, 1982).

SOUTHAM, B. C. (ed.), *Critical Essays on Jane Austen*, 2nd edn. (London: Routledge & Kegan Paul, 1970).

SPURGEON, CAROLINE, *Shakespeare's Imagery: And What it Tells us* (Cambridge: Cambridge University Press, 1935).

STEINER, GEORGE, *Language and Silence* (London: Faber & Faber, 1967).

STRAWSON, P. F. (ed.), *Studies in the Philosophy of Thought and Action* (Oxford: Oxford University Press, 1968).

STURROCK, JOHN, *Structuralism* (London: Paladin, 1986).

TAYLOR, CHARLES, *The Explanation of Behaviour* (London: Routledge & Kegan Paul, 1964).

THOMAS, R. S., *Between Here and Now: Poems by R. S. Thomas* (London: Macmillan, 1981).

TRILLING, LIONEL, *The Liberal Imagination: Essays on Literature and Society*, uniform edn. (Oxford: Oxford University Press, 1978).

—— *A Gathering of Fugitives*, uniform edn. (Oxford: Oxford University Press, 1980).

VESEY, GODFREY (ed.), *Philosophy and the Arts: Royal Institute of Philosophy Lectures*, vi: 1971/72 (London: Macmillan, 1973).

WALSH, DOROTHY, *Literature and Knowledge* (Middletown, Conn.: Wesleyan University Press, 1969).

WALTON, KENDALL, 'Pictures and Make-Believe', *Philosophical Review*, 82/3 (July 1973), 283–319.

—— 'Are Representations Symbols?', *Monist*, 58/2 (Apr. 1974), 285–93.

—— 'Points of View in Narrative and Depictive Representation', *Noûs*, 10/1 (Mar. 1976), 49–61.

—— 'Fearing Fictions', *Journal of Philosophy*, 73/1 (Jan. 1978), 5–27.

—— 'How Remote are Fictional Worlds from the Real World?', *Journal of Aesthetics and Art Criticism*, 37/1 (Autumn 1978), 11–24.

WARNOCK, G. J., *The Object of Morality* (London: Methuen, 1971).

WEIL, SIMONE, *Waiting on God*, trans. Emma Crawford, 2nd edn. (London: Collins/Fontana, 1959).

—— *On Science, Necessity and the Love of God*, trans. and ed. Richard Rees (Oxford: Oxford University Press, 1968).

—— *First and Last Notebooks*, trans. Richard Rees (Oxford: Oxford University Press, 1968).

—— *The Need for Roots: Prelude to a Declaration of Duties towards Mankind*, trans. A. F. Wills, with a Preface by T. S. Eliot, 2nd edn. (London: Routledge & Kegan Paul, 1978).

—— *Intimations of Christianity among the Early Greeks*, 2nd edn. (London: Ark Paperbacks, 1987).

WHITE, ALAN, *The Language of Imagination* (Oxford: Blackwell, 1990).

—— (ed.), *The Philosophy of Action*, 2nd edn. (Oxford: Oxford University Press, 1970).

WILDE, OSCAR, *The Complete Works of Oscar Wilde*, introd. Vyvyan Holland, 2nd edn. (London: Collins, 1966).

—— *Selected Letters of Oscar Wilde*, ed. Rupert Hart-Davis (Oxford: Oxford University Press, 1979).

WILSON, CATHERINE, 'Literature and Knowledge', *Philosophy*, 58/226 (Oct. 1983), 489–96.

WILSON-KNIGHT, G., *The Wheel of Fire: Essays in Interpretation of Shakespeare's Sombre Tragedies* (Oxford: Oxford University Press, 1930).

WINCH, PETER, *Ethics and Action* (London: Routledge & Kegan Paul, 1972).

—— *Trying to Make Sense* (Oxford: Blackwell, 1987).

WITTGENSTEIN, LUDWIG, *Philosophical Investigations*, trans. G. E. M. Anscombe, 2nd edn. (Oxford: Blackwell, 1967).

—— *Zettel*, ed. G. E. M. Anscombe and G. H. von Wright, trans. G. E. M. Anscombe, 2nd edn. (Oxford: Blackwell, 1981).

—— *Culture and Value*, ed. G. H. von Wright in collaboration with Heikki Nyman, trans. Peter Winch, 2nd edn. (Oxford: Blackwell, 1980).

WOLLHEIM, RICHARD, *Painting as an Art* (London: Thames & Hudson, 1980).

WOOLF, VIRGINIA, *Moments of Being: Unpublished Autobiographical Writings of Virginia Woolf*, ed. Jeanne Schulkind (London: Sussex University Press, 1976).

INDEX